Top Stocks 2012

A Sharebuyer's Guide to Leading Australian Companies

Martin Roth

16
EasyRead Large

RHYW

Copyright Page from the Original Book

Martin Roth is also the author of novel *Prophets and Loss*.

The author and publisher would like to thank Alan Hull (author of *Active Investing*, Revised Edition and *Trade My Way*; <www.alanhull.com>) for generating the five-year share-price graphs.

This eighteenth edition first published 2012 by Wrightbooks
an imprint of John Wiley & Sons Australia, Ltd
42 McDougall Street, Milton Qld 4064

Office also in Melbourne

Typeset in 10/11.5 pt Berkeley

First edition published as *Top Stocks* by Wrightbooks in 1995
New edition published annually

ISBN: 9780730377276

Cover design by Rob Cowpe

Printed in Australia by Ligare Book Printer

10 9 8 7 6 5 4 3 2 1

Set in 16 pt. Verdana

TABLE OF CONTENTS

Preface

In the midst of a weak economy one company, BHP Billiton, reported the largest profit ever in Australian corporate history. Many other businesses, too, have been seeing strong growth in their profits. At a time of slowing corporate profitability, many fine companies continue to raise dividends. And despite a limping stock market, plenty of individual stocks continue to see solid share-price appreciation.

Welcome to *Top Stocks 2012.*

Despite the title, *Top Stocks,* now in its 18th year of publication, is actually a book about companies. Right from the first edition it has been an attempt to help investors find the best public companies in Australia, using strict criteria.

These criteria are explained fully later. But, in essence, all companies in the book must have been publicly listed for at least five years and must have been making a profit and paying a dividend for each of those five years. They must also meet tough benchmarks of profitability and debt levels. Share prices have never been relevant.

The words I wrote a year ago still ring true: The economy may be fragile. The stock market remains volatile. The direction of the currency seems uncertain. And yet a surprisingly large number of Australian companies continue to race ahead with surging profits.

It is exactly companies like these that form the core of *Top Stocks.* Of the 102 companies in this latest edition of the book, 84 saw after-tax profits rise in their latest full-year reporting period, despite the weak economy, and 78 saw EPS rise.

Of the 84 companies reporting higher profits, 51 achieved double-digit profit growth, with a further three reporting a triple-digit increase. In addition, 61 of them saw profits growing at a faster rate than revenues, implying that their profit margins were expanding.

And, as it happens, 25 of the companies in the book have provided investor returns—share-price appreciation plus dividends—of at least 20 per cent a year for five straight years.

Trends among the top stocks

Each year I try to discern some of the trends that are moving our stocks. Last year I pointed to the rise and rise of Australian high-tech stocks. Just 11 years ago only one high-tech company—Computershare—made it into *Top Stocks.* Two years ago there were eight, and last year 11 companies from the Information Technology (IT) sector and two from Telecommunications Services were in the book.

The tend has continued, with 12 IT companies and three from Telecommunications Services in *Top Stocks 2012.*

Of the 11 broad sectors that comprise the Australian stock market, IT is by far the smallest, accounting for less than 1 per cent of total market capitalisation. (By contrast, IT is the largest sector in the United States, representing around 18 per cent of the market there.) So for 12 IT stocks—plus three from Telecommunications Services—to be among the 102 companies in the book suggests that something is happening.

Last year I cited two examples. Let's look at them again. The first is Brisbane-based IT consultant Data#3. It has just reported its ninth straight record profit. It has no debt and more than $53 million in cash holdings, and looks set for continued growth. Last year it was in the book with a share price of $9.23. This year it is $13.32.

Melbourne company M2 Telecommunications has sales that have grown nearly 13 times in five years, and it continues to expand. It is forecasting that profits will rise a further 15 per cent in its June 2012 year. Its return to investors over those five years—share-price appreciation plus dividends—is an annual average of an astonishing 63.5 per cent.

Some years ago I noted the steady entry to the book of pharmaceuticals companies. This was at a time when stocks such as CSL and Cochlear were much smaller, and were not the superstars they are today. Perhaps something similar is starting to occur in high-tech.

A smaller, related trend—a sub-trend, if you like—is the entry to the book of online retailers and service providers. The jobseeker website Seek entered *Top Stocks* last year. This year it is joined by flights booking agency Webjet and hotel specialist W otif.com.

With our resources boom still continuing, it is also worth noting the continuing admission to the book of mining support companies, with new entries Industrea, Mermaid Marine Australia, Mineral Resources and Sedgman.

Small stocks

A particular attraction of *Top Stocks* is the manner in which the editions regularly place the spotlight on smaller, emerging companies that have just ascended into the rankings of the top 500 stocks. Some of these companies continue to rise, offering extraordinary gains to astute investors.

The classic example is the Perth engineering company Monadelphous, which first appeared in *Top Stocks '99,* at a share price (adjusted for a subsequent share split) of $0.66. Last year it was in the book at $15.06. In this edition it is priced at $20.10, and it has been as high as $22.40.

Here are more examples of other high-flying stocks that have appeared in *Top Stocks* well before they hit the radar screens of most small investors. Remember that, along with superb share-price appreciation, they have all also paid regular dividends.

- Campbell Brothers, now enjoying booming profits from its laboratory business, appeared in the very first edition of the book (though it has not appeared in every edition)—when its main business was making soap—with a share price of $3.70. Last year it was in the book at $31.86. This year it is in at $45.89, having been as high as $57.00.

- Four-wheel-drive specialist ARB entered *Top Stocks '99* with a share price of (adjusted) $1.00. It has been in every edition since, and in last year's edition of the book had a price of $6.80. In this edition it is $8.56.
- Austin Engineering is a leader in the engineering and fabricating of specialist products for the mining sector, with a rapidly growing overseas business. It entered the book only two years ago with its shares priced at $2.20. In this edition of the book they are $4.23, and have reached $5.45.
- Caravan and mobile home manufacturer Fleetwood made its debut in *Top Stocks 2003* with a share price of $2.90. Now it is $11.00, and it has been to $14.25.

Who is Top Stocks written for?

Top Stocks is written for all those investors wishing to exercise a degree of control over their portfolios. It is for those just starting out as well as for those with plenty of experience but who still feel the need for some guidance through the thickets of more than 2200 listed stocks.

It is not a how-to book. It does not give step-by-step instructions to 'winning' in the stock market. Rather, it is an independent and objective evaluation of leading companies, based on rigid criteria, with the intention of yielding a large selection of stocks that can become the starting point for investors wishing to do their own research.

A large amount of information is presented on each company, and another key feature of the book is that the data is presented in a common format, to allow readers to make easy comparisons between companies.

It is necessarily a conservative book. All stocks must have been listed for five years even to be considered for inclusion. It is especially suited for those seeking out value stocks for longer term investment.

Yet, perhaps ironically, the book is also being used by short-term traders seeking a goodly selection of financially sound and reliable companies whose shares they can trade. In addition, there are many regular readers, who buy the book each year, and to them in particular I express my thanks.

What are the entry criteria?

The criteria for inclusion in *Top Stocks* are strict:

- All companies must be included in the All Ordinaries index, which comprises Australia's 500 largest stocks (out of more than 2200). The reason for excluding smaller companies is that there is often little investor information available on many of them and some are so thinly traded as to be almost illiquid. In fact, the 500 All Ordinaries companies comprise, by market capitalisation, more than 95 per cent of the entire market. (For the sake of continuity, an exception is made for two companies, Infomedia and Treasury Group, that were in *Top Stocks 2011,* and which were formerly in the All Ordinaries index but have since been excluded.)

- It is necessary that all companies be publicly listed since at least the end of 2006, and have a five-year record of profits and dividend payouts each year.
- All companies are required to post a return-on-equity ratio of at least 10 per cent in their latest financial year.
- No company should have a debt-to-equity ratio of more than 70 per cent.
- It must be stressed that share-price performance is *not* one of the criteria for inclusion in this book. The purpose is to select companies with good profits and a strong balance sheet. These may not offer the spectacular share-price returns of a biotech start-up or a promising gold miner, but they should also present far less risk.
- There are several notable exclusions. Listed managed investments—as defined by the Australian Securities Exchange—are out, as these mainly buy other shares or investments. Examples are Australian Foundation Investment Company and all the property trusts.

• A further exclusion are the foreign stocks listed on the Australian Securities Exchange. There is sometimes a lack of information available about such companies. In addition, their stock prices tend to move on events and trends in their home countries, making it difficult at times for local investors to follow them.

It is surely a tribute to the strength and resilience of Australian corporations that, despite the volatility of the past few years, so many companies have qualified for the book.

Changes to this edition

A total of 22 companies from *Top Stocks 2011* have been omitted from this new edition.

One company, Mitchell Communications, was acquired during the year and delisted. Two others, Downer EDI and Macmahon Holdings, were excluded for not paying any dividend in the June 2011 financial year.

Four companies from *Top Stocks 2011* were excluded because they had debt-to-equity ratios that rose higher than 70 per cent:

- Aristocrat Leisure
- JB Hi-Fi
- The Reject Shop
- Salmat.

The remaining 15 excluded companies fell into the red or otherwise had return-on-equity figures that fell below the required 10 per cent:

- Amalgamated Holdings
- Austal
- Billabong International
- CSR

- Energy Resources of Australia
- Hastie Group
- Independence Group
- K&S Corporation
- Leighton Holdings
- Macquarie Group
- New Hope Corporation
- Pro Medicus
- Spotless Corporation
- TFS Corporation
- Watpac.

There are 19 new companies in this book (although four of them have appeared in earlier editions of the book, but were not in *Top Stocks 2011)*. The companies are:

- APN News & Media
- Consolidated Media Holdings
- Country Road*
- DWS Advanced Business Solutions*
- iiNet*
- IMF (Australia)*
- Industrea*
- IOOF Holdings*
- Mermaid Marine Australia*
- Mineral Resources*
- National Australia Bank
- Nick Scali*
- Patties Foods*
- Retail Food Group*
- Sedgman*

- Ten Network Holdings
- Thorn Group*
- Webjet*
- Wotif.com Holdings.*

* Companies that have not appeared in any previous edition of *Top Stocks.*

Companies in every edition of Top Stocks

Just five companies have appeared in every edition of *Top Stocks:*

- ANZ Banking
- Commonwealth Bank of Australia
- Harvey Norman Holdings
- QBE Insurance
- Westpac Banking.

Once again it is my hope that *Top Stocks* will serve you well.

Martin Roth
Melbourne
September 2011

Introduction

The 102 companies in this book have been placed as much as possible into a common format, for ease of comparison. Please study the following explanations in order to get as much as possible from the large amount of data.

The tables have been made as concise as possible, though they repay careful study, as they contain large amounts of information. Note that the tables for the banks have been arranged a little differently from the others. Details of these are later in this Introduction.

Entry head

At the head of each entry is the company name, with its three-letter ASX code and the website address.

Share-price chart

Under the company name is a five-year share-price chart, to September 2011, provided by Alan Hull, <w ww.alanhullbooks.com.au>, author of *Trade My Way* and *Active Investing,* revised edition.

Small table

Under the share-price chart is a small table with the following data.

Share price

This is the closing price on 31 August 2011. Also included are the 12-month high and low prices, as of the same date.

Market capitalisation

This is the size of the company, as determined by the stock market. It is the share price (again, as of 31 August 2011) multiplied by the number of shares in issue. All companies in this book must be in the All Ordinaries index, which comprises Australia's 500 largest stocks, as measured by market capitalisation.

Price-to-NTA-per-share ratio

The NTA-per-share figure expresses the worth of a company's net tangible assets—that is, its assets minus its liabilities and intangible assets—for each share of the company. The price-to-NTA-per-share ratio relates this figure to the share price.

A ratio of one means that the company is valued exactly according to the value of its assets. A ratio below one suggests that the shares are a bargain, though usually there is a good reason for this. Profits are more important than assets.

Some companies in this book have a negative NTA-per-share figure—as a result of having intangible assets valued at more than their remaining net assets—and a price-to-NTA-per-share ratio cannot be calculated.

See table M, in the second part of this book, for more detail on this ratio.

share-price return

This is the total return you could have received from the stock in the five years to 31 August 2011. It includes reinvested dividends, bonus stock, rights issues and capital gain from the stock's appreciation. It is expressed as a compounded annual rate of return.

Dividend reinvestment plan

A dividend reinvestment plan (DRP) allows shareholders to receive additional shares in their company in place of the dividend. Usually—though not always—these shares are provided at a small discount to the prevailing price, which can make them quite attractive. And of course no broking fees apply.

Around half of all large companies offer such plans. However, they come and go. When a company needs finance it may introduce a DRP When its financing requirements become less pressing it may withdraw it.

The information in this book is based on up-to-date information from the companies at the time of writing. But if you are investing in a particular company in expectation of a DRP be sure to check that it is still on offer. The company's own website will often provide this information.

Price/earnings ratio

The price/earnings ratio (PER) is one of the most popular measures of whether a share is cheap or expensive. It is calculated by dividing the share price—in this case the closing price for 31 August 2011—by the earnings per share figure. Obviously the share price is continually changing, so the PER figures in this book are for guidance only. Many newspapers publish each morning the latest PER for every stock.

Dividend yield

This is the latest full-year dividend expressed as a percentage of the share price. Like the price/earnings ratio, it changes as the share price moves. It is a useful figure, especially for investors who are buying shares for income, as it allows you to compare this income with alternative investments, such as a bank term deposit or a rental property.

Sector comparisons

It is sometimes useful to compare a company's price/earnings ratio and its dividend yield with those of its sector. Figures used in this book are those of the S&P/ASX sectors, again as of 31 August 2011.

Company commentary

Each commentary begins with a brief introduction to the company and its activities. Then follow the highlights of its latest business results. For the majority of the companies these are their June 2011 results, which were issued during July and August 2011. Finally, there is a section on the outlook for the company.

Main table

Here is what you can find in the main table.

Revenues

These are the company's revenues from its business activities, generally the sale of products or services. It includes the revenues from discontinued businesses. However, it does not usually include additional income from such sources as investments, bank interest or the sale of assets. If the information is available, the revenues figure has been broken down into the major product areas.

Earnings before interest and taxation

Earnings before interest and taxation (EBIT) is the firm's profit from its operations before the payment of interest and tax. This figure is often used by analysts examining a company. The reason is that some companies have borrowed extensively to finance their activities, while others have opted for alternative means. By expressing profits before interest payments it is possible to compare more precisely the performance of these companies. The net interest figure—interest payments minus interest receipts—has been used for this calculation.

EBIT margin

This is the company's EBIT expressed as a percentage of its revenues. It is a gauge of a company's efficiency. A high EBIT margin suggests that a company is achieving success in keeping its costs low.

Gross margin

The gross margin is the company's gross profit as a percentage of its sales. The gross profit is the amount left over after deducting from a company's sales figure its cost of sales; that is, its manufacturing costs or, for a retailer, the cost of purchasing the goods it sells. The cost of goods sold figure does not usually include marketing or administration costs.

As there are different ways of calculating the cost of goods sold figure, this ratio is best used for year-to-year comparisons of a single company's efficiency, rather than in comparing one company with another.

Not all companies present a cost of goods sold figure, so a gross margin ratio is not given for every stock in this book.

The revenues for some companies include a mix of sales and services. Where a breakdown is possible, the gross profit figure will relate to sales only.

Profit before tax/profit after tax

The profit before tax figure is simply the EBIT figure minus net interest payments. The profit after tax figure is, of course, the company's profit after the payment of tax, and also after the deduction of minority interests. Minority interests are that part of a company's profit that is claimed by outside interests, usually the other shareholders in a subsidiary which is not fully owned by the company. Many companies do not have any minority interests, and for those that do it is generally a tiny figure. The figures also incorporate the profits (or losses) from discontinued businesses.

Where possible, I have adjusted the profit figures to exclude non-recurring profits and losses, which are often referred to as significant items. It is for this reason that the profit figures in *Top Stocks* sometimes differ from those in the financial media or on financial websites, where profit figures normally include significant items.

Significant items are those that have an abnormal impact on profits, even though they happen in the normal course of the company's operations.

Examples are the profit from the sale of a business, or losses from a business restructuring, the write-down of property, an inventory write-down, a bad-debt loss or a write-off for research and development expenditure.

Significant items are controversial. It is often a matter of subjective judgement as to what is included and what is excluded. After analysing the accounts of hundreds of companies, while writing the various editions of this book, it is clear that different companies use quite widely varying interpretations of what is significant.

Further, when they do report a significant item there is no consistency as to whether they use pre-tax figures or after-tax figures. Some report both, making it easy to adjust the profit figures in the tables in this book. But difficulties arise when only one figure—generally pre-tax—is given for significant items.

In normal circumstances most companies do not report significant items. But investors should be aware of this issue. It sometimes causes consternation for readers of *Top Stocks* to find that a particular profit figure in this book is substantially different from that given by some other source. My publisher occasionally receives anguished emails from readers enquiring why a profit figure in this book is so different from that reported elsewhere. In virtually all cases the reason is that I have stripped out a significant item.

Earnings per share

Earnings per share is the after-tax profit divided by the number of shares. Because the profit figure is for a 12-month period the number of shares used is a weighted average of those on issue during the year. This number is provided by the company in its annual report and its results announcements.

Cash flow per share

The cash flow per share ratio tells—in theory—how much actual cash the company has generated from its operations.

In fact, the ratio in this book is not exactly a true measure of cash flow. It is simply the company's depreciation and amortisation figures for the year added to the after-tax profit, and then divided by a weighted average of the number of shares. Depreciation and amortisation are expenses that do not actually utilise cash, so can be added back to after-tax profit to give a kind of indication of the company's cash flow.

By contrast, a true cash flow—including such items as newly raised capital and money received from the sale of assets—would require quite complex calculations based on the company's statement of cash flows.

However, many analysts use the ratio as I present it, because it is easy to calculate, and it is certainly a useful guide to how much funding the company has available from its operations.

Dividend

The dividend figure is the total for the year, interim and final. It does not include special dividends. The level of franking is also provided.

Net tangible assets per share

The NTA-per-share figure tells the theoretical value of the company—per share—if all assets were sold and then all liabilities paid. It is very much a theoretical figure, as there is no guarantee that corporate assets are really worth the price put on them in the balance sheet. Intangible assets such as goodwill, newspaper mastheads and patent rights are excluded because of the difficulty in putting a sales price on them, and also because they may in fact not have much value if separated from the company.

As already noted, some companies in this book have a negative NTA, due to the fact that their intangible assets are so great, and no figure can be listed for them.

Where a company's most recent financial results are the half-year figures, these are used to calculate this ratio.

Interest cover

The interest cover ratio indicates how many times a company could make its interest payments from its pre-tax profit. A rough rule of thumb says a ratio of at least three times is desirable. Below that and fast-rising interest rates could imperil profits. The ratio is derived by dividing the EBIT figure by net interest payments. Some fortunate companies have interest receipts that are higher than their interest payments, which turns the interest cover into a negative figure, and so it is not listed.

Return on equity

Return on equity is the after-tax profit expressed as a percentage of the shareholders' equity. In theory, it is the amount that the company's managers have made for you—the shareholder—on your money. The shareholders' equity figure used is an average for the year.

Debt-to-equity ratio

This ratio is one of the best-known measures of a company's debt levels. It is total borrowings minus the company's cash holdings, expressed as a percentage of the shareholders' equity. Some companies have no debt at all, or their cash position is greater than their level of debt, which results in a negative ratio, so no figure is listed for them.

Where a company's most recent financial results are the half-year figures, these are used to calculate this ratio.

Current ratio

The current ratio is simply the company's current assets divided by its current liabilities. Current assets are cash or assets that can, in theory, be converted quickly into cash. Current liabilities are normally those payable within a year. Thus, the current ratio measures the ability of a company to repay in a hurry its short-term debt, should the need arise. The surplus of current assets over current liabilities is referred to as the company's working capital.

Where a company's most recent financial results are the half-year figures, these are used to calculate this ratio.

Banks

The tables for the banks are somewhat different from those for most other companies. EBIT and debt-to-equity ratios have little relevance for them, as they have such high interest payments (to their customers). Other differences are examined below.

Operating income

Operating income is used instead of sales revenues. Operating income is the bank's net interest income—that is, its total interest income minus its interest expense—plus other income, such as bank fees, fund management fees and income from businesses such as corporate finance and insurance.

Net interest income

Banks borrow money—that is, they accept deposits from savers—and they lend it to businesses, home buyers and other borrowers. They charge the borrowers more than they pay those who deposit money with them, and the difference is known as net interest income.

Operating expenses

These are all the costs of running the bank. Banks have high operating expenses, and one of the keys to profit growth is cutting these expenses. Add the provision for doubtful debts to operating expenses, then deduct the total from operating income, and you get the pre-tax profit.

Non-interest income to total income

Banks have traditionally made most of their income from savers and from lending out money.

But increasingly this is becoming a commodity business, with a growing number of entrants offering higher interest rates to savers and lower rates to borrowers. In response the big banks are working to diversify into new fields, and this ratio is an indication of their success.

Cost-to-income ratio

As noted, the banks have high costs—numerous branches, expensive computer systems, many staff and so on—and they are all striving to reduce these. The cost-to-income ratio expresses their expenses as a percentage of their operating income, and is one of the ratios most often used as a gauge of efficiency. The lower the ratio drops the better.

Return on assets

Banks have enormous assets, in sharp contrast to, say, a high-tech start-up whose main physical assets may be little more than a set of computers. So the return on assets—the after-tax profit expressed as a percentage of the year's average total assets—is another measure of efficiency.

Part I

The companies

Adelaide Brighton Limited

ABC

<www.adbri.com.au>

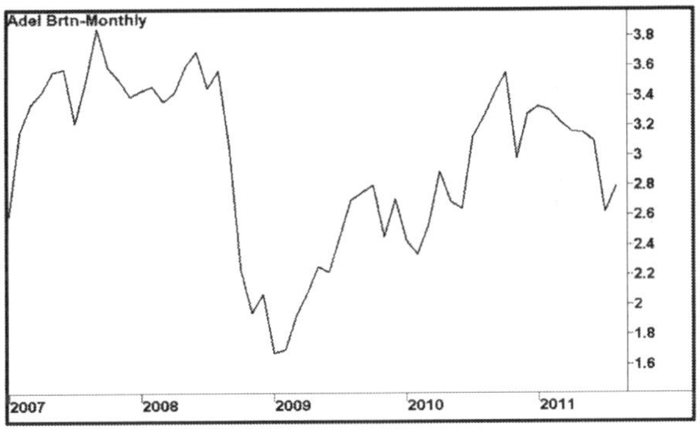

Share price ($)	2.79
12-month high ($)	3.69
12-month low ($)	2.22
Market capitalisation ($mn)	1775.3
Price-to-NTA-per-share ratio	2.4
5-year share price return (% p.a.)	10.4
Dividend reinvestment plan	No

Sector: Materials	Company	Sector
Price/earnings ratio (times)	11.7	12.3
Dividend yield (%)	5.9	2.2

Adelaide-based Adelaide Brighton, established in 1882, is one of Australia's leaders in the production and supply of construction materials, notably cement and lime. In addition, its Hy-Tec business and its Mawson Group joint venture are suppliers of pre-mixed concrete, and it has a business as a supplier of aggregates, through Mawson Group and Hurd Haulage. The Adbri Masonry operation is a leading producer of concrete masonry products. Adelaide Brighton's major customers include the residential, non-residential and engineering construction sectors, as well as the infrastructure, alumina, steel and mining industries.

Latest business results (June 2011, half year)

Sales and profits fell as the company was hit by a combination of a weak housing construction market, the loss of sales of 100000 tonnes of cement to a major customer in Western Australia and the temporary suspension of operations by a major lime customer in the Northern Territory. Cement and lime together comprise about 70 per cent of the company's turnover. Partially offsetting the decline was strong demand from the mining sector. Concrete and aggregates demand was generally firm, in line with an improving east coast market, and the company was able to raise some prices. But demand for concrete masonry products was down, with continued weakness in Queensland exacerbated by the impact of floods. During the period the company paid $47 million for four acquisitions in the concrete, quarry and aggregate businesses.

Outlook

Adelaide Brighton is a key supplier to the construction industry, and its fortunes are heavily dependent on trends in this sector, with mining and engineering also important. It says that it expects a modest recovery in business in the 2011 second half, and forecasts a 2011 after-tax profit of $144 million to $152 million. It also believes it will be able to realise price increases in the 2011 second half in lime, concrete, aggregates and concrete masonry. Looking longer term, it is hopeful that any interest rate cut might stimulate housing demand. However, it sees a possible $5 million negative impact on after-tax profit from the first year of a new carbon tax. It is spending $60 million to expand cement-milling capacity in South Australia by 750000 tonnes annually. This initiative is expected to generate annual EBIT of $10 million to $12 million from 2013. A $34 million project in Western Australia will boost annual lime capacity by 10000 tonnes and improve efficiency.

Year to 31 December	2009	2010
Revenues ($mn)	987.2	1072.9
EBIT ($mn)	185.3	216.2
EBIT margin (%)	18.8	20.2
Gross margin (%)	35.7	37.8
Profit before tax ($mn)	168.6	202.2
Profit after tax ($mn)	123.1	151.4
Earnings per share (¢)	20.4	23.8
Cash flow per share (¢)	29.8	32.2
Dividend (¢)	13.5	16.5
Percentage franked	100	100
Interest cover (times)	11.1	15.4
Return on equity (%)	15.5	16.6

Half year to 30 June	2010	2011
Revenues ($mn)	519.4	507.9
Profit before tax ($mn)	92.1	84.5
Profit after tax ($mn)	68.8	61.5
Earnings per share (¢)	10.8	9.7
Dividend (¢)	7.5	7.5
Percentage franked	100	100
Net tangible assets per share ($)	1.16	1.17
Debt-to-equity ratio (%)	19.8	23.9
Current ratio	2.2	2.5

5

Amcom Telecommunications Ltd

AMM

<www.amcom.com.au>

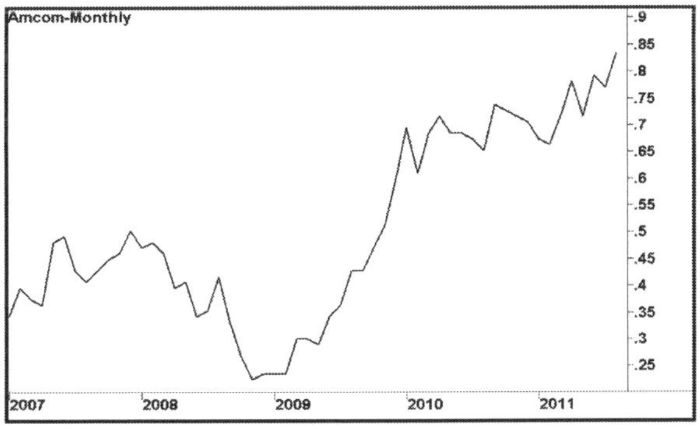

Share price ($)	0.84
12-month high ($)	0.90
12-month low ($)	0.57
Market capitalisation ($mn)	605.7
Price-to-NTA-per-share ratio	4.3
5-year share price return (% p.a.)	25.9
Dividend reinvestment plan	No

Sector: Telecommunication services	Company	Sector
Price/earnings ratio (times)	23.2	12.5
Dividend yield (%)	1.9	8.7

Perth-based Amcom Telecommunications, founded in 1988, owns and operates over 2100 kilometres of fibre optic network in Perth, Adelaide, Darwin and Alice Springs, with additional links to Melbourne, Sydney, Canberra and Brisbane, providing high-speed data, voice and internet services. Its Amnet business provides broadband internet services to domestic companies and the small business sector, and the company also offers a range of IT-related business services. It has sold or distributed to its own shareholders its 20.4 per cent stake in the internet and telephone service provider iiNet.

Latest business results (June 2011, full year)

Amcom posted another strong rise in revenues and profits. Some of this reflected dividends and capital gain from the sale of part of the company's holding in iiNet. However, even excluding this, the after-tax profit from the company's own operations rose a healthy 31 per cent. The result also incorporated a full year of business from Amcom IP Tel—formerly IP Systems, a provider of voice, video and data communication services—which the company acquired in May 2010. Amcom makes the bulk of its profits from its Fibre business, which provides high-speed data transmission products to companies and government agencies, with revenues up 23 per cent and profits up 22 per cent. The smaller Business Services division also enjoyed very strong growth. However, the Amnet business was hit by the intense competition in the residential broadband market, with revenues down 7 per cent and profits tumbling 30 per cent.

Outlook

Amcom occupies a small but strong position in the high-growth fibre optic business, and is forecasting further double-digit profit growth in the June 2012 year. In particular, it expects a solid contribution from a $20 million, five-year contract with the Northern Territory government to provide high-speed services to government agencies and schools in Darwin and Alice Springs. In mid 2011 it announced a $9 million contract to provide hosted cloud computer services to the University of Western Australia, and it views this as providing a platform for some sustained strong growth in the high-potential cloud computing market. The company also sees the new National Broadband Network as offering more growth opportunities, though with the risk that it will also permit new competitors into the market. Amcom has been cited as a possible takeover target for a larger telecommunications company, which has helped boost the share price.

Year to 30 June	2010	2011
Revenues ($mn)	62.2	86.7

Year to 30 June	2010	2011
Fibre (%)	72	63
Business Services (%)	8	23
Amnet (%)	20	13
EBIT ($mn)	23.4	32.2
EBIT margin (%)	37.7	37.1
Profit before tax ($mn)	22.7	31.0
Profit after tax ($mn)	18.4	26.1
Earnings per share (¢)	2.9	3.6
Cash flow per share (¢)	4	4.8
Dividend (¢)	1.4	1.6
Percentage franked	100	100
Net tangible assets per share ($)	0.16	0.20
Interest cover (times)	33.1	27.4
Return on equity (%)	14.3	16.7
Debt-to-equity ratio (%)	0.6	–
Current ratio	1.3	3.5

Ansell Limited

ANN

<www.ansell.com>

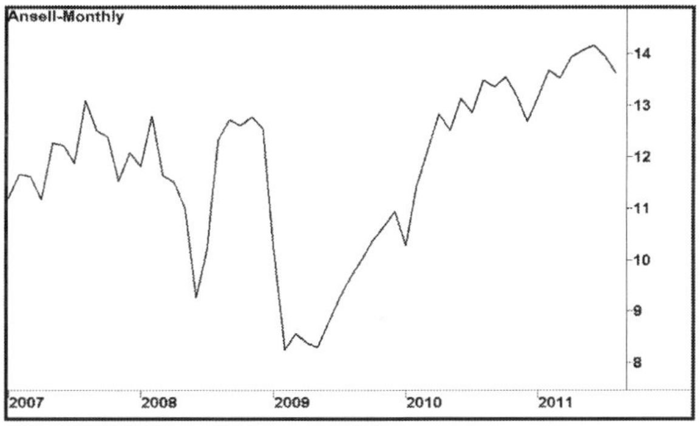

Share price ($)	13.62
12-month high ($)	14.70
12-month low ($)	11.82
Market capitalisation ($mn)	1811.6
Price-to-NTA-per-share ratio	5.6
5-year share price return (% p.a.)	10.5
Dividend reinvestment plan	No

Sector: Health care	Company	Sector
Price/earnings ratio (times)	14.7	17.5
Dividend yield (%)	2.4	2.6

Melbourne-based Ansell has roots that stretch back to the manufacture of pneumatic bicycle tyres in the

19th century. It is today a global leader in a variety of safety and healthcare products. It makes a wide range of examination and surgical gloves for the medical profession. It also makes gloves and other hand and arm protective products for industrial applications, along with household gloves. In addition, it is a prominent global producer of condoms. It has production facilities in many countries, and more than 85 per cent of company revenue derives from abroad. Though based in Australia, the company has its operational headquarters in the US.

Latest business results (June 2011, full year)

Ansell reports its results in US dollars, and on that basis sales and profits recorded a double-digit increase. It also provides Australian-dollar figures—used in this book—and on that basis sales were down and the after-tax profit only edged up. This was an excellent result in the face of a US$50 million hit from rising raw material prices, especially natural rubber latex. The Industrial division—which generated 39 per cent of revenues and 56 per cent of EBIT—was especially strong, with sales jumping 19 per cent on the back of buoyant demand from Europe, Brazil and China, and a big jump in sales to Australian mining companies. However, the second-largest division,

Medical, achieved just a 2 per cent rise in sales, and profits fell, with the company unable to offset rising rubber costs. The Sexual Wellness division saw sales up 18 per cent, with EBIT soaring 59 per cent, although this partly reflected a rebound from manufacturing and marketing problems in the previous year. The New Verticals division is responsible for a wide range of innovative high-tech gloves for specific applications, such as food processing, construction and military. Sales rose 6 per cent, but EBIT crashed 77 per cent, blamed particularly on raw material price rises and development costs.

Outlook

Ansell sees its growth momentum continuing, despite the pressure of high commodity prices, and forecasts a June 2012 EPS rise of 6 per cent to 12 per cent, in US dollars. In particular, emerging markets are providing excellent opportunities. The company has been steadily withdrawing from low-margin businesses, and it continues a major restructure of its global operations. It is working to reduce latex consumption. With no net debt, it is also seeking strategic acquisitions.

Year to 30 June	2010	2011
Revenues ($mn)	1230.6	1219.8
Industrial (%)	37	39
Medical (%)	32	30

Year to 30 June	2010	2011
Sexual Wellness (%)	16	17
New Verticals (%)	15	14
EBIT ($mn)	143.1	138.8
EBIT margin (%)	11.6	11.4
Gross margin (%)	41.6	38.9
Profit before tax ($mn)	133.4	134.7
Profit after tax ($mn)	119.4	122.7
Earnings per share (¢)	89.6	92.4
Cash flow per share (¢)	109.1	106.9
Dividend (¢)	30.5	33
Percentage franked	0	0
Net tangible assets per share ($)	2.22	2.44
Interest cover (times)	14.8	33.9
Return on equity (%)	18.7	18.7
Debt-to-equity ratio (%)	8.8	–
Current ratio	2.1	1.5

ANZ Banking Group Limited

ANZ

<www.anz.com.au>

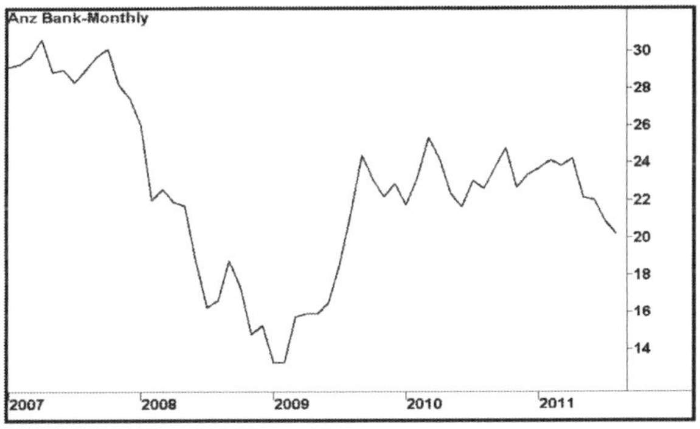

Share price ($)	20.18
12-month high ($)	25.96
12-month low ($)	17.63
Market capitalisation ($mn)	52395.9
Price-to-NTA-per-share ratio	1.8
5-year share price return (% p.a.)	−0.3
Dividend reinvestment plan	Yes

Sector: Financials	Company	Sector
Price/earnings ratio (times)	11.3	10.8
Dividend yield (%)	6.2	6.8

Melbourne-based ANZ has its roots in the establishment of the Bank of Australasia in London in 1835.

It is today one of Australia's four banking giants. It owns the finance companies Esanda and Landmark, and the online stockbroker E*Trade Australia. It is a market leader in New Zealand banking, and it is also active throughout Asia and the Pacific region. Altogether it has a presence in more than 30 countries, including a major technology and back-office operation in Bangalore, India.

Latest business results (March 2011, half year)

ANZ maintained the rebound of a year earlier, with another rise in profits. This in part reflected a further decline in the bank's provisioning for bad debts, along with some tight cost control, which more than offset a slowdown in growth in many of its mainline operations. Total customer deposits were up 4 per cent, while lending grew 2 per cent. The bank's domestic business was generally firm, with single-digit growth across most areas of retail operations, although commercial business was mixed, and Australia-region profits rose just 2 per cent. International business (excluding New Zealand) saw a 12 per cent rise in profits, with customer deposits up 22 per cent and lending up 19 per cent. ANZ enjoyed a particularly vibrant result from its institutional global markets business. Economic recovery in New Zealand helped business there to a 19 per cent jump in profits.

Outlook

ANZ has adopted a strategy of growth through expansion in Asia, with an eventual aim that the region should provide 30 per cent of revenues and $1.5 billion in annual after-tax profit. In 2009 it paid Royal Bank of Scotland $687 million for a string of Asian banking assets that included 54 bank branches, doubling its network in the region and bringing customer numbers there from one million to three million. This strategy has the added advantage of providing access to funding, thanks to strong growth in Asian customer deposits, at a time when new funds are not always easy to acquire. As a result ANZ enjoys a higher net interest margin than rivals—2.47 per cent, compared with an average of 2.26 per cent for the major banks. However, the bank lags its three major rivals in wealth management. A new relationship with UBS is intended to leverage the Swiss financial giant's global expertise in investment management, research, asset allocation and advisory services to boost ANZ's domestic operations.

Year to 30 September	2009	2010
Operating income ($mn)	13610.0	15692.0
Net interest income ($mn)	9808.0	10869.0
Operating expenses ($mn)	6225.0	7304.0
Profit before tax ($mn)	4380.0	6601.0
Profit after tax ($mn)	2943.0	4501.0

Year to 30 September	2009	2010
Earnings per share (¢)	132.5	179.4
Dividend (¢)	102	126
Percentage franked	100	100
Non-interest income to total income (%)	27.9	30.7
Cost-to-income ratio (%)	45.7	46.5
Return on equity (%)	10.0	13.5
Return on assets (%)	0.6	0.9

Half year to 31 March	2010	2011
Operating income ($mn)	7217.0	8605.0
Profit before tax ($mn)	2753.0	3904.0
Profit after tax ($mn)	1925.0	2664.0
Earnings per share (¢)	76.8	104.2
Dividend (¢)	52	64
Percentage franked	100	100
Net tangible assets per share ($)	10.34	10.95

APN News & Media Limited

APN

<www.apn.com.au>

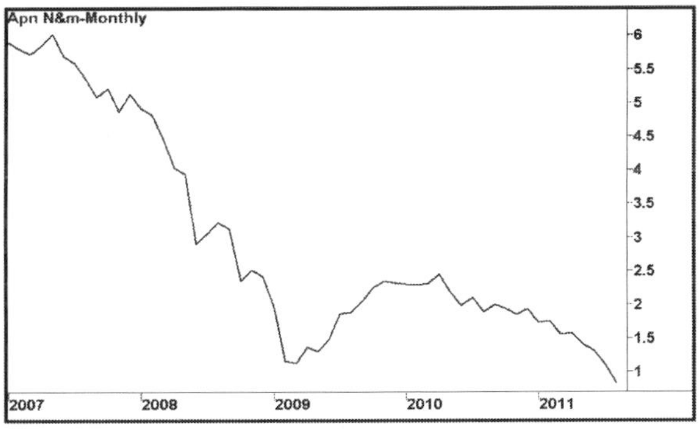

Share price ($)	0.83
12-month high ($)	2.06
12-month low ($)	0.74
Market capitalisation ($mn)	513.4
Price-to-NTA-per-share ratio	–
5-year share price return (% p.a.)	–24.6
Dividend reinvestment plan	Yes

Sector: Consumer discretionary	Company	Sector
Price/earnings ratio (times)	5.1	13.1
Dividend yield (%)	14.5	3.5

Sydney-based APN is a 32 per cent-owned subsidiary of Independent News & Media plc of Ireland.

It is a leading publisher of newspapers in Australia and New Zealand, with 22 daily and more than 100 non-daily titles. These include the *New Zealand Herald,* New Zealand's largest newspaper. It is also a prominent radio broadcaster involved in two joint venture companies, Australian Radio Network and New Zealand's The Radio Network, with leading US broadcaster Clear Channel Communications. APN is also a leader in outdoor advertising—including advertising on buses and trams, street furniture and billboards—with operations in Australia, New Zealand, Hong Kong and Indonesia. In addition, it operates a growing internet business in Australia and New Zealand.

Latest business results (June 2011, half year)

Profits plunged with revenues little changed, as the company's businesses were hit by rocky economies and a slowdown in consumer spending. Both its Australian and New Zealand newspaper operations saw revenues edge down, with profits sharply lower. The company's Australian titles are concentrated in regional Queensland and northern New South Wales, where business was hit by floods and by declining tourist inflows. New Zealand titles were hurt by a weak economy and the Christchurch earthquakes, despite a growing circulation for the flagship *New Zealand Herald.*

The New Zealand radio business recorded a modest rise in profits, though Australian radio edged down. The main bright spot for the company was its outdoor advertising, responsible for nearly a quarter of total turnover. Revenues rose 11 per cent and profits soared more than 80 per cent, with particular strength in billboards and public transport advertising. In addition to the results in the table, APN announced a $156 million writedown of its New Zealand newspapers.

Outlook

APN is one of several media companies that are struggling as people are buying fewer newspapers, and, at the same time, much classified advertising is migrating to the internet. Meanwhile, other advertising suffers from the decline in consumer spending. In response, the company has been working to rationalise its operations, including the closure of some loss-making titles, staff layoffs and a reorganisation of its printing facilities. It sees good growth continuing in its outdoor advertising business, and plans the introduction of a strong pipeline of new digital products. It also expects solid growth to continue for its online businesses, especially in New Zealand where it is a market leader.

Year to 31 December	2009	2010
Revenues ($mn)	1030.7	1059.1
EBIT ($mn)	189.0	205.4

Year to 31 December	2009	2010
EBIT margin (%)	18.3	19.4
Profit before tax ($mn)	138.4	155.6
Profit after tax ($mn)	92.9	98.2
Earnings per share (¢)	16.8	16.4
Cash flow per share (¢)	24.1	22.9
Dividend (¢)	4	12
Percentage franked	100	17
Interest cover (times)	3.7	4.1
Return on equity (%)	10.6	10.4

Half year to 30 June	2010	2011
Revenues ($mn)	507.4	508.1
Profit before tax ($mn)	62.2	38.8
Profit after tax ($mn)	39.5	21.8
Earnings per share (¢)	6.6	3.6
Dividend (¢)	5	3.5
Percentage franked	0	100
Net tangible assets per share ($)	–	–
Debt-to-equity ratio (%)	58.6	60.6
Current ratio	1.5	1.2

ARB Corporation Limited

ARP

<www.arb.com.au>

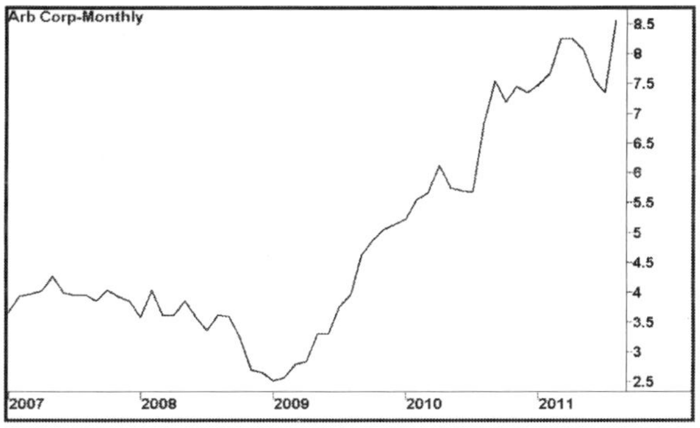

Share price ($)	8.56
12-month high ($)	8.60
12-month low ($)	6.54
Market capitalisation ($mn)	620.4
Price-to-NTA-per-share ratio	5.3
5-year share price return (% p.a.)	26.5
Dividend reinvestment plan	No

Sector: Consumer discretionary	Company	Sector
Price/earnings ratio (times)	16.4	13.1
Dividend yield (%)	2.7	3.5

Melbourne-based ARB is a prominent manufacturer of specialty automotive accessories, and an international leader in the design and production of specialised equipment for four-wheel-drive (4WD) vehicles. It has gained particular renown for its Air Locker air-operated locking differential system. It also makes or distributes a wide range of other products, including bull bars, roof racks, tow bars, canopies, the Old Man Emu range of suspension products and a variety of touring and camping accessories. It operates a network of 40 ARB-brand stores throughout Australia. It has established manufacturing facilities in Thailand and a sales and distribution company in the US. It also exports to more than 100 countries.

Latest business results (June 2011, full year)

Once again ARB produced a superb result, despite the challenging economy and a global slowdown in discretionary consumer spending. Domestic business was the key, with 15 per cent growth in sales, following 29 per cent growth in the previous year. In addition, it expanded its retail network, with the opening of a new ARB-brand store in Queensland. Export sales rose by nearly 13 per cent, twice as fast as in the previous year, but once again the strong dollar meant that revenues received by the company were on par with the previous year, and the company's US operation moved from a small profit to a small loss. Altogether, the domestic aftermarket accounted for 64 per cent of total sales, with exports 23 per cent and OEM sales to vehicle manufacturers 13 per cent.

Outlook

ARB has become a superb performer in the small stock sector, thanks to its ability to sail through the economic storms with enhanced profits. It is a particular beneficiary of the firm Australian car market, and, in particular, growing demand for 4WD vehicles. In the year to June 2011, domestic 4WD sales rose 6 per cent, while total vehicle sales fell 1 per cent. Such is their popularity that 4WD vehicles now represent nearly a third of new car sales in Australia. ARB continues to boost its research and development spending and, with its plants in both Australia and Thailand operating at close to full capacity, it is working to increase production ability. With no debt and more than $30 million in cash holdings—up from $20 million a year earlier—it is considering a range of growth opportunities.

Year to 30 June	2010	2011
Revenues ($mn)	228.0	254.2
EBIT ($mn)	44.6	50.4
EBIT margin (%)	19.6	19.8
Gross margin (%)	39.9	41.3
Profit before tax ($mn)	44.8	51.3

Year to 30 June	2010	2011
Profit after tax ($mn)	32.6	37.9
Earnings per share (¢)	46.3	52.2
Cash flow per share (¢)	54.3	60.6
Dividend (¢)	19.5	23
Percentage franked	100	100
Net tangible assets per share ($)	1.39	1.63
Interest cover (times)	–	–
Return on equity (%)	32.1	31.5
Debt-to-equity ratio (%)	–	–
Current ratio	2.5	3.0

ASG Group Limited

ASZ

<www.asggroup.com.au>

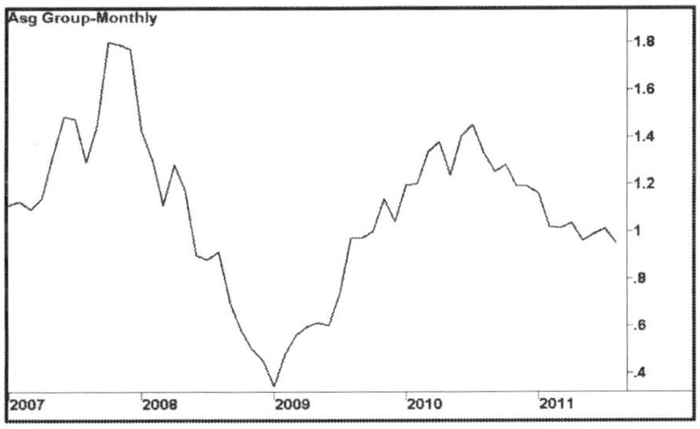

Share price ($)	0.95
12-month high ($)	1.42
12-month low ($)	0.75
Market capitalisation ($mn)	160.7
Price-to-NTA-per-share ratio	–
5-year share price return (% p.a.)	10.5
Dividend reinvestment plan	Yes

Sector: Information technology	Company	Sector
Price/earnings ratio (times)	9.8	18.2
Dividend yield (%)	7.9	3.9

Perth-based ASG, founded in 1996, provides information technology consulting services to corporations and government agencies throughout Australia. Its particular strengths are in application development, IT outsourcing, computer infrastructure, systems integration and the provision of specialist technical services and support.

Latest business results (June 2011, full year)

In an uncertain business environment, ASG reported its 11th straight year of record profits. With profit growth slightly higher than revenues growth, the result indicated the company's continuing success in boosting margins, and this was particularly evident in the second half. There was an excellent contribution from long-term recurring contracts secured in the previous year, as well as from new contracts in strategic growth areas such as the mining and the oil and gas sectors. The company reported that three acquisitions made in the previous year—Capiotech, Courtland Business Solutions and Dowling Consulting—performed well, though did not meet their revenue targets, due to the weak operating environment of these particular businesses. During the year the company completed and commissioned its new data centre in Perth, and it reported that this was already performing ahead of expectations.

Outlook

Much of ASG's income is derived from long-term contracts with blue-chip clients, and is steady and reliable in nature, providing a solid and long-term base of recurring income. Government departments and agencies are particularly prominent among the client base. Nevertheless, in times of economic uncertainty many companies cut back sharply on their IT spending, often postponing major upgrades or new projects, and IT consultants can be among the first to suffer when the economy turns down. Despite the uncertain outlook, ASG expects continuing strong revenue growth from the public sector, especially the federal government, and it also believes it is well placed to win new business from the resources sector, as well as from areas of IT business such as Oracle application services and SAP (systems, applications, products) services. Consequently, the company believes it can deliver further growth in the June 2012 year. It says its recent acquisitions are now fully integrated into its operations, and as a result it is now in a position to bid for larger contracts—those worth up to $500 million—rather than the smaller contracts—up to $100 million in value—that were previously its focus. With just modest debt, the company continues to seek new acquisitions.

Year to 30 June	2010	2011
Revenues ($mn)	120.8	153.3
EBIT ($mn)	16.6	22.4
EBIT margin (%)	13.8	14.6
Profit before tax ($mn)	16.1	21.3
Profit after tax ($mn)	12.3	15.7
Earnings per share (¢)	8.8	9.7
Cash flow per share (¢)	12.3	13.2
Dividend (¢)	6.5	7.5
Percentage franked	100	100
Net tangible assets per share ($)	–	–
Interest cover (times)	28.7	20.8
Return on equity (%)	16.4	16.1
Debt-to-equity ratio (%)	6.8	10.6
Current ratio	1.2	1.4

ASX Limited

ASX

<www.asxgroup.com.au>

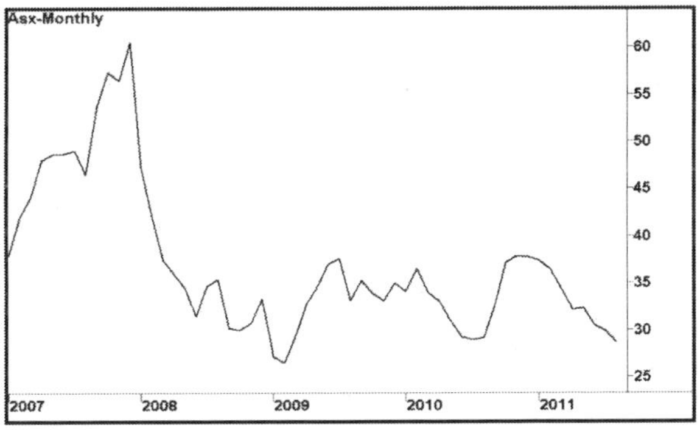

Share price ($)	28.64
12-month high ($)	43.89
12-month low ($)	25.83
Market capitalisation ($mn)	5015.9
Price-to-NTA-per-share ratio	7.1
5-year share price return (% p.a.)	2.2
Dividend reinvestment plan	No

Sector: Financials	Company	Sector
Price/earnings ratio (times)	14.0	10.8
Dividend yield (%)	6.4	6.8

ASX (Australian Securities Exchange) was formed in 1987 through the amalgamation of six independent stock exchanges that formerly operated in the state capital cities. Each of those exchanges had a history of share trading dating back to the 19th century. Though originally a mutual organisation of stockbrokers, in 1998 ASX became a listed company, with its shares traded on its own market. It expanded in 2006 when it merged with the Sydney Futures Exchange. Today it provides primary, secondary and derivative market services, along with clearing, settlement and compliance services. It is also a provider of a range of comprehensive market data.

Latest business results (June 2011, full year)

In a rough year for the markets ASX saw its revenues and profits rise modestly for the second straight year. The company was a beneficiary of the volatility in global financial markets, with a 16.5 per cent jump in revenues for its derivatives businesses. This was particularly due to a sharp rise in futures trades on debt contracts such as the 30-day interbank cash rate futures contract.

The listings and issuer services saw revenues up 3 per cent. There was a big jump in initial public offerings business, with 160 new listings, compared with 93 in the previous year. Cash market revenues—from the trading, clearing and settlement of equities, warrants and interest rate securities—fell 11 per cent. The total number of trades rose 9.1 per cent to 144.3 million, but total turnover of $1.34 trillion was 1.5 per cent down on the previous year.

Outlook

ASX's profits are highly geared to levels of stock market activity, and it is a beneficiary of market volatility, which it expects to continue, possibly for several years. It had hoped to merge with the Singapore Exchange—essentially an $8 billion takeover of ASX by Singapore Exchange—but this was blocked by the government. It is now seeking new directions for its businesses in an era of expanded competition and global consolidation. A new exchange, Chi-X, owned by Japanese stockbroker Nomura Securities, is due to launch in Australia in late 2011. Initially, however, this new exchange will compete directly with ASX only in equity trading, which is around 10 per cent of ASX's revenues. Meanwhile, ASX is exploring new trading instruments, and hopes to play an active role in the government's carbon trading scheme.

Year to 30 June	2010	2011
Revenues ($mn)	588.2	617.6
Derivatives (%)	25	28
Listings and Issuer Services (%)	25	24
Cash Market (%)	26	22

Year to 30 June	2010	2011
Information Services (%)	12	11
EBIT ($mn)	436.8	468.6
EBIT margin (%)	74.3	75.9
Profit before tax ($mn)	466.2	506.2
Profit after tax ($mn)	328.1	356.6
Earnings per share (¢)	190.4	204.0
Cash flow per share (¢)	204.1	218.7
Dividend (¢)	173.1	183.2
Percentage franked	100	100
Net tangible assets per share ($)	3.49	4.01
Interest cover (times)	–	–
Return on equity (%)	11.5	12.0
Debt-to-equity ratio (%)	–	–
Current ratio	1.2	1.3

Ausdrill Limited

ASL

<www.ausdrill.com.au>

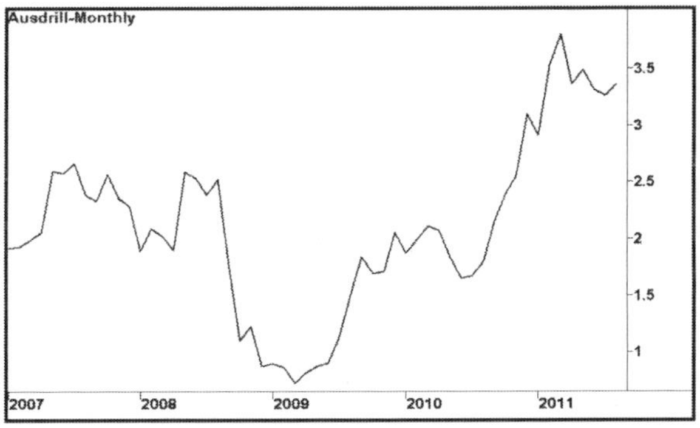

Share price ($)	3.36
12-month high ($)	3.94
12-month low ($)	1.77
Market capitalisation ($mn)	1012.9
Price-to-NTA-per-share ratio	1.6
5-year share price return (% p.a.)	23.5
Dividend reinvestment plan	Yes

Sector: Industrials	Company	Sector
Price/earnings ratio (times)	12.4	11.9
Dividend yield (%)	3.6	5.5

Perth-based Ausdrill, founded in 1987, is a prominent drilling and contract mining company serving the resources industry. Through its Supply Direct subsidiary it is also involved in mining equipment supplies and logistics support, and its Diamond Communications subsidiary is engaged in cable ploughing, horizontal boring and the repair and maintenance of communications networks. It also has a manufacturing business, producing a wide range of drilling accessories. Its MinAnalytical business provides geochemical and precious metals analysis services. As well as its domestic activities it is active in Africa, particularly Ghana.

Latest business results (June 2011, full year)

Ausdrill enjoyed another excellent result, its seventh consecutive record profit. The company's expanding activities, designed to take advantage of the mining boom, lay behind much of the good result, although there was also a full year's contribution from the drilling and blasting company Brandrill, acquired in December 2009. With some 60 per cent of its business geared towards the gold mining sector, Ausdrill is a beneficiary of a soaring gold price and flourishing activity by gold mining companies. It is also winning increased work in the iron ore sector, particularly in the Pilbara. Its contract mining operations in Africa—more than a quarter of total company business—enjoyed a good year, with revenues up 16 per cent and profits doubling, despite the impact of the strong dollar. Ausdrill's manufacturing operations, representing about 12 per cent of its total business, also saw a substantial improvement in revenues and profits, with strong sales of drilling consumables and truck tray bodies.

Outlook

Ausdrill's contract mining services are in high demand and it continues to see its order inflow grow. With a continuing focus on the gold and iron ore sectors, it is targeting June 2012 revenues of $1 billion, with a commensurate increase in profits. It has entered the coal seam gas drilling business through its subsidiary Energy Drilling Australia, and hopes to increase its participation. In July 2011 Ausdrill moved from 50 per cent to 100 per cent ownership of Energy Drilling. It is also considering an entry to the underground contract mining business, possibly through an acquisition. It continues to enjoy growing business in West Africa, and from a base in Tanzania it is working to win contracts in East Africa. However, skill shortages and delays in procuring equipment are hampering some operations, and the high dollar is also denting profits.

Year to 30 June	2010	2011
Revenues ($mn)	631.0	834.6
EBIT ($mn)	80.5	112.9
EBIT margin (%)	12.8	13.5
Profit before tax ($mn)	64.7	99.5
Profit after tax ($mn)	48.3	73.4

Year to 30 June	2010	2011
Earnings per share (¢)	23.7	27.1
Cash flow per share (¢)	58.0	57.6
Dividend (¢)	11	12
Percentage franked	100	100
Net tangible assets per share ($)	1.78	2.06
Interest cover (times)	5.1	8.4
Return on equity (%)	12.0	12.7
Debt-to-equity ratio (%)	19.6	12.7
Current ratio	1.7	1.7

Austbrokers Holdings Limited

AUB

<www.austbrokers.com.au>

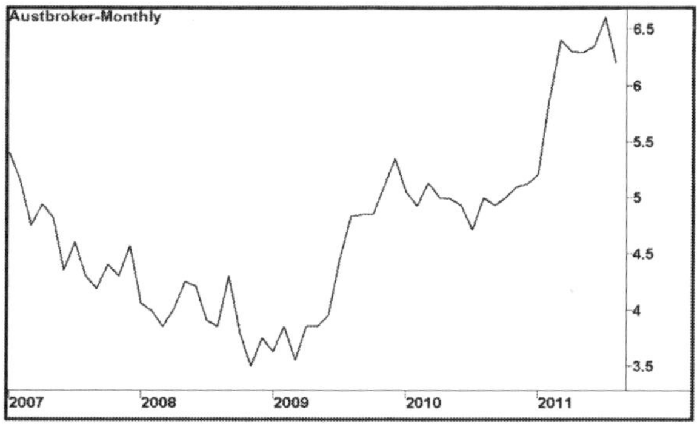

Share price ($)	6.20
12-month high ($)	6.60
12-month low ($)	4.72
Market capitalisation ($mn)	338.9
Price-to-NTA-per-share ratio	5.1
5-year share price return (% p.a.)	20.4
Dividend reinvestment plan	No

Sector: Financials	Company	Sector
Price/earnings ratio (times)	15.6	10.8
Dividend yield (%)	4.1	6.8

Sydney-based Austbrokers was established in 1985 and operates a network of 41 insurance brokers at more than 110 locations throughout Australia. It holds an equity stake of at least 50 per cent in each business, usually in partnership with the original owners. As well as insurance broking it is also involved in related financial services activity, including financial planning. It also operates the Austagencies underwriting agency business, which operates in many specialised areas of the insurance business. It has become one of the four largest insurance broking networks in Australia.

Latest business results (June 2011, full year)

Once again Austbrokers reported an excellent result, with a further solid rise in revenues and profits, thanks to business growth initiatives and to the impact of 13 bolt-on acquisitions during the year. Total commission and fee income was up 9 per cent, with broker network expenses up 7.9 per cent. The company's small underwriting business boosted fee and commission income by 32.2 per cent and achieved profit growth of 23.5 per cent, thanks especially to acquisitions.

Outlook

Austbrokers has achieved considerable success with its model of buying a stake in a broking house, but, in most cases, continuing to operate it with the original owners. This has allowed the businesses to preserve their local identity and management, while benefiting from the support of being part of a large group. The company is able to help its members develop their businesses through growth initiatives, including the addition of new products, and sometimes through appropriate bolt-on acquisitions. It has established the Austbrokers Business Centre to provide back-office services, and this is now servicing many of its businesses. Austbrokers' revenues are largely derived from fees and commissions on the insurance policies it arranges, so its profits are geared to premium rates, the amounts insured and general economic activity. The company has expressed concern that a slowing economy could damage business confidence, especially among the small-company sector, leading to a decline in its activity. Nevertheless, it believes its operations are generally quite resistant to changing economic conditions, and it expects continuing organic growth and further acquisitions, along with some premium increases, to deliver after-tax profit growth of 5 per cent to 10 per cent in the June 2012 year. The company had more than $67 million in net cash holdings at June 2011.

Year to 30 June	2010	2011
Revenues ($mn)	87.1	92.3
EBIT ($mn)	26.9	30.1
EBIT margin (%)	30.9	32.6

Year to 30 June	2010	2011
Profit before tax ($mn)	27.2	32.1
Profit after tax ($mn)	18.2	21.4
Earnings per share (¢)	35.3	39.6
Cash flow per share (¢)	43.5	47.0
Dividend (¢)	22.5	25.5
Percentage franked	100	100
Net tangible assets per share ($)	0.95	1.21
Interest cover (times)	–	–
Return on equity (%)	16.1	16.2
Debt-to-equity ratio (%)	–	–
Current ratio	1.2	1.2

Austin Engineering Limited

ANG

<www.austineng.com.au>

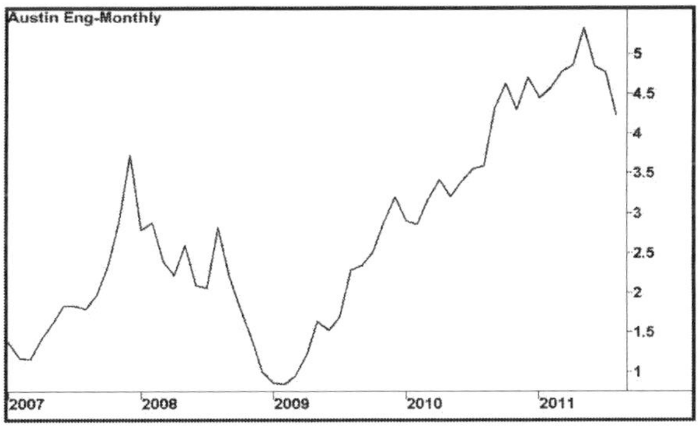

Share price ($)	4.23
12-month high ($)	5.45
12-month low ($)	3.14
Market capitalisation ($mn)	304.0
Price-to-NTA-per-share ratio	9.3
5-year share price return (% p.a.)	59.9
Dividend reinvestment plan	No

Sector: Industrials	Company	Sector
Price/earnings ratio (times)	13.9	11.9
Dividend yield (%)	2.7	5.5

Austin Engineering, based in Brisbane and founded in 1982, is a leader in the engineering and fabrication of products for the mining, energy and aluminium industries. Its JEC-brand products include excavator buckets, wheel loaders, water tanks, fuel modules and tyre handling equipment, and its Pilbara Hire business provides repair and maintenance services. Since the 2007 acquisition of Westech in the US it has become one of the world's largest designers and manufacturers of mining dump truck bodies. It also manufactures dump trucks in Chile, and is expanding this business elsewhere. In addition, it has started operations in Indonesia, and it runs a joint venture in Oman supplying the aluminium industry.

Latest business results (June 2011, full year)

A strengthening mining services sector, along with several acquisitions during the year, delivered another solid result to Austin. Australian operations, responsible for about three-quarters of company turnover, generated some excellent profit growth, with particular strength in the Bowen Basin. However, Hunter Valley operations were affected by a loss-making performance from the new Phillips Engineering business. The company continues to make inroads to key Western Australian markets, and the July 2010 acquisition of Pilbara Hire has helped it win several large contracts. The US delivered a strong result in a weak economy, but the new Chilean business struck production problems, and profits there slumped.

Mideast profits also fell sharply, due to the completion in the previous year of some major work.

Outlook

Austin's business is heavily geared to the resources industry, and it continues to see orders rise strongly, especially as it operates in niche markets, with just limited global competition. It sees particular potential in South America, and reports that, although its strategy there has fallen behind schedule, it expects eventually that South American profits will exceed those derived in Australia. It is expanding its Chilean operations and is building a new plant in Colombia. It is also in negotiations concerning a planned expansion to Peru, where it has already won a major contract, and to Brazil, where it also has business. In Indonesia it has been constructing a new facility, and has already won a large contract for the supply of 60 dump truck trays. It continues to seek out further acquisition opportunities, though at the same time Austin has been spoken of as a possible takeover target for heavy engineering company Bradken.

Year to 30 June	2010	2011
Revenues ($mn)	143.3	205.9
EBIT ($mn)	26.5	31.5
EBIT margin (%)	18.5	15.3
Profit before tax ($mn)	26.5	30.3
Profit after tax ($mn)	19.3	21.5
Earnings per share (¢)	28.3	30.4
Cash flow per share (¢)	32.0	35.5

Year to 30 June	2010	2011
Dividend (¢)	9.5	11.5
Percentage franked	100	100
Net tangible assets per share ($)	0.65	0.46
Interest cover (times)	616.6	25.0
Return on equity (%)	27.8	22.5
Debt-to-equity ratio (%)	2.5	13.2
Current ratio	2.1	1.4

BHP Billiton Limited

BHP

<www.bhpbilliton.com>

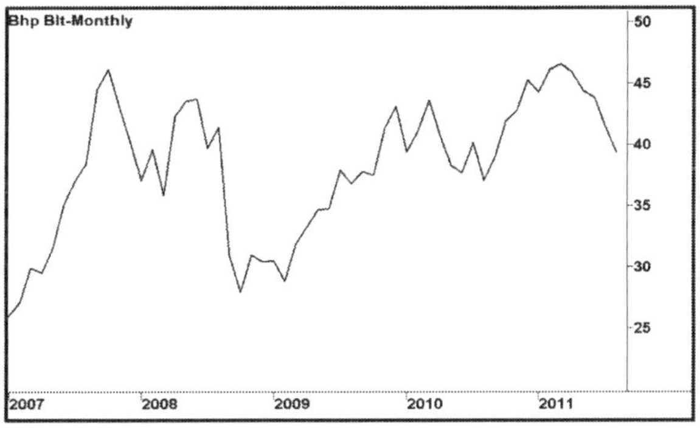

Share price ($)	39.35
12-month high ($)	49.81
12-month low ($)	34.81
Market capitalisation ($mn)	126372.2
Price-to-NTA-per-share ratio	4.0
5-year share price return (% p.a.)	9.8
Dividend reinvestment plan	No

Sector: Materials	Company	Sector
Price/earnings ratio (times)	9.4	12.3
Dividend yield (%)	2.5	2.2

BHP Billiton is the world's largest diversified resources company. It has more than 100 operations in approximately 25 countries, and occupies industry leader or near industry leader positions in major commodity businesses, including aluminium, energy coal and metallurgical coal, copper, manganese, iron ore, uranium, nickel, silver and titanium minerals, along with substantial interests in oil, gas, liquefied natural gas and diamonds. It has acquired US shale gas group Petrohawk Energy.

Latest business results (June 2011, full year)

BHP announced a stupendous result, with the largest profit ever recorded in Australian corporate history. Note that BHP reports its results in US dollars. The Australian dollar figures in this book—converted at prevailing exchange rates—are for guidance only. The boom in Chinese steel production was the major contributing factor, with iron ore revenues up 83.2 per cent and EBIT soaring 122.1 per cent. Though just 28 per cent of company turnover, iron ore represented more than 40 per cent of profit. Energy coal was also strong, with sales up 29.1 per cent and EBIT jumping 54.7 per cent. Base metals, petroleum, metallurgical coal and diamonds all also reported double-digit increases in sales and profits. However, three categories—aluminium, stainless steel materials and manganese—recorded profit declines.

Outlook

BHP expects commodities demand to remain strong in the medium term, underpinned by the industrialisation and urbanisation of China, India and other emerging economies, and it plans capital spending of US$20 billion in the June 2012 year—a big jump from the US$12.8 billion of June 2011—aimed at boosting output. But it is also seeking to ensure that it remains well diversified, and in particular it is working to boost its energy businesses. Its mid 2011, $14.2 billion acquisition of Petrohawk Energy will help it become a major participant in the high-potential shale gas sector. It has also been actively acquiring other shale gas assets, and has now become the world's seventh-largest independent oil and gas company. It expects that by 2020 it will have tripled its energy products output. Having failed in its bid to acquire Canada's Potash Corporation, the company is considering launching its own multi-billion-dollar Canadian potash project. However, it has warned that costs tend to lag the commodity price cycle, and that it is facing an increasingly tight market for skilled labour and equipment across most of its businesses.

Year to 30 June	2010	2011
Revenues ($mn)	59997.7	70332.4
Iron Ore (%)	20	28
Base Metals (%)	14	20
Petroleum (%)	14	15
Metallurgical Coal (%)	16	11
Energy Coal (%)	13	8
EBIT ($mn)	22762.5	31192.2
EBIT margin (%)	37.9	44.3
Profit before tax ($mn)	22240.9	30642.2
Profit after tax ($mn)	14456.8	23184.3
Earnings per share (¢)	259.8	420.7
Cash flow per share (¢)	357.0	510.3
Dividend (¢)	95.12	97.95
Percentage franked	100	100
Net tangible assets per share ($)	10.11	9.93
Interest cover (times)	43.6	56.7
Return on equity (%)	27.8	42.1
Debt-to-equity ratio (%)	6.7	10.1
Current ratio	1.9	1.3

Blackmores Limited

BKL

<www.blackmores.com.au>

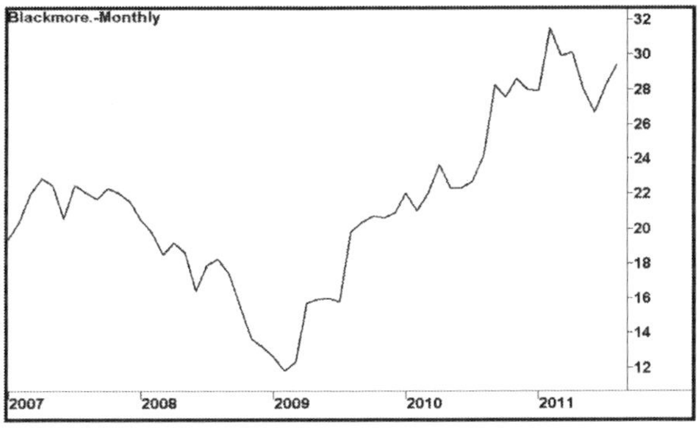

Share price ($)	29.40
12-month high ($)	32.10
12-month low ($)	24.05
Market capitalisation ($mn)	492.3
Price-to-NTA-per-share ratio	6.4
5-year share price return (% p.a.)	20.9
Dividend reinvestment plan	No

Sector: Health care	Company	Sector
Price/earnings ratio (times)	18.0	17.5
Dividend yield (%)	4.2	2.6

Founded in Queensland in the 1930s, and now based in Sydney, Blackmores is a leading manufacturer and distributor of a wide range of natural healthcare products, nutritional supplements and cosmetics, with a high market share. It has an expanding export business, mainly to Asia and New Zealand, and these sales now represent more than 20 per cent of company turnover. In 2010 Blackmores acquired Pure Animal Wellbeing (PAW), which specialises in natural dietary supplements for dogs and cats.

Latest business results (June 2011, full year)

Blackmores overcame a slowdown in consumer spending to report its ninth straight year of record sales and profits. There was another excellent performance from the company's fast-growing Asian operations, despite the strength of the dollar. Australian sales and after-tax profit each rose 3 per cent, to $185.1 million and $22.2 million respectively. Thai revenues were up 20.8 per cent to $20.3 million, with profits jumping 81.7 per cent to $4.2 million. Malaysian sales rose 16.6 per cent to $13.4 million, with profits up 66 per cent to $1.2 million. There was also a big jump in sales to other Asian countries, particularly South Korea, although this business remained in the red. New Zealand profits fell for the fourth straight year, with sales there also down. The company introduced 68 new products during the year. There was an initial contribution from Pure Animal Wellbeing.

Outlook

Blackmores is a beneficiary of several trends, including an ageing population that requires more health products and a move towards natural medications. It has also benefited from its reputation for quality, which in some cases enables it to charge higher prices than competitors, and which has enabled it to maintain a high market share. It has an intensive research and development capability, and is continually launching new products. However, with domestic demand now sluggish, the company is seeking new areas of growth, and it is finding this particularly in Asia, where it works with a variety of local partners. Its entry to South Korea in December 2010, working with a TV shopping network, is already proving profitable. Its new animal health business has introduced 21 new products, with distribution in over 800 veterinary clinics and 300 pet stores, and with sales up 60 per cent in the first year of operations. Blackmores has been launching websites in all its major markets to provide online healthcare advice.

Year to 30 June	2010	2011
Revenues ($mn)	215.8	235.3
EBIT ($mn)	36.7	41.5

Year to 30 June	2010	2011
EBIT margin (%)	17.0	17.7
Gross margin (%)	62.4	66.4
Profit before tax ($mn)	34.7	39.3
Profit after tax ($mn)	24.3	27.3
Earnings per share (¢)	146.8	163.2
Cash flow per share (¢)	171.8	190.2
Dividend (¢)	112	124
Percentage franked	100	100
Net tangible assets per share ($)	4.27	4.57
Interest cover (times)	18.2	18.8
Return on equity (%)	37.3	36.2
Debt-to-equity ratio (%)	36.0	37.7
Current ratio	2.4	2.4

Bradken Limited

BKN

<www.bradken.com>

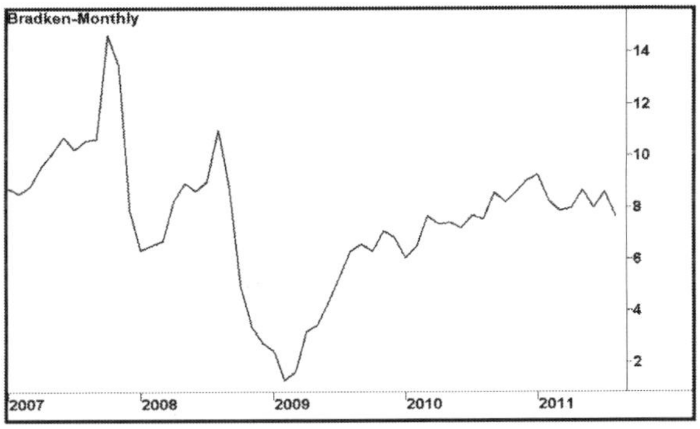

Share price ($)	7.62
12-month high ($)	9.60
12-month low ($)	6.82
Market capitalisation ($mn)	1233.2
Price-to-NTA-per-share ratio	2.6
5-year share price return (% p.a.)	11.8
Dividend reinvestment plan	Yes

Sector: Industrials	Company	Sector
Price/earnings ratio (times)	12.4	11.9
Dividend yield (%)	5.2	5.5

Newcastle-based Bradken was established in 1922 by two BHP employees who used their racecourse winnings to launch a new steel foundry business. It is today a leading heavy engineer and designer and manufacturer of products for the mining, rail, steel, smelting, transportation, cement, oil and gas, power generation and sugar industries. It operates more than 30 manufacturing and service facilities in Australia, New Zealand, the US, Canada, China and Britain.

Latest business results (June 2011, full year)

A booming domestic mining environment helped power Bradken to a solid rise in sales and profits. The Mining Products division achieved a strong turnaround from the slump of the previous year, with sales up 33 per cent. There was particularly strong demand for the company's crawler systems for mining shovels and excavators. The US-based Engineered Products division also saw a recovery from the previous year's weakness, with sales soaring 61 per cent, thanks to strong demand from the mining, locomotive and energy markets. Stringent cost control led to a big increase in the division's profit margins. The Industrial division realised sales up 28 per cent, thanks to solid domestic demand. However, the Rail division, strong in the previous year, saw revenues down 34 per cent, with profits also hit, due especially to some tough competition from Chinese rivals.

Outlook

With most of its businesses now enjoying strong demand, Bradken has said that it believes its June 2012 after-tax profit will be 35 per cent to 40 per cent higher than in June 2011. It is particularly optimistic about its Mining Products division, which it believes should see 10 per cent sales growth, despite the loss of up to $50 million in business from losing, from July 2011, the Australian licence to produce an American ground-engaging tool. Capacity upgrades are expected to lead to continuing good business for the Engineered Products division. Strong growth is also expected for the Rail division, with targeted production of 2000 wagons, compared with 1444 in June 2011, and with higher profit margins. In July 2011 Bradken announced the $209 million acquisition of Canadian mining consumables company Norcast, which it sees as providing considerable synergies with its existing business. Bradken holds a 19 per cent equity stake in mining products company Austin Engineering, and there has been speculation that it might launch a full takeover bid.

Year to 30 June	2010	2011
Revenues ($mn)	1003.7	1147.5
Mining Products (%)	34	40
Engineered Products (%)	21	30
Rail (%)	32	19
Industrial (%)	6	7
EBIT ($mn)	126.8	156.1

Year to 30 June	2010	2011
EBIT margin (%)	12.6	13.6
Gross margin (%)	22.8	23.4
Profit before tax ($mn)	96.5	119.2
Profit after tax ($mn)	70.4	87.1
Earnings per share (¢)	54.1	61.4
Cash flow per share (¢)	85.0	92.4
Dividend (¢)	34	39.5
Percentage franked	100	100
Net tangible assets per share ($)	2.15	2.92
Interest cover (times)	4.2	4.2
Return on equity (%)	17.2	15.5
Debt-to-equity ratio (%)	51.8	34.7
Current ratio	1.9	2.8

Cabcharge Australia Limited

CAB

<www.cabcharge.com.au>

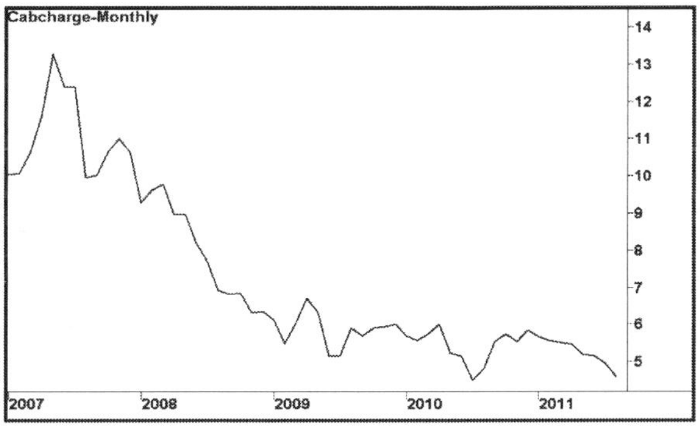

Share price ($)	4.58
12-month high ($)	6.38
12-month low ($)	4.25
Market capitalisation ($mn)	551.9
Price-to-NTA-per-share ratio	2.4
5-year share price return (% p.a.)	−5.3
Dividend reinvestment plan	No

Sector: Industrials	Company	Sector
Price/earnings ratio (times)	12.0	11.9
Dividend yield (%)	6.6	5.5

Sydney-based Cabcharge, founded in 1976, manages a charge-card system that allows taxi users to pay fares without requiring cash. The system is used by most Australian taxis, and also by other companies, such as limousine services. Cabcharge has tens of thousands of account customers, ranging from large corporations and government departments to small businesses and individuals. Cabcharge also owns Australia's largest taxi company, Sydney-based Combined Communications Network, and other taxi companies in Sydney, Melbourne and Newcastle. It has established a presence in the UK, named CityFleet, with a joint venture operation in several cities. In another joint venture, with Singapore's ComfortDelGro Corporation, it has become the largest private bus operator in New South Wales.

Latest business results (June 2011, full year)

Cabcharge's profits fell for a second straight year, although the result incorporated a $15 million court fine imposed for anti-competitive conduct. Excluding this, profits rose, reflecting some solid underlying business. A total of $1.033 billion in fares was processed through Cabcharge terminals, which the company said was up from $1.005 billion in the previous year, thanks to growth from Cabcharge accounts and bank-issued cards, offsetting a decline in revenues from third-party cards. The company's own taxi services saw revenues up 8.4 per cent to $83.6 million, largely attributable to fleet number increases. The ComfortDelGro Cabcharge joint venture contributed $13.2 million to after-tax profit, up from $10.9 million in the previous year and $7.8 million in the year before that. But British business remained weak, with a $1.7 million contribution to after-tax profit, down from $1.8 million in June 2010 and $3.3 million in June 2009.

Outlook

Despite a weak economy and the arrival of some rival operators, Cabcharge has expressed confidence about the prospects for continuing growth. It sees particularly strong potential for its new contactless cards, which have been distributed to all account holders. It is also working to expand consumer access to its terminals, and it can now accept the Unionpay card from China, of which more than one billion are on issue. It expects its taxi services business to continue its steady growth as new taxi licences are issued in both Sydney and Melbourne. It is also boosting its bus services, with new buses and new routes, and expects its bus joint venture to expand further. It believes the London Olympics will provide a boost to British operations.

Year to 30 June	2010	2011
Revenues ($mn)	161.7	171.0
EBIT ($mn)	81.1	70.8

Year to 30 June	2010	2011
EBIT margin (%)	50.2	41.4
Profit before tax ($mn)	75.4	64.4
Profit after tax ($mn)	57.6	46.1
Earnings per share (¢)	47.8	38.3
Cash flow per share (¢)	56.5	48.7
Dividend (¢)	34	30
Percentage franked	100	100
Net tangible assets per share ($)	1.82	1.89
Interest cover (times)	14.3	11.1
Return on equity (%)	20.0	15.3
Debt-to-equity ratio (%)	32.6	40.4
Current ratio	1.5	1.0

Caltex Australia Limited

CTX

<www.caltex.com.au>

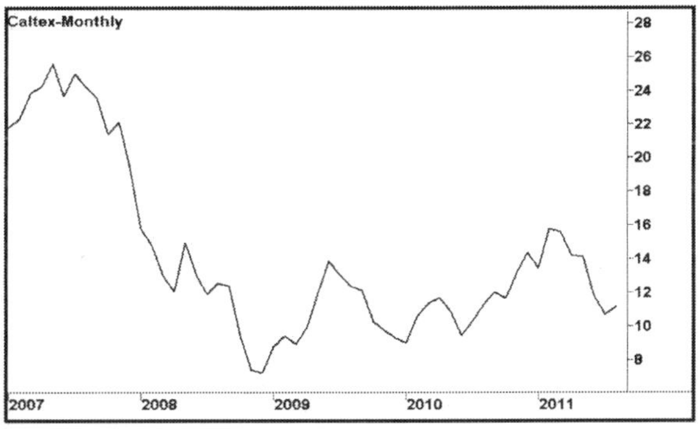

Share price ($)	11.13
12-month high ($)	16.44
12-month low ($)	8.76
Market capitalisation ($mn)	3005.1
Price-to-NTA-per-share ratio	0.9
5-year share price return (% p.a.)	−9.9
Dividend reinvestment plan	No

Sector: Energy	Company	Sector
Price/earnings ratio (times)	9.5	20.4
Dividend yield (%)	5.4	2.7

Caltex Australia formally got its start in 1941, although it has roots dating back to 1900 and the initial marketing of Texaco products in this country. Based in Sydney, the company is today 50 per cent owned by Chevron Corporation of the US. It is Australia's largest oil refiner, with two petroleum refineries in Sydney and Brisbane offering a combined daily capacity of more than 35 million litres. It also operates a 600000-litre-per-day lubricating oil refinery, 11 seaboard storage terminals and a 200-kilometre pipeline from the Kurnell refinery in Sydney to the Wickham terminal in Newcastle. It operates its own fleet of road tankers and also maintains the country's largest oil company retail network. The network incorporates more than 2000 Caltex and Ampol sites, including several hundred that are jointly branded with Woolworths.

Latest business results (June 2011, half year)

Profits rose sharply, thanks to product and crude oil inventory gains of approximately $157 million, due to the significant rise in the price of crude oil during the half. This compares with product and crude oil inventory losses of approximately $8 million in the June 2010 half, when the crude price was more stable. However, the company also presents what it calls a replacement cost operating profit, which excludes the impact of volatile crude oil prices, and uses replacement costs, rather than historical costs. On this basis, its after-tax profit actually fell from $163 million to $113 million. The Caltex Refiner Margin, a key measure of profitability, fell from US$9.67 to US$7.82, due to higher crude oil prices and the stronger dollar. Total fuel sales rose 4.3 per cent, underpinned by growth in commercial diesel, jet and retail premium fuels.

Outlook

Caltex occupies a key position in the Australian economy. However, its business has been hit by problems of refinery over-capacity in the Asian region, with big new plants in countries like India and China far more efficient and competitive than Australia's four refineries. Consequently there has been growing speculation about the future of the two refineries owned by Caltex, with a suggestion that the Caltex and the BP Brisbane refineries might merge. Another possibility is that the refineries could be converted to import terminals. The company estimates that a new carbon tax will cost it $5 million to $10 million in the first year of the scheme.

Year to 31 December	2009	2010
Revenues ($mn)	17740.3	18671.9
EBIT ($mn)	475.7	499.7
EBIT margin (%)	2.7	2.7
Gross margin (%)	6.3	5.7

Year to 31 December	2009	2010
Profit before tax ($mn)	447.7	442.3
Profit after tax ($mn)	314.8	317.0
Earnings per share (¢)	116.6	117.4
Cash flow per share (¢)	189.4	194.8
Dividend (¢)	25	60
Percentage franked	100	100
Interest cover (times)	17.0	8.7
Return on equity (%)	11.4	10.6

Half year to 30 June	2010	2011
Revenues ($mn)	9036.5	10845.9
Profit before tax ($mn)	201.7	382.1
Profit after tax ($mn)	141.2	269.7
Earnings per share (¢)	52.3	99.9
Dividend (¢)	30	17
Percentage franked	100	100
Net tangible assets per share ($)	10.76	11.73
Debt-to-equity ratio (%)	19.2	20.7
Current ratio	1.6	1.5

Campbell Brothers Limited

CPB

<www.campbell.com.au>

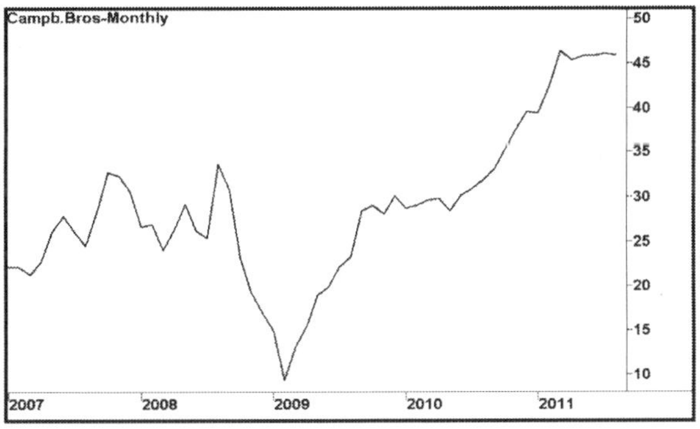

Share price ($)	45.89
12-month high ($)	57.00
12-month low ($)	30.99
Market capitalisation ($mn)	3097.7
Price-to-NTA-per-share ratio	9.7
5-year share price return (% p.a.)	25.4
Dividend reinvestment plan	No

Sector: Industrials	Company	Sector
Price/earnings ratio (times)	22.6	11.9
Dividend yield (%)	3.1	5.5

Brisbane-based Campbell Brothers, established in 1863, has become one of the world's largest providers of laboratory analysis services to the environmental, minerals, coal, tribology (used oil), food, industrial and metallurgical markets, and its ALS Laboratory Group operates some 270 laboratories in 44 countries. A second business, Campbell Chemicals, incorporates two separate units, Deltrex Chemicals and Panamex Pacific, and is responsible for supplying a wide range of industrial, commercial and consumer products and engineering services throughout Australia, New Zealand and the South Pacific. The third division, Reward Distribution, supplies chemicals, paper goods, tableware, kitchenware and other non-food consumables to motels, hotels, nursing homes, hospitals, restaurants, fast-food chains, sporting clubs and the retail sector.

Latest business results (March 2011, full year)

Campbell resumed its high growth trajectory, after the profit slump of the previous year. The star was its ALS Minerals division, thanks to strong global mineral exploration activity. This business saw sales up 63 per cent, while profits more than doubled, making a sharp recovery from the plunge of the previous year. Excellent growth was also recorded by ALS Environmental, with revenues up 26 per cent and profits jumping by more than 50 per cent. These two business units alone accounted for 58 per cent of total company sales and more than 80 per cent of profits. The newly formed ALS Industrial division also recorded strong growth, but this largely reflected the acquisition in the previous year of industrial services company PearlStreet. The low-margin Campbell Chemicals operation saw sales and profits down, following the sale of the Cleantec chemical and cleaning solutions business. Reward Distribution boosted sales, but volatile markets caused it to fall into the red.

Outlook

Campbell is looking to further strong growth as it continues to expand its laboratory operations. In July 2011 it acquired Britain's Stewart Group for approximately $222 million. Stewart Group operates 26 laboratories and offices globally, with three main divisions: geochemical, inspection and metallurgical. Its Canadian laboratories operate one of North America's largest metallurgical businesses. Following the 2010 acquisition of Ammtec, this now helps Campbell in its quest to become a global leader in the metallurgical market. The company is also targeting the coal market as a growth area, and in 2011 it opened a new facility in Brisbane it claims is the world's most technologically advanced coal testing facility.

Year to 31 March	2010	2011
Revenues ($mn)	825.5	1108.3

Year to 31 March	2010	2011
ALS Minerals (%)	25	30
ALS Environmental (%)	30	28
Campbell Chemicals (%)	18	11
Reward Distribution (%)	14	11
ALS Industrial (%)	2	10
EBIT ($mn)	117.0	195.4
EBIT margin (%)	14.2	17.6
Profit before tax ($mn)	105.9	185.1
Profit after tax ($mn)	74.9	132.3
Earnings per share (¢)	128.4	203.1
Cash flow per share (¢)	196.8	267.8
Dividend (¢)	100	140
Percentage franked	50	50
Net tangible assets per share ($)	3.74	4.75
Interest cover (times)	10.5	19.1
Return on equity (%)	14.4	18.2
Debt-to-equity ratio (%)	23.3	13.5
Current ratio	2.5	1.9

Cardno Limited

CDD

<www.cardno.com>

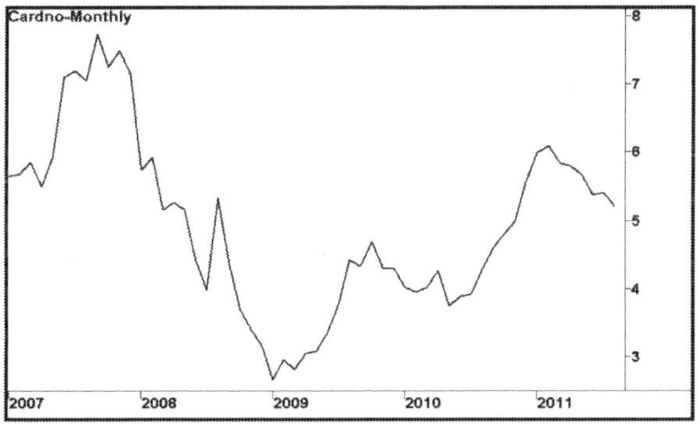

Share price ($)	5.21
12-month high ($)	6.31
12-month low ($)	4.10
Market capitalisation ($mn)	572.3
Price-to-NTA-per-share ratio	376.3
5-year share price return (% p.a.)	7.9
Dividend reinvestment plan	Yes

Sector: Industrials	Company	Sector
Price/earnings ratio (times)	9.3	11.9
Dividend yield (%)	6.5	5.5

Brisbane-based engineering consultancy Cardno was formed in 1945 to provide services to the

Queensland public and private sectors. In 1999 it merged with a New South Wales engineering practice that dated back to 1936, and it has since expanded steadily through both organic growth and a series of acquisitions of local practices. Today it offers a wide range of professional engineering services to clients locally and overseas, including civil and structural engineering, materials testing, international development assistance and environmental management services. It also provides water engineering software and stormwater drainage design software to the engineering industry. It operates from more than 160 offices in numerous countries.

Latest business results (June 2011, full year)

Sales and profits jumped, with an excellent contribution from two mid-2010 American acquisitions. These were the 615-person environmental consultant ENTRIX and the 155-person soil and groundwater remediation specialist Environmental Resolutions. Both companies have significantly boosted Cardno's exposure to the growing oil and gas sector, and ENTRIX has been involved in Gulf of Mexico oil spill clean-up work. The result would have been even better but for the strength of the dollar. Cardno groups its operations into three broad segments. By far the best-performing of these was Professional Services Americas and Software, which provides a wide range of consulting services throughout North and South America, and also undertakes global software sales. This division, now the company's largest, saw revenues up more than threefold with EBIT surging more than fourfold. Professional Services Australia and New Zealand, previously the largest division, achieved a 17 per cent rise in sales, but with EBIT slightly down. The International Development Assistance division, responsible for governmental and private aid projects around the world, saw revenues down for a second straight year, though EBIT edged up. On a regional basis, the Americas contributed 58 per cent of revenues, with Australia and New Zealand at 37 per cent.

Outlook

Cardno's strengths have been in public works, with much of its business coming from government departments and related organisations, especially in the fields of environment and water consultancy. By contrast, it has been relatively weak in the resources industry, and it is now working to boost its presence in this sector. It continues to expand. In the June 2011 year it acquired the 150-person US environmental consultancy JFNew, the Perth-based 100-person electrical engineering services firm BEC and the 60-person Queensland engineering firm Roadtest.

Year to 30 June	2010	2011
Revenues ($mn)	473.8	827.7

Year to 30 June	2010	2011
Prof. Services Americas and Software (%)	24	53
Prof. Services Australia and NZ (%)	46	31
Int. Development Assistance (%)	30	16
EBIT ($mn)	45.3	86.9
EBIT margin (%)	9.6	10.5
Profit before tax ($mn)	43.6	84.3
Profit after tax ($mn)	37.6	58.8
Earnings per share (¢)	43.9	56.3
Cash flow per share (¢)	53.8	67.2
Dividend (¢)	29	34
Percentage franked	100	70
Net tangible assets per share ($)	–	0.01
Interest cover (times)	26.1	34.0
Return on equity (%)	13.3	17.9
Debt-to-equity ratio (%)	39.7	6.3
Current ratio	1.3	1.4

Cash Converters International

CCV

<www.cashconverters.com>

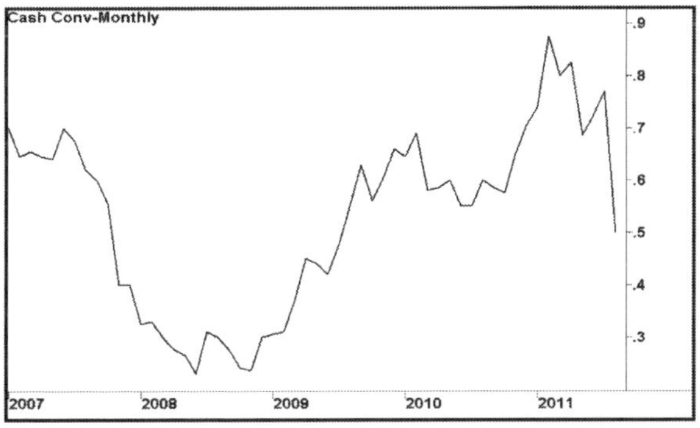

Share price ($)	0.50
12-month high ($)	0.91
12-month low ($)	0.47
Market capitalisation ($mn)	191.2
Price-to-NTA-per-share ratio	2.2
5-year share price return (% p.a.)	6.3
Dividend reinvestment plan	No

Sector: Consumer discretionary	Company	Sector
Price/earnings ratio (times)	6.9	13.1
Dividend yield (%)	7.0	3.5

Perth-based Cash Converters began life in 1984 as a single secondhand store. It has since expanded into a chain of over 130 company-owned and franchised secondhand stores nationwide. In 1991 it opened a store in the UK, and it now operates more than 190 outlets there. It also operates a flourishing and highly profitable consumer finance business offering cash advances and personal loans. In addition, it has launched a global network of franchised stores, and in mid 2011 its operations incorporated a network of more than 600 stores in 21 countries. However, stores outside Australia and the UK contribute little to its overall business. Cash Converters is also listed on the London Stock Exchange, and about a third of its revenues derive from Britain. The large US pawnbroker EZCorp owns a third of Cash Converters' equity.

Latest business results (June 2011, full year)

Cash Converters enjoyed another excellent result as it continued to expand its businesses. Once again the key was the company's consumer finance business, which represented 28 per cent of revenues but contributed around 47 per cent of company profits. The personal loan book in Australia grew 36.1 per cent to $52.7 million and in the UK it soared 746 per cent to £5 million. Business at company-owned secondhand stores grew well, with profits also up, although profit margins were well below those for the loans business. Franchise Operations grew, but with profits down.

Outlook

Cash Converters faces the possibility of a sharp decline in its business, due to proposed government legislation that will place severe limits on short-term loans, sometimes known as payday loans. Cash Converters is one of the largest such lenders in Australia, and this business is hugely profitable and has been growing rapidly. The company is fighting the proposed changes, and the outcome remains unclear. However, because of the uncertainty, the company's big US shareholder EZCorp has abandoned its plans to move to a 53 per cent shareholding. In response, Cash Converters has said it might divert more resources towards building up its operations in the UK, where it has been starting to enjoy some high growth for both its cash advance and its personal loans businesses. It has also embarked on a strategy of buying stores from its franchisees and turning them into company-owned businesses, believing this will maximise profits.

Year to 30 June	2010	2011
Revenues ($mn)	127.8	186.1
Store Operations (%)	47	51

Year to 30 June	2010	2011
Financial Services—personal loans (%)	28	28
Franchise Operations (%)	17	14
Financial Services—administration (%)	8	7
EBIT ($mn)	30.9	39.2
EBIT margin (%)	24.2	21.1
Profit before tax ($mn)	31.2	39.2
Profit after tax ($mn)	21.6	27.6
Earnings per share (¢)	6.6	7.3
Cash flow per share (¢)	7.1	8.2
Dividend (¢)	3	3.5
Percentage franked	100	100
Net tangible assets per share ($)	0.24	0.23
Interest cover (times)	–	1353.2
Return on equity (%)	17.7	16.4
Debt-to-equity ratio (%)	–	–
Current ratio	5.0	3.1

Cedar Woods Properties Limited

CWP

<www.cedarwoods.com.au>

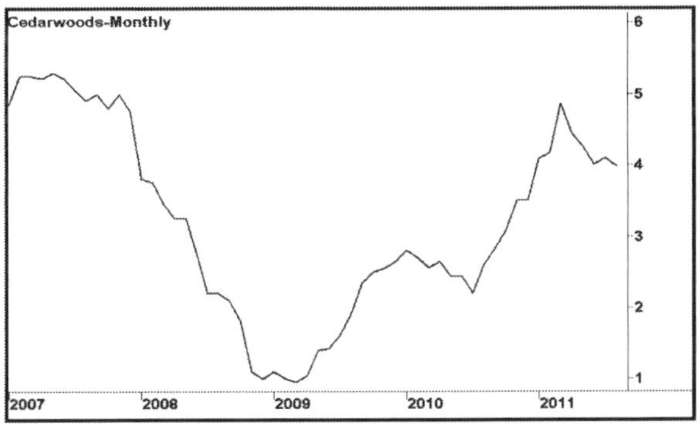

Share price ($)	3.98
12-month high ($)	5.15
12-month low ($)	2.60
Market capitalisation ($mn)	246.0
Price-to-NTA-per-share ratio	1.9
5-year share price return (% p.a.)	1.8
Dividend reinvestment plan	Yes

Sector: Financials	Company	Sector
Price/earnings ratio (times)	8.7	10.8
Dividend yield (%)	5.8	6.8

Perth-based Cedar Woods, founded in 1987, is a prominent property developer in Western Australia. Its main interests are in urban land subdivision for residential, commercial and industrial purposes. Its work includes apartment projects, integrated housing developments, business parks, mixed use developments and several large-scale master planned communities. It is also active in Melbourne.

Latest business results (June 2011, full year)

Profits jumped for the second successive year, thanks especially to strong business for the company's Melbourne developments. It recorded more than 200 settlements for its major suburban development at Williams Landing, which has become one of the fastest growing municipalities in Australia. At Banbury Village, in Melbourne's Footscray, construction and settlement for several stages of housing have been completed. With demand for its Melbourne developments generally remaining strong, the company was able to raise some prices. In Western Australia the company recorded some steady sales, despite a weakening market environment. Construction of the final stage at The Kestrels in Tapping was completed. Sales at the Emerald Park project in Wellard were firm, and there was also solid demand for the second release of properties at the company's joint venture Harrisdale Green development.

Outlook

By August 2011 Cedar Woods had received pre-sales of $130 million for projects to be settled during the June 2012 year. If sales continued at the same rate it was forecasting a June 2012 after-tax profit of approximately $34 million. Nevertheless, the company's business has been hit by a marked slowdown in housing demand and an easing in consumer confidence. In Melbourne the enquiry and sales rates have slowed, with weaker clearance rates, and the company doubts that it can achieve pricing growth during the June 2012 year. In Western Australia the company has reported that it is taking longer than before to sell properties. However, its major 2200-lot development at Williams Landing, which is due to become a town of 10000 residents, continues to generate solid demand. In May 2011 Cedar Woods signed a 20-year leasing deal with Woolworths for the development of three large stores at Williams Landing, as part of a 50-hectare town centre, due to open by mid 2014. In Western Australia it has acquired 68 hectares of land in Baldivis for $21 million and it plans an 800-lot residential estate to complement the company's nearby Emerald Park and The Rivergums developments.

Year to 30 June	2010	2011
Revenues ($mn)	106.9	129.8
EBIT ($mn)	25.3	39.4
EBIT margin (%)	23.7	30.4

Year to 30 June	2010	2011
Gross margin (%)	45.2	46.1
Profit before tax ($mn)	24.7	40.2
Profit after tax ($mn)	17.2	28.1
Earnings per share (¢)	29.0	45.8
Cash flow per share (¢)	29.4	46.3
Dividend (¢)	13	23
Percentage franked	100	100
Net tangible assets per share ($)	1.80	2.10
Interest cover (times)	44.7	–
Return on equity (%)	17.1	23.5
Debt-to-equity ratio (%)	36.5	42.5
Current ratio	0.8	1.4

Coal & Allied Industries Limited

CNA

<www.coalandallied.com.au>

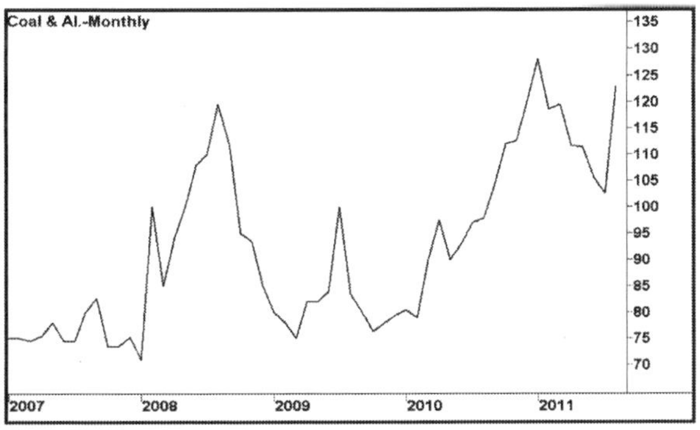

Share price ($)	122.80
12-month high ($)	134.99
12-month low ($)	89.80
Market capitalisation ($mn)	10632.6
Price-to-NTA-per-share ratio	6.7
5-year share price return (% p.a.)	14.1
Dividend reinvestment plan	No

Sector: Energy	Company	Sector
Price/earnings ratio (times)	15.1	20.4
Dividend yield (%)	4.8	2.7

Brisbane-based Coal & Allied, a 76 per cent-owned subsidiary of Rio Tinto, was formally established in 1960 from the merger of three coal companies. It mines coal from three regions of New South Wales: the Hunter Valley, Mount Thorley Warkworth and Bengalla.

Latest business results (June 2011, half year)

Higher production and a 25 per cent increase in the US-dollar coal price offset inclement weather and the strong dollar, to hand Coal & Allied a healthy rise in sales revenues and profits. Production was up 11 per cent, thanks especially to the company's investment in heavy mobile equipment, which boosted mine productivity. However, wet weather led to a 20 per cent loss in hours worked during June. Profits were also dented by a reduction in the proportion of high-margin semi-soft coal in the company's total sales. In addition, the company was hit by a 25 per cent increase in mine production costs, with higher fuel prices a particular burden. It experienced just a modest detrimental impact from the Japanese earthquake and tsunami, with the postponement of some shipments.

Outlook

Coal & Allied is a beneficiary of booming Asian demand for Australian coal. As contracts are renewed it is continually seeing the benefits of higher prices flow through to revenues and profits. It anticipates that Japanese demand could eventually rise as the country seeks alternatives to its nuclear power plants. It is investing heavily in future growth, with expansion projects at each of its existing mine sites. It has also launched a feasibility study into a new Mount Pleasant project, adjacent to its Bengalla operations. If this project goes ahead it could cost as much as $1 billion, with the first coal produced in 2014. The company is benefiting from the expansion of the Port of Newcastle coal terminals, which have boosted capacity by 10 per cent to 113 million tonnes per year, with further expansion to 145 million tonnes expected by the end of 2012. However, the strong dollar remains a check on profits, and the company is threatened by continuing rises in its operating costs. It has also expressed its concern that the new carbon price scheme could have a detrimental impact on business, together with a loss of the diesel fuel rebate and a minerals resource rent tax. Rio Tinto, working together with Japan's Mitsubishi, is moving towards a full takeover of Coal & Allied.

Year to 31 December	2009	2010
Revenues ($mn)	2319.0	2098.3
EBIT ($mn)	781.7	980.9
EBIT margin (%)	33.7	46.7
Profit before tax ($mn)	791.4	987.1
Profit after tax ($mn)	585.5	703.6
Earnings per share (¢)	676.2	812.6
Cash flow per share (¢)	813.1	949.9

Year to 31 December	2009	2010
Dividend (¢)	510	588
Percentage franked	100	100
Interest cover (times)	–	–
Return on equity (%)	39.2	46.6

Half year to 30 June	2010	2011
Revenues ($mn)	909.6	1155.8
Profit before tax ($mn)	218.0	315.6
Profit after tax ($mn)	160.7	227.4
Earnings per share (¢)	185.6	262.6
Dividend (¢)	450	120
Percentage franked	100	100
Net tangible assets per share ($)	19.26	18.41
Debt-to-equity ratio (%)	–	–
Current ratio	2.1	1.3

Cochlear Limited

COH

<www.cochlear.com/au>

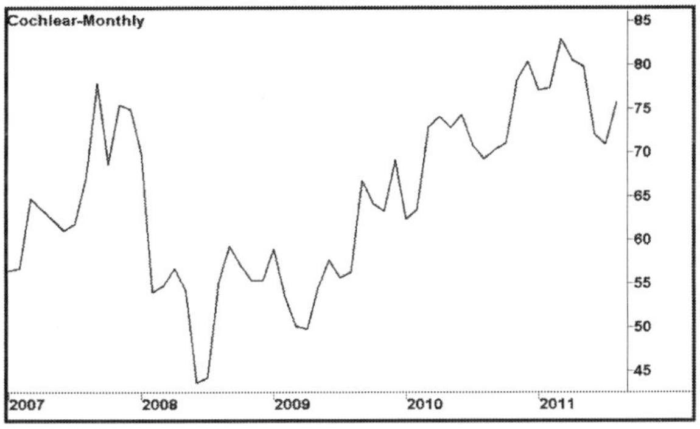

Share price ($)	75.74
12-month high ($)	85.00
12-month low ($)	63.05
Market capitalisation ($mn)	4300.2
Price-to-NTA-per-share ratio	14.6
5-year share price return (% p.a.)	11.5
Dividend reinvestment plan	No

Sector: Health care	Company	Sector
Price/earnings ratio (times)	23.8	17.5
Dividend yield (%)	3.0	2.6

Sydney-based Cochlear, founded in 1981, has more than two-thirds of the world market for cochlear bionic-ear implants, which are intended to assist the communication ability of people suffering from severe hearing impediments. It also sells the Baha bone-anchored hearing implant. It has sales in over 100 countries, and overseas business accounts for more than 90 per cent of sales and profits.

Latest business results (June 2011, full year)

Cochlear enjoyed another sparkling result, with revenues and profits rising. Because of the overwhelming proportion of overseas business in its sales mix, currency movements and the company's own extensive hedging policies played a prominent role in the results. Cochlear implant sales of $648 million were up 7 per cent, or 20 per cent when excluding the foreign currency impact. Baha implant sales of $84.2 million fell 9 per cent on a reported basis, though rose 2 per cent on a constant-currency basis. The company also reported hedging revenues of $77.4 million, double the figure of the previous year. The company divides its operations into three broad regions, and all reported gains. The best was Asia Pacific, with sales of $121.9 million, up 26 per cent (31 per cent in constant currency), followed by the Americas, up 3 per cent (16 per cent in constant currency) and Europe, Middle East,

Africa, up 1 per cent (14 per cent in constant currency).

Outlook

Cochlear enjoys a tight grip on the global cochlear implant market, with high margins, growing sales, and apparent resistance to financial market turmoil. It continues to drive its market forward, with high R&D spending and a continual stream of innovations. Consequently, the company's shares have been superb long-term performers. It is enjoying success with the Nucleus 5 system, which represents a new generation of cochlear implants. It is considerably smaller and stronger than earlier models, with significant advances in performance and ease of use. The company's comprehensive hedging program has helped insulate it from much of the impact of the surging dollar, although it says its June 2011 after-tax profit would have been about $15 million higher with a stable currency. Cochlear has moved its global headquarters to Sydney's Macquarie University campus, as part of the establishment there of a major new Hearing Health Precinct employing over 2000 people, and believes this new location will help drive future innovation for the company.

Year to 30 June	2010	2011
Revenues ($mn)	734.8	809.6

Year to 30 June	2010	2011
EBIT ($mn)	219.4	240.2
EBIT margin (%)	29.9	29.7
Gross margin (%)	72.3	71.6
Profit before tax ($mn)	209.4	235.1
Profit after tax ($mn)	155.2	180.1
Earnings per share (¢)	275.7	318.2
Cash flow per share (¢)	316.7	366.6
Dividend (¢)	200	225
Percentage franked	79	65
Net tangible assets per share ($)	4.01	5.20
Interest cover (times)	21.9	47.5
Return on equity (%)	38.7	38.3
Debt-to-equity ratio (%)	26.0	–
Current ratio	2.1	1.9

Codan Limited

CDA

<www.codan.com.au>

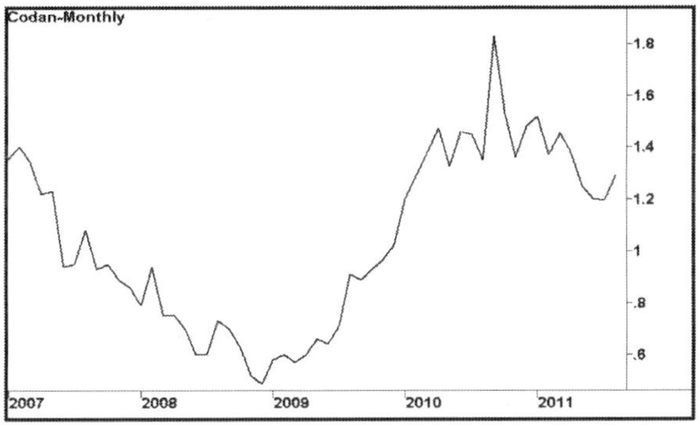

Share price ($)	1.29
12-month high ($)	1.83
12-month low ($)	1.00
Market capitalisation ($mn)	211.7
Price-to-NTA-per-share ratio	15.1
5-year share price return (% p.a.)	7.5
Dividend reinvestment plan	No

Sector: Information technology	Company	Sector
Price/earnings ratio (times)	9.0	18.2
Dividend yield (%)	7.0	3.9

Adelaide electronics company Codan was founded in 1959. Its main products are high-frequency radios, satellite communications systems and mine and metal detectors. It has sold its Parketronics printed circuit board business. Its customers range from individual consumers to telecommunications corporations, major international aid agencies and security and military organisations, and it enjoys good market shares for its products. It sells to more than 150 countries, and overseas sales comprise around 85 per cent of company revenues.

Latest business results (June 2011, full year)

After the boom of the previous year, when sales of metal detection equipment soared more than 150 per cent, Codan's business retreated, with June 2011 sales and profits down. Both of the company's major profit groups saw sales fall. In the high-margin Metal Detection division, responsible for around 90 per cent of company profit, earnings slid about 13 per cent, in line with the decline in revenues. However, a restructuring program helped move the Communications division from loss to profit. In addition to the figures in the table, the company also reported one-off profits from business and investment sales, offset by restructuring expenses and a $6 million write-down of its satellite communications product business.

Outlook

Codan's $70 million acquisition in 2008 of the metal detector company Minelab continues to power the company's business. It is enjoying particularly strong demand in Africa, where small-scale gold mining takes place, and it has consolidated its position with the launch of new and improved products with deeper ground penetration. A high-profile marketing campaign has generated good business in Europe and the US for coin and treasure detectors. The company is now working to develop new markets for these products. The transfer of consumer metal detection machine production to Malaysia is expected to bring cost benefits. Codan's communications products are aimed at the global security and protection, peacekeeping and military market sectors. The company's strategy is to package third-party technology with its own high-frequency radio products, and it enjoyed a notable pick-up in demand in the June 2011 second half. Its satellite communications products are aimed at the US market, and the strong dollar has forced it to lower its sales prices and led to the June 2011 writedown in this division. Having cut its debt levels, Codan is now seeking acquisition opportunities in industries that will complement its existing businesses.

Year to 30 June	2010	2011
Revenues ($mn)	189.3	169.6
Metal Detection (%)	56	54
Communications (%)	37	41
EBIT ($mn)	45.8	35.0
EBIT margin (%)	24.2	20.7
Gross margin (%)	51.8	53.3
Profit before tax ($mn)	42.7	32.0
Profit after tax ($mn)	31.1	23.4
Earnings per share (¢)	18.9	14.3
Cash flow per share (¢)	25.2	19.8
Dividend (¢)	8	9
Percentage franked	100	100
Net tangible assets per share ($)	0.02	0.09
Interest cover (times)	14.6	11.5
Return on equity (%)	48.2	34.2
Debt-to-equity ratio (%)	46.7	35.5
Current ratio	1.5	1.4

Commonwealth Bank of Aust.

CBA

<www.commbank.com.au>

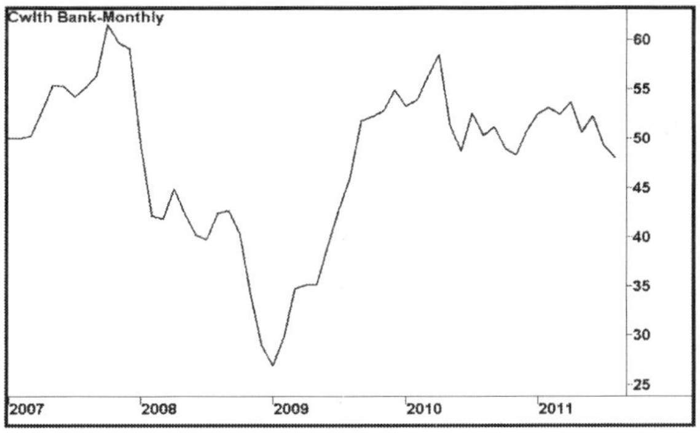

Share price ($)	47.93
12-month high ($)	55.77
12-month low ($)	43.41
Market capitalisation ($mn)	74400.5
Price-to-NTA-per-share ratio	2.7
5-year share price return (% p.a.)	7.1
Dividend reinvestment plan	Yes

Sector: Financials	Company	Sector
Price/earnings ratio (times)	11.6	10.8
Dividend yield (%)	6.7	6.8

The Commonwealth Bank, based in Sydney, was founded in 1911. It is today one of Australia's largest banks, and one of the country's top providers of home loans, personal loans and credit cards, and the largest holder of deposits. It is also Australia's largest retail fund manager, with operations that include Colonial First State, and one of the largest life insurers in Australia. Commonwealth Securities has become Australia's largest online stockbroker. It has significant interests in New Zealand, through ASB Bank, and a growing network of businesses in Asia. It owns Bankwest in Western Australia.

Latest business results (June 2011, full year)

Profits enjoyed another year of solid gains, thanks especially to strength in the core retail and business banking businesses. The bank's Retail Banking Services division saw profits up 16 per cent, only slightly less than the gain of the previous year, thanks in part to the decision by the bank to raise interest rates by more than the Reserve Bank. However, the bank's dominant position in home loans slipped to a market share of 25.7 per cent, from 26.1 per cent a year earlier. The Business and Private Banking division also achieved 16 per cent profit growth. New Zealand business rebounded strongly, with a 21 per cent rise in profits, despite the impact of the Christchurch earthquakes, and Bankwest moved from loss to profit. However, the Wealth Management and the Institutional Banking and Markets divisions both recorded double-digit profit declines, although funds under administration rose 5 per cent to total $196 billion.

Outlook

Commonwealth Bank occupies a powerful position in the domestic economy as well as in the domestic banking industry, and this has helped it weather the financial storms afflicting the worldwide banking sector. However, it now believes that it is facing the slowest growth rate for the domestic home loan market in more than 30 years. In addition, it sees global financial turmoil as pushing up the cost of its funds. Consequently, it is embarking on an ambitious but risky strategy of offshore expansion, with Asia the main target. It has taken equity stakes in banks in China, Indonesia and Vietnam, and has CBA branch offices in Hong Kong, Shanghai, Ho Chi Minh City, Mumbai, Tokyo and Singapore. The bank has also expressed interest in pursuing small bolt-on acquisitions in the British wealth management sector.

Year to 30 June	2010	2011
Operating income ($mn)	19288.0	19397.0
Net interest income ($mn)	11922.0	12607.0

Year to 30 June	2010	2011
Operating expenses ($mn)	8716.0	9060.0
Profit before tax ($mn)	8193.0	9057.0
Profit after tax ($mn)	5664.0	6394.0
Earnings per share (¢)	370.9	413.9
Dividend (¢)	290	320
Percentage franked	100	100
Non-interest income to total income (%)	38.2	35.0
Net tangible assets per share ($)	16.62	17.49
Cost-to-income ratio (%)	45.2	46.7
Return on equity (%)	17.2	17.8
Return on assets (%)	0.9	1.0

Computershare Limited

CPU

<www-au.computershare.com>

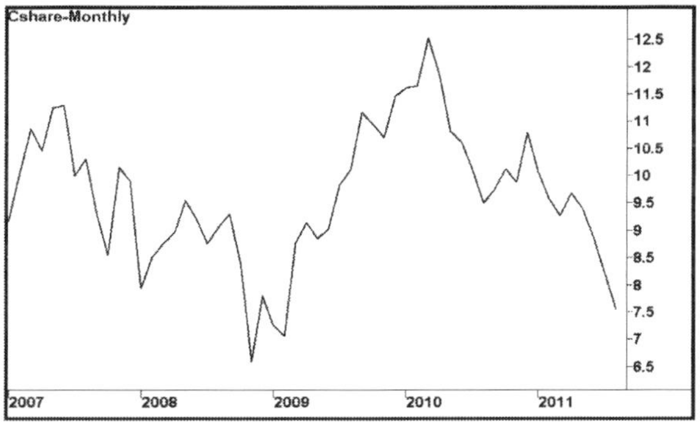

Share price ($)	7.55
12-month high ($)	11.37
12-month low ($)	6.55
Market capitalisation ($mn)	4196.3
Price-to-NTA-per-share ratio	–
5-year share price return (% p.a.)	2.2
Dividend reinvestment plan	No

Sector: Information technology	Company	Sector
Price/earnings ratio (times)	16.2	18.2
Dividend yield (%)	3.7	3.9

Melbourne-based Computershare, established in 1978, is one of the world's leading financial services and technology providers for the global securities industry, offering services to listed companies, investors, employees, exchanges and other financial institutions. These offerings include share registration, employee equity plans, proxy solicitation and other specialised financial, governance and stakeholder communication services. It manages more than 100 million shareholder accounts for over 30000 clients in 20 countries. In Australia it arranges registry services for more than half of all companies, and it has significant market shares in other countries. About 80 per cent of revenue comes from abroad.

Latest business results (June 2011, full year)

Profits took a hit as subdued global levels of merger and acquisition activity and of public floats bit into the company's business. Computershare now reports its results in US dollars, so benefited from the relative weakness of that currency. Thus the actual profit decline was not as dire as suggested by the figures in this book, which have been converted to Australian dollars. In US-dollar terms revenues were largely flat. American operations, responsible for nearly a third of total turnover, saw revenues and profits decline by double-digit amounts, due especially to a significant decline in both the company's mutual fund proxy solicitation business and its bankruptcy administration business. Asia, responsible for about 8 per cent of company turnover, also experienced lower profits. However, other regions were generally firm, with Australia and New Zealand (about 22 per cent of company turnover) benefiting from the strong Australian dollar, and British and African business (about 18 per cent of turnover) a beneficiary of a full year's contribution from the HBOS employee share scheme acquisition.

Outlook

Computershare is a major beneficiary of robust worldwide equity markets, and especially of merger and acquisition activity and of new public floats. Conversely, it can suffer once this activity falters. It holds a considerable amount of clients' funds in various forms, and is a notable beneficiary of rising interest rates. It also has a high percentage of recurring revenue. The company is wary about the outlook for June 2012, noting that high levels of volatility and uncertainty have sometimes—but not always—benefited the company, as they can generate elevated levels of secondary fundraisings and Chapter 11 bankruptcy filings. It is seeking regulatory approval for the US$550 million acquisition of New York Mellon's shareowner services business.

Year to 30 June	2010	2011
Revenues ($mn)	1817.7	1567.6

Year to 30 June	2010	2011
EBIT ($mn)	488.3	388.3
EBIT margin (%)	26.9	24.8
Profit before tax ($mn)	466.7	361.2
Profit after tax ($mn)	335.0	258.9
Earnings per share (¢)	60.3	46.6
Cash flow per share (¢)	75.5	61.1
Dividend (¢)	28	28
Percentage franked	55	60
Net tangible assets per share ($)	–	–
Interest cover (times)	22.6	14.3
Return on equity (%)	29.1	21.6
Debt-to-equity ratio (%)	66.7	53.5
Current ratio	1.3	1.4

Consolidated Media Holdings Ltd

CMJ

<www.cmh.com.au>

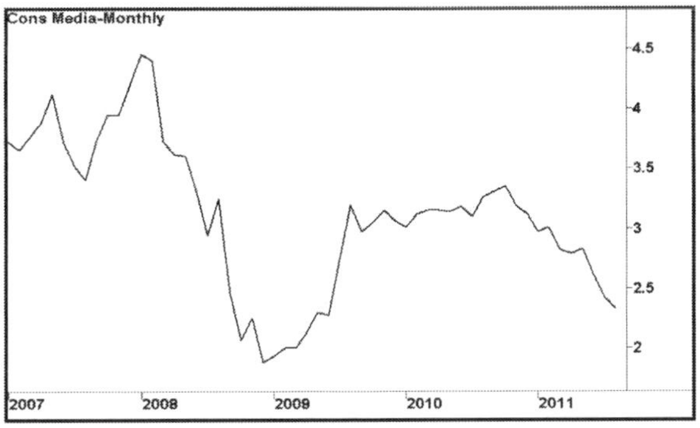

Share price ($)	2.33
12-month high ($)	3.43
12-month low ($)	2.10
Market capitalisation ($mn)	1309.1
Price-to-NTA-per-share ratio	4.0
5-year share price return (% p.a.)	−2.9
Dividend reinvestment plan	No

Sector: Consumer discretionary	Company	Sector
Price/earnings ratio (times)	14.0	13.1
Dividend yield (%)	7.1	3.5

Sydney-based Consolidated Media, formerly known as Publishing and Broadcasting, is a holding company. After a complex restructuring it now holds two key investments. In a joint venture with News Corporation it owns 50 per cent of Premier Media Group, which runs the Fox Sports, Fuel TV and How To subscription television channels. In another joint venture, with Telstra and News Corporation, it owns 25 per cent of the Foxtel subscription television service. It has also invested in SEEKAsia, part of Australia's Seek online employment business. James Packer's Consolidated Press Holdings owns 50.1 per cent of the company's equity, and Kerry Stokes's Seven Group Holdings owns 24.4 per cent.

Latest business results (June 2011, full year)

Profits rose, thanks especially to buoyant business at Foxtel. As a holding company, Consolidated Media receives a share of the after-tax profit from its investments, and the contribution from Foxtel of $37.6 million was 26 per cent up on the previous year. During the year Foxtel recorded a 1 per cent rise in its subscriber base to 1.65 million, with a 6 per cent rise in subscriber revenues to $1.81 billion. Its annualised churn rate fell from 13.5 per cent to 12.5 per cent. By contrast, Premier Media Group suffered from a slowdown in subscriber growth at Foxtel and Austar, as well as from increased costs for certain sports rights, and its contribution dipped 5 per cent to $51.5 million.

Outlook

Consolidated Media's fortunes are tied strongly to the pay television business, which is showing signs of reaching maturity, with just limited scope for further growth. Much could change should Foxtel be allowed to acquire regional provider Austar United Communications. This has been delayed by the Australian Competition and Consumer Commission, on the grounds that the takeover would substantially reduce competition in the two companies' markets. The company expects Premier Media to benefit from the 2011 Rugby World Cup, as well as from the 2012 AFL season, when it will launch a new dedicated television channel. It will also introduce eight dedicated channels for the 2012 London Olympics. Foxtel is working to introduce new delivery methods for its programming, including the On Demand library of programs and movies, which can be accessed through an IQ set top unit. Some Foxtel channels are also now accessible through the Telstra T-Box and the Microsoft Xbox 360 console.

Year to 30 June	2010	2011
Revenues ($mn)	97.2	104.0
EBIT ($mn)	71.1	89.7
EBIT margin (%)	73.2	86.2
Profit before tax ($mn)	83.1	95.7
Profit after tax ($mn)	89.5	94.8

Year to 30 June	2010	2011
Earnings per share (¢)	14.0	16.6
Cash flow per share (¢)	14.0	16.6
Dividend (¢)	16.5	16.5
Percentage franked	64	0
Net tangible assets per share ($)	0.73	0.59
Interest cover (times)	–	–
Return on equity (%)	19.9	24.4
Debt-to-equity ratio (%)	–	–
Current ratio	4.9	0.7

Count Financial Limited

COU

<www.count.com.au>

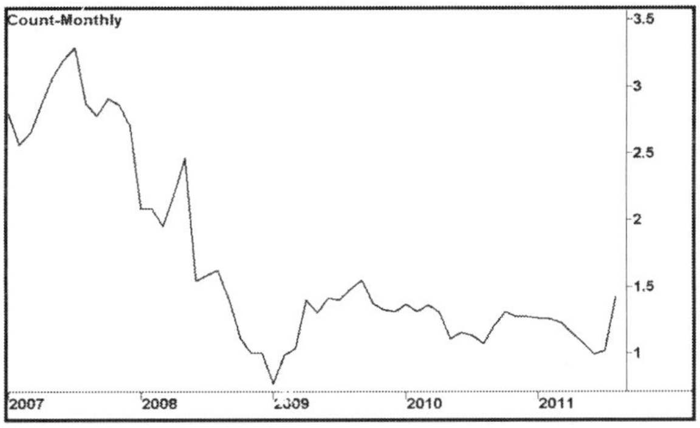

Share price ($)	1.42
12-month high ($)	1.43
12-month low ($)	0.81
Market capitalisation ($mn)	372.4
Price-to-NTA-per-share ratio	3.9
5-year share price return (% p.a.)	−3.6
Dividend reinvestment plan	No

Sector: Financials	Company	Sector
Price/earnings ratio (times)	14.5	10.8
Dividend yield (%)	7.0	6.8

Sydney-based financial services specialist Count Financial was established in 1980, and has since grown into Australia's largest independently owned network of financial planning accountants and advisers. It consists of a franchise network of more than 400 mainly accountancy practices, employing some 900 financial advisers. It provides traditional accounting services, and offers advice in such areas of financial planning as wealth creation, wealth protection, superannuation, home and investment loans, business loans and leasing. It also holds investment funds under management. Its Finconnect operation is a lending referral business. Its Countplus subsidiary, which owns a network of accounting and financial planning practices, was listed on the ASX in December 2010. Count continues to hold 39.1 per cent of the Countplus equity. Count also owns 17.3 per cent of the equity of Mortgage Choice, a mortgage broking firm, and 7.4 per cent of the equity of DKN Financial Group, which is expected to be acquired by IOOF Holdings. In August 2011 Commonwealth Bank made a takeover bid for Count.

Latest business results (June 2011, full year)

In an increasingly volatile market the after-tax profit edged up. Revenues also grew modestly, thanks especially to rising retail fees and commissions. Total funds under advice fell 4 per cent to $9.86 billion. Residential lending edged up 0.2 per cent but the company's portfolio of loans outstanding fell 5 per cent to $3.59 billion. About 29 per cent of revenues were related to superannuation, with non-superannuation investments comprising 24 per cent of revenues, residential and commercial lending at 20 per cent and insurance representing 15 per cent. The company also reported a $37 million pre-tax profit from the listing of Countplus.

Outlook

Count's future is now tied up with Commonwealth Bank's $1.40-a-share takeover bid, which values the company at $373 million. The Count founder and executive chairman Barry Lambert and his family have accepted the offer, and will sell their 20 per cent holding. Lambert has said that proposed government reforms to the financial advice industry were forcing smaller financial advisory groups to seek mergers in order to remain competitive. However, the takeover offer must be approved by shareholders, and it is possible other financial institutions may come in with higher bids. Meanwhile, Count says it has been strengthening its software, platforms and advice offerings in advance of the proposed government reforms.

Year to 30 June	2010	2011
Revenues ($mn)	123.9	126.0

Year to 30 June	2010	2011
EBIT ($mn)	33.2	44.2
EBIT margin (%)	26.8	35.1
Profit before tax ($mn)	33.7	42.1
Profit after tax ($mn)	24.0	25.6
Earnings per share (¢)	9.3	9.8
Cash flow per share (¢)	9.4	10.3
Dividend (¢)	8	10
Percentage franked	100	100
Net tangible assets per share ($)	0.22	0.37
Interest cover (times)	–	21.1
Return on equity (%)	45.3	32.5
Debt-to-equity ratio (%)	11.6	15.4
Current ratio	1.2	1.1

Country Road Limited

CTY

<www.countryroad.com.au>

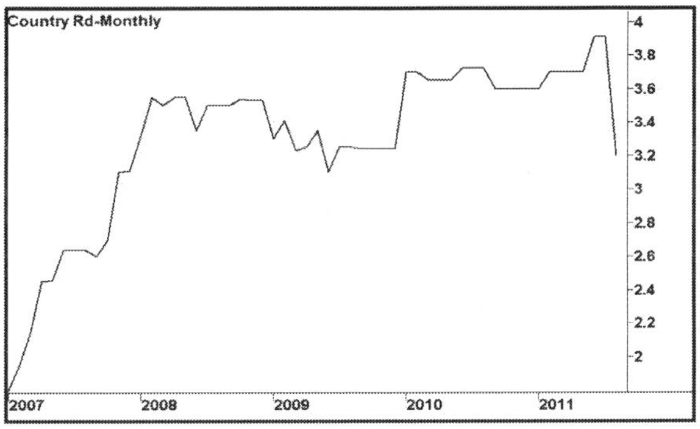

Share price ($)	3.20
12-month high ($)	3.95
12-month low ($)	3.20
Market capitalisation ($mn)	221.0
Price-to-NTA-per-share ratio	2.7
5-year share price return (% p.a.)	12.4
Dividend reinvestment plan	No

Sector: Consumer discretionary	Company	Sector
Price/earnings ratio (times)	12.1	13.1
Dividend yield (%)	5.8	3.5

Melbourne-based Country Road started life in 1974 as a niche shirt business. It has since evolved into a prominent fashion clothing and accessories designer and retailer, under the Country Road and Trenery brands. It sells through some 60 stores and a further 80 concession outlets in Australia, New Zealand and South Africa. It is an 88 per cent-owned subsidiary of Woolworths South Africa, with Australian retail magnate Solomon Lew holding a further 11 per cent of the equity.

Latest business results (June 2011, full year)

The company reported a strong increase in revenues and profits, although the former figure mainly reflected accounting changes. Australia and New Zealand sales fell 2 per cent during the year, including even the contribution from new store openings. Australian retail conditions were particularly weak, with sales down 10.9 per cent on a same-store basis. However, the company began adding South African sales to the revenues figure, whereas previously these had been recorded, under a licence agreement, as royalty income. The good profit result came from a series of significant cost-saving initiatives from the company, including the enforcement of strict inventory control and cash management. The result was also aided by the restructuring of Country Road's South African operations and by an expansion in the company's product range. During the year the company opened seven new Trenery and three new Country

Road stores in Australia and New Zealand, and two new concession stores in South Africa. Australia was responsible for 80 per cent of total turnover, South Africa contributed 13 per cent and New Zealand the remainder.

Outlook

With its operations concentrated in Australia, Country Road has been hit by the slowdown in consumer spending that has also been affecting rival fashion-related retail groups. In response, it is seeking to introduce further cost-reduction measures and to maintain tight inventory control. It is also introducing new product lines. In addition, it is working towards an expansion of its small South African chain of 18 stores, together with its parent company Woolworths South Africa. In response to the growth in internet sales, Country Road has launched its own popular online presence, and is also introducing a range of smartphone applications. In a bid to compete with cheap internet retailers it has been trialling a free delivery service for orders received online. The company is a beneficiary of the strong dollar.

Year to 30 June	2010	2011
Revenues ($mn)	381.0	420.1
EBIT ($mn)	17.9	23.1
EBIT margin (%)	4.7	5.5
Gross margin (%)	55.7	58.4
Profit before tax ($mn)	17.5	22.7
Profit after tax ($mn)	12.3	18.2

Year to 30 June	2010	2011
Earnings per share (¢)	17.9	26.4
Cash flow per share (¢)	34.1	50.0
Dividend (¢)	8.81	18.57
Percentage franked	100	100
Net tangible assets per share ($)	1.06	1.16
Interest cover (times)	44.4	55.5
Return on equity (%)	15.4	20.6
Debt-to-equity ratio (%)	0.6	–
Current ratio	1.3	1.4

Credit Corp Group Limited

CCP

<www.creditcorp.com.au>

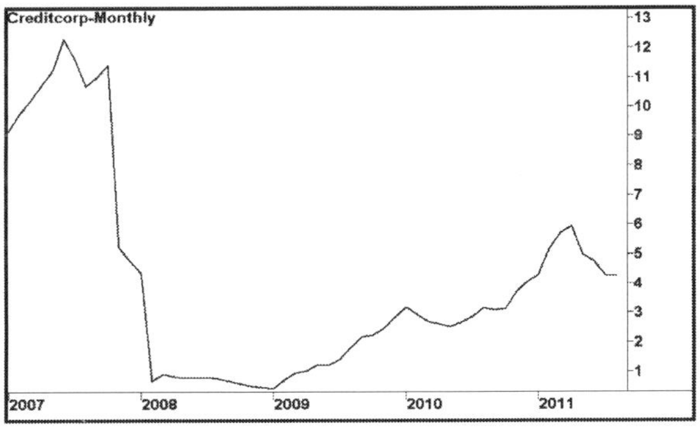

Share price ($)	4.25
12-month high ($)	6.37
12-month low ($)	2.85
Market capitalisation ($mn)	192.1
Price-to-NTA-per-share ratio	1.9
5-year share price return (% p.a.)	−8.7
Dividend reinvestment plan	No

Sector: Industrials	Company	Sector
Price/earnings ratio (times)	9.1	11.9
Dividend yield (%)	4.7	5.5

Sydney-based Credit Corp was formed in 1992, although it has its origins in companies that started in the early 1970s. It provides debt collection services to companies in numerous industries, including the finance, insurance, legal and government sectors, though with a specialty in credit card and unsecured personal loan debt.

Latest business results (June 2011, full year)

A combination of organic growth and new business initiatives helped Credit Corp to a big jump in its profits. Credit Corp buys parcels of debt in the form of purchased debt ledgers (PDLs), and purchases of these during the year jumped 42 per cent to $92.6 million—following a 75 per cent rise in the previous year—thanks to the company's ability to offer attractive pricing to its clients. Actual PDL collections and fee income rose 14 per cent to $206.8 million. The company reported a 26 per cent rise in recurring payment arrangements, and these accounts now comprise some 70 per cent of its collections. During the year Credit Corp made its first significant purchases in New Zealand, it acquired its first portfolio of telecommunications receivables and it secured its first insolvency purchases. It also opened its first overseas collection facility, in Manila. This operation has grown to 80 staff members and became profitable in its fifth month, well ahead of schedule.

Outlook

Credit Corp's business effectively involves buying consumer debt at a discount to its face value from debt providers, and then seeking to recover an amount in excess of the purchase price. Often this recovery takes the form of phased payments over an extended period, and Credit Corp thus has substantial recurring income. Setting an appropriate price for the acquisition of PDLs is one of the keys to success, and Credit Corp has acquired expertise in this. However, competition can force PDL prices up, with Collection House and Baycorp among rivals also bidding for debt parcels. Though a weak economy suggests that more people will enter into credit repayment arrangements, it can also mean that more people are unable to repay their debts, hurting business. The company believes its new Manila office has established a platform for expansion into new markets and services. With signs of intensifying competition in its markets, Credit Corp is tentatively forecasting that June 2012 after-tax profit will be little changed from June 2011.

Year to 30 June	2010	2011
Revenues ($mn)	93.3	113.5
EBIT ($mn)	27.7	35.4
EBIT margin (%)	29.7	31.2
Profit before tax ($mn)	19.9	30.1

Year to 30 June	2010	2011
Profit after tax ($mn)	13.0	21.0
Earnings per share (¢)	29.3	46.9
Cash flow per share (¢)	32.2	49.6
Dividend (¢)	8	20
Percentage franked	100	100
Net tangible assets per share ($)	1.97	2.29
Interest cover (times)	3.5	6.6
Return on equity (%)	16.0	21.8
Debt-to-equity ratio (%)	47.6	22.8
Current ratio	2.7	1.2

CSL Limited

CSL

<www.csl.com.au>

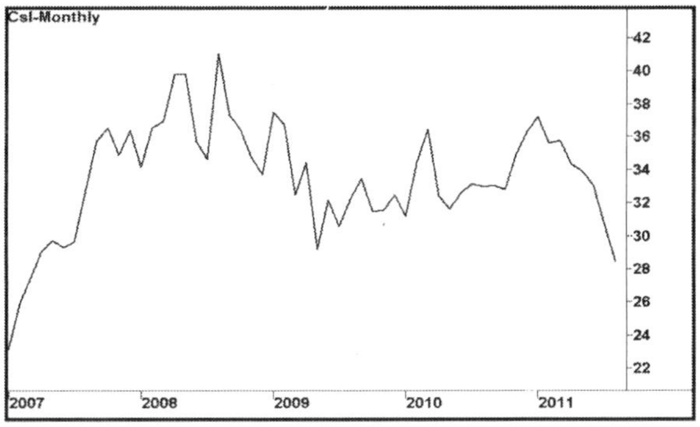

Share price ($)	28.44
12-month high ($)	38.07
12-month low ($)	26.23
Market capitalisation ($mn)	14926.5
Price-to-NTA-per-share ratio	5.5
5-year share price return (% p.a.)	13.1
Dividend reinvestment plan	No

Sector: Health care	Company	Sector
Price/earnings ratio (times)	16.3	17.5
Dividend yield (%)	2.8	2.6

Melbourne-based CSL, formerly the state-owned Commonwealth Serum Laboratories, was founded in

1916. It has grown through acquisition to become a global company, with operations in 27 countries and more than 85 per cent of revenues derived from outside Australia. Its principal business now is the provision of a range of plasma therapies and services through its CSL Behring division. Its CSL Biotherapies business is prominent in the development of a wide variety of vaccines. The CSL Bioplasma business works in the plasma therapeutics business. It has high margins and high market shares for many of its products.

Latest business results (June 2011, full year)

For a second straight year CSL was hit by the strong dollar, and sales and profits fell. However, the company reported that on a constant-currency basis the operational after-tax profit was up 14 per cent. The core CSL Behring division, responsible for about 80 per cent of company turnover, saw sales up 10 per cent on a constant-currency basis. Immunoglobulins and specialty products once again underpinned this growth, with transition programs to new-generation products well under way. The much smaller CSL Biotherapies business saw sales up 4 per cent on a constant-currency basis, a big decline from the 21 per cent jump of the previous year, when the company benefited from a sharp rise in demand for its swine flu vaccine.

Outlook

CSL was for many years a stock market superstar, with businesses that seemed largely impervious to the economic slowdown. However, despite a strong underlying performance, it has been hit hard by the strong dollar, and the company has conceded that the currency threatens its forecast of a 10 per cent rise in profits in the June 2012 year. It could also suffer as a key rival, Octapharma, returns to the lucrative US plasma market later in 2011, following a period when regulators forced it to withdraw its Octagam product due to health concerns. CSL is enjoying particular success with its immunoglobulin products. Its Privigen liquid intravenous product is attracting growing demand. Also gaining in popularity is Hizentra, which can be self-administered. Both these carry higher margins than their predecessor products. With high R&D spending—$325 million in the June 2011 year, up a little from the previous year—CSL expects to see a continuing stream of new products.

Year to 30 June	2010	2011
Revenues ($mn)	4455.8	4187.6
EBIT ($mn)	1357.1	1184.2
EBIT margin (%)	30.5	28.3
Gross margin (%)	51.0	49.2
Profit before tax ($mn)	1379.5	1198.1
Profit after tax ($mn)	1052.9	940.6
Earnings per share (¢)	185.8	174.0
Cash flow per share (¢)	213.4	206.0
Dividend (¢)	80	80

Year to 30 June	2010	2011
Percentage franked	7	3
Net tangible assets per share ($)	5.93	5.20
Interest cover (times)	–	–
Return on equity (%)	21.8	23.9
Debt-to-equity ratio (%)	–	–
Current ratio	4.2	2.9

Data#3 Limited

DTL

<www.data3.com.au>

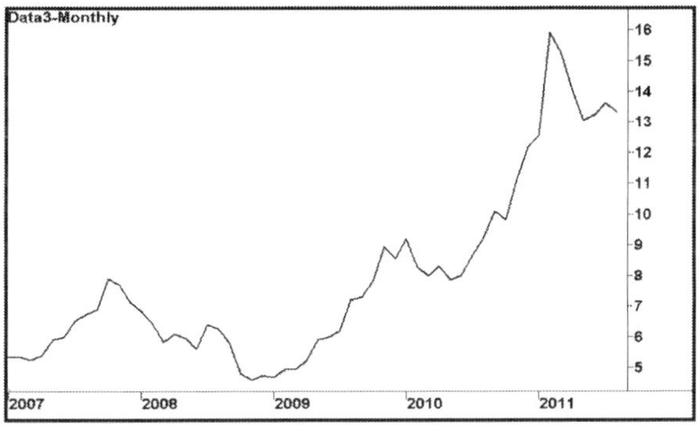

Share price ($)	13.32
12-month high ($)	16.38
12-month low ($)	8.85
Market capitalisation ($mn)	205.1
Price-to-NTA-per-share ratio	8.0
5-year share price return (% p.a.)	33.8
Dividend reinvestment plan	No

Sector: Information technology	Company	Sector
Price/earnings ratio (times)	13.7	18.2
Dividend yield (%)	5.8	3.9

Brisbane-based IT consultant Data#3 was formed in 1984 from the merger of computer software consultancy Powell, Clark and Associates with IBM typewriter dealer Albrand Typewriters and Office Machines. Today it operates from offices around Australia, providing information and communication technology services, notably software licensing and software asset management, to a wide range of businesses that include banking and finance, mining, tourism and leisure, legal, healthcare, manufacturing, distribution, government and utilities.

Latest business results (June 2011, full year)

Data#3 reported an excellent result, with its ninth straight record profit. With profits growing at a substantially faster rate than revenues, the company achieved notable success in boosting margins. Hardware and software product revenues grew 14 per cent to $586.4 million, thanks to a significant number of contracts with new customers. Software licensing fees grew 12 per cent, their 16th consecutive year of growth. Services revenues jumped 29 per cent to $109.8 million. During the year the number of company contractors rose from 277 to 352, while the number of permanent staff rose from 502 to 638.

Outlook

Data#3 is a beneficiary of a recovery in corporate IT spending, which fell sharply during the global financial crisis, and it anticipates that it will be able to deliver further growth in the June 2012 year. However, it is wary of continuing global economic volatility, as IT projects are among the first to be cut or postponed when business conditions worsen. As it continues to strengthen its operations it also faces the twin problems of skill shortages and escalating wage demands. It continues to invest in new premises and automated systems and it expects to launch new and expanded business services, particularly in asset management and workplace productivity. It also expects strong growth in integration services. The company is engaged in a three-year restructuring of its Microsoft reseller program. Much of Data#3's profits come from software licensing, with the provision of Microsoft software a particular strength, and the company could be threatened by moves to cloud computing. This would mean that customers might no longer need to buy their software needs, but could access appropriate applications online. In response, the company is providing its own cloud computing consultancy services, advising clients on how best to adopt this new business model. With more than $53 million in net cash holdings, the company continues to seek new acquisition or expansion opportunities.

Year to 30 June	2010	2011
Revenues ($mn)	598.6	696.2
EBIT ($mn)	15.2	20.4
EBIT margin (%)	2.5	2.9

Year to 30 June	2010	2011
Gross margin (%)	9.2	10.2
Profit before tax ($mn)	15.8	21.8
Profit after tax ($mn)	10.9	15.0
Earnings per share (¢)	70.9	97.4
Cash flow per share (¢)	77.5	101.8
Dividend (¢)	56	77
Percentage franked	100	100
Net tangible assets per share ($)	1.36	1.66
Interest cover (times)	–	–
Return on equity (%)	44.2	53.3
Debt-to-equity ratio (%)	–	–
Current ratio	1.1	1.2

David Jones Limited

DJS

<www.davidjones.com.au>

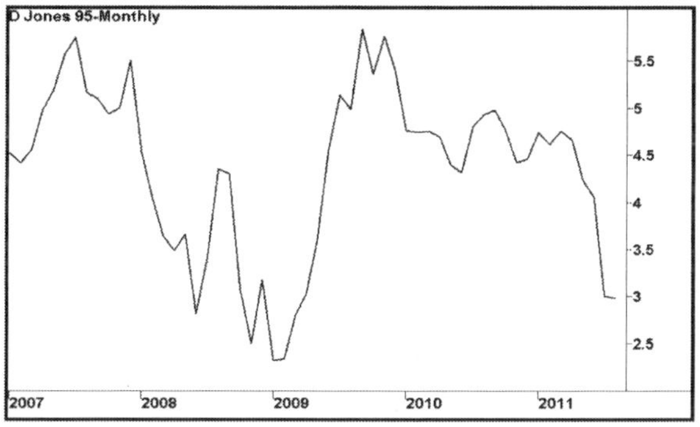

Share price ($)	2.98
12-month high ($)	5.29
12-month low ($)	2.44
Market capitalisation ($mn)	1521.5
Price-to-NTA-per-share ratio	2.0
5-year share price return (% p.a.)	2.9
Dividend reinvestment plan	Yes

Sector: Consumer discretionary	Company	Sector
Price/earnings ratio (times)	8.8	13.1
Dividend yield (%)	10.1	3.5

Retailer David Jones dates back to 1838 and the opening of the David Jones & Company general store in Sydney. It is Australia's oldest department store chain and claims to be the oldest in the world still trading under its original name. It operates 36 stores throughout Australia.

Latest business results (January 2011, half year)

Sales edged down from the January 2010 half, but profits showed a modest gain, in what was a solid result for the company in a sluggish retail environment. Facing particularly strong competition, including heavy promotional activity from rivals and some significant discounting, the company responded with continued re-allocation of space to high-margin categories and an increase in the promotion of its own exclusive brands. Nevertheless, its gross profit margin fell slightly from 40.0 per cent to 39.7 per cent. The addition of 30 per cent more selling space to the key David Jones Melbourne CBD store helped it gain market share in the city. The company also benefited from its financial services activities, with EBIT for this business up 7.5 per cent to $22.8 million.

Outlook

David Jones is being battered by fragile consumer sentiment—a result of uncertainty over the impact of the new carbon tax, rising interest rates and volatile European economies—and it has described trading conditions as the worst since 2001. The June and July 2011 clearance sales showed a sharp deterioration in business, and the company expected July 2011 second-half sales revenues to be down 11 per cent from July 2010, with profits down by as much as 12 per cent. For the January 2012 half the company anticipated that profits will fall 15 per cent to 20 per cent from January 2011. Nevertheless, it maintains a strong expansion program that it feels will deliver solid long-term growth. It has entered into an agreement to launch a new 14000-square-metre store in the Highpoint Shopping Centre in Melbournes west. This will open in 2013, and is expected to generate annual sales of $50 million to $60 million. The company has four other new stores in the pipeline, in New South Wales, Queensland and Western Australia, and it also maintains an active program of refurbishing existing stores. It continues to add new brands to its portfolio, and it has also introduced its own online store.

Year to 31 July*	2009	2010
Revenues ($mn)	1985.5	2053.1
EBIT ($mn)	225.6	248.8
EBIT margin (%)	11.4	12.1
Gross margin (%)	39.6	39.7
Profit before tax ($mn)	217.4	242.0
Profit after tax ($mn)	156.5	170.8

Year to 31 July*	2009	2010
Earnings per share (¢)	31.5	34.0
Cash flow per share (¢)	40.3	42.7
Dividend (¢)	28	30
Percentage franked	100	100
Interest cover (times)	27.6	36.6
Return on equity (%)	23.9	23.9

* 25 July 2009

Half year to 29 January**	2010	2011
Revenues ($mn)	1086.1	1083.4
Profit before tax ($mn)	143.5	150.1
Profit after tax ($mn)	100.5	105.7
Earnings per share (¢)	20.0	20.8
Dividend (¢)	12	13
Percentage franked	100	100
Net tangible assets per share ($)	1.36	1.46
Debt-to-equity ratio (%)	9.7	9.8
Current ratio	1.0	1.1

** 23 January 2010

Domino’s Pizza Enterprises Ltd

DMP

<www.dominos.com.au>

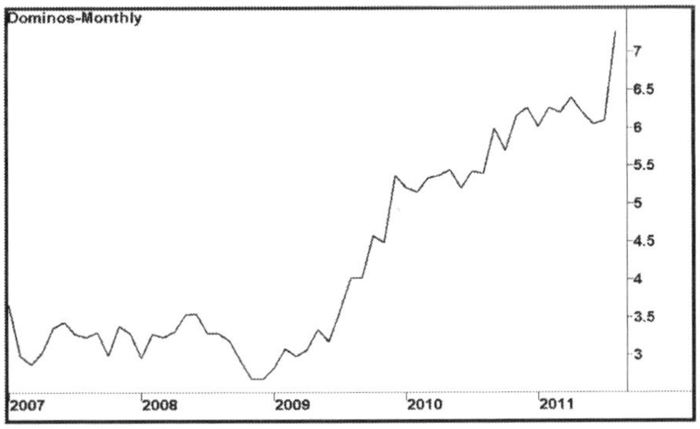

Share price ($)	7.26
12-month high ($)	7.45
12-month low ($)	5.10
Market capitalisation ($mn)	496.6
Price-to-NTA-per-share ratio	10.2
5-year share price return (% p.a.)	17.8
Dividend reinvestment plan	No

Sector: Consumer discretionary	Company	Sector
Price/earnings ratio (times)	23.2	13.1
Dividend yield (%)	3.0	3.5

Brisbane-based Domino's Pizza Enterprises has its roots in the establishment of Australia's first Domino's store in Springwood, Queensland, in 1983. Today it holds the exclusive master franchise rights for the Domino's pizza brand and system—owned by Domino's Pizza in the US—for Australia, New Zealand, France, Belgium, the Netherlands and Monaco, and has become the largest Domino's franchisee in the world. Its network incorporates more than 865 stores, with about 12 per cent of these—mainly in Australia and New Zealand—company owned, and the remainder held by franchisees. In Australia it is the sixth-largest fast-food chain. More than a quarter of the company's revenue derives from Europe.

Latest business results (July 2011, full year)

Domino's announced another sparkling result as it continued to expand. During the year it added 28 stores to its network in Australia and New Zealand, and a further 25 in Europe. It also closed or removed from the network 10 European stores. Australia and New Zealand recorded 11.3 per cent growth, or 13.2 per cent on a same-store basis. Europe achieved sales growth of 14.9 per cent, or 5.9 per cent on a same-store basis. However, European profit—already low—fell further, although in local currencies it edged up.

Outlook

Domino's continues on its strong expansion path, and it forecasts the addition of 60 to 70 new stores in the June 2012 year, with after-tax profit growth of around 15 per cent. Looking longer term, it has revised up its Australia and New Zealand store target from 620 to 750—the present number is 550—to be achieved within six years. Its target is for 2000 stores in Europe, up from 316 at present, to be realised over 15 years. As part of its European growth strategy it aims to boost the number of company-owned stores, believing these provide leadership structure and support to the entire network. In Australia and New Zealand it has embarked on a $24 million store refurbishment program. It has also launched, late in 2010, an advanced online ordering system, and already 40 per cent of Australian orders are received online or through mobile devices. It plans to expand this innovation to its European businesses. However, the company has expressed deep concern about the rising cost of labour, which it describes as one of its biggest challenges, and about the prospects for higher food commodity prices.

Year to 3 July*	2010	2011
Revenues ($mn)	234.7	245.3
EBIT ($mn)	23.1	29.0
EBIT margin (%)	9.8	11.8
Profit before tax ($mn)	23.7	29.7

Year to 3 July*	2010	2011
Profit after tax ($mn)	17.8	21.4
Earnings per share (¢)	26.2	31.3
Cash flow per share (¢)	38.0	44.1
Dividend (¢)	17.8	21.9
Percentage franked	100	100
Net tangible assets per share ($)	0.70	0.71
Interest cover (times)	–	–
Return on equity (%)	18.2	20.9
Debt-to-equity ratio (%)	–	–
Current ratio	1.6	1.1

* 4 July 2010

DWS Advanced Bus. Solutions Ltd

DWS

<www.dws.com.au>

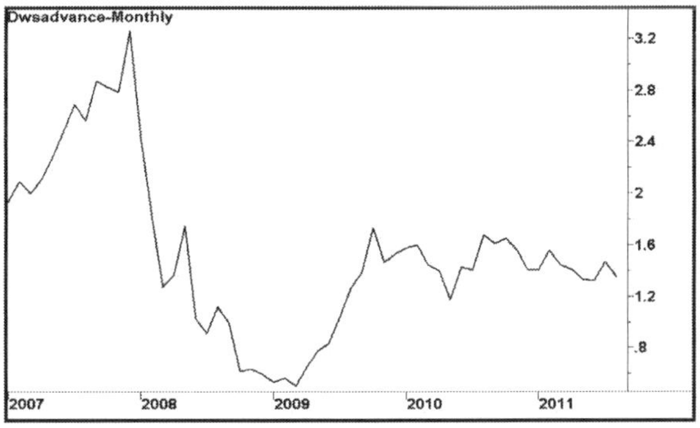

Share price ($)	1.35
12-month high ($)	1.73
12-month low ($)	1.14
Market capitalisation ($mn)	179.3
Price-to-NTA-per-share ratio	5.9
5-year share price return (% p.a.)	9.6
Dividend reinvestment plan	No

Sector: Information technology	Company	Sector
Price/earnings ratio (times)	10.3	18.2
Dividend yield (%)	8.9	3.9

Melbourne-based DWS is an IT services company established in 1991. It specialises in the design, development and maintenance of software for a range of clients across many industries. It operates from offices in Melbourne, Sydney, Adelaide, Geelong, Canberra and Brisbane.

Latest business results (June 2011, full year)

Revenues edged up but profits were down, with DWS's costs rising as it boosted staff numbers, launched two new specialist business operations and opened a new office. The average utilisation rate for its consultants fell 3 per cent to 75 per cent, which the company attributed to disruptions caused by federal and Victorian state elections, natural disasters in Queensland and a decision by Telstra to stand down contractors for an extended period over Christmas. Despite disruptions from the elections, the company continued to win significant business in the government sector, which rose from 17 per cent of revenues in the June 2010 year to 24 per cent. A conclusion to some large projects led to the information and communications technology sector dropping from 33 per cent to 24 per cent of revenues. Banking and finance added clients, to rise from 13 per cent to 18 per cent of turnover, while the utilities sector fell from 20 per cent to 17 per cent. During the year the total number of consultants rose from 504 to 540, with total staff numbers up from 550 to 594, and employee costs increased 7 per cent.

Outlook

With margins now stabilised, DWS believes that it has laid the foundations for renewed profit growth. It has also embarked on an aggressive long-term expansion strategy, and is seeking to hire more staff, although it is constrained by skills shortages and by escalating wage demands. It is also working to expand its number of offices. Its latest office is in Geelong, Victoria, and is intended to service a growth in regional client demand. The company is also seeking to expand business with existing clients. Its two new specialist business operations are in the fields of business intelligence and cloud computing, where it sees great potential. It believes government business will continue to grow, and it is also experiencing solid demand in the banking and finance and the utilities sectors. DWS has no debt and around $11 million in cash holdings, and is seeking appropriate acquisitions or growth opportunities. It believes its mid 2011 acquisition of Taten Pty Ltd will strengthen it in the financial services and cloud computing sectors.

Year to 30 June	2010	2011
Revenues ($mn)	95.7	98.4

Year to 30 June	2010	2011
EBIT ($mn)	26.5	24.5
EBIT margin (%)	27.7	24.9
Profit before tax ($mn)	26.8	25.1
Profit after tax ($mn)	18.5	17.4
Earnings per share (¢)	14.0	13.1
Cash flow per share (¢)	14.3	13.4
Dividend (¢)	11.25	12
Percentage franked	100	100
Net tangible assets per share ($)	0.23	0.23
Interest cover (times)	–	–
Return on equity (%)	34.2	30.6
Debt-to-equity ratio (%)	–	–
Current ratio	3.7	4.0

•

Equity Trustees Limited

EQT

<www.equitytrustees.com.au>

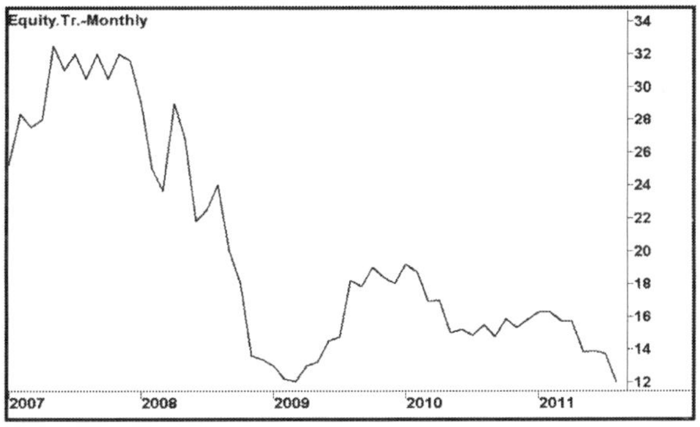

Share price ($)	12.00
12-month high ($)	17.30
12-month low ($)	11.60
Market capitalisation ($mn)	102.8
Price-to-NTA-per-share ratio	4.6
5-year share price return (% p.a.)	−2.2
Dividend reinvestment plan	Yes

Sector: Financials	Company	Sector
Price/earnings ratio (times)	12.4	10.8
Dividend yield (%)	8.3	6.8

Melbourne-based Equity Trustees dates back to its establishment by a special Act of Parliament in 1888 as a trustee and executor service provider. It is today a diversified financial services company with businesses that include estate management services, trustee services, legal and financial advice, superannuation and personal investment services and responsible entity services for external fund managers. In August 2011 it acquired Lifetime Planning and Tender Living Care, an advisory business in the aged care sector.

Latest business results (June 2011, full year)

Revenues rose, but profits were little changed as volatile markets and higher costs hit the company's operations. The company's biggest business unit is Corporate Fiduciary and Fund Services, which manages the company's wholesale and retail funds. It saw revenues up 6.4 per cent, with a growth in responsible entity clients and some strong fund inflows. Funds under management and administration rose 20.5 per cent to $19.48 billion. Superannuation has become the second-largest business unit, partly reflecting the acquisition during the year of OAMPS Superannuation, now renamed Apex Super. Revenues were up 34.9 per cent, and funds under management leapt 56.9 per cent to $979 million. The third business unit, Private Clients, provides personal asset management services. An increase in client numbers helped boost revenues 12.2 per cent, and funds under management and administration rose 4 per cent to $1.31 billion.

The company's profits were affected by a 19.2 per cent rise in operating expenses, in part due to acquisition costs and duplicated staff costs during the implementation of a new investment management system.

Outlook

Equity Trustees is intimately geared to trends in financial markets, and it has expressed concern that volatility and challenging business conditions that became especially evident during the June 2011 fourth quarter appear set to continue. Nevertheless, it continues to invest for long-term growth, working to restructure its operations to enhance client relationship management and to focus on risk management and compliance. It has also boosted its marketing efforts, at a time when some rivals have been cutting back, and it has completed a new IT platform project. It sees the aged care advisory business as an attractive market sector, and believes its new Lifetime Planning and Tender Living Care acquisition will be a strong complement to its existing wealth management and personal estates and trusts operations. The company also continues to seek out further acquisitions.

Year to 30 June	2010	2011
Revenues ($mn)	33.6	38.6
Corporate Fiduciary and Fund Services (%)	48	45
Superannuation (%)	25	29
Private Clients (%)	25	25

Year to 30 June	2010	2011
EBIT ($mn)	10.9	11.2
EBIT margin (%)	32.6	29.0
Profit before tax ($mn)	11.5	11.5
Profit after tax ($mn)	8.0	8.2
Earnings per share (¢)	96.6	97.0
Cash flow per share (¢)	110.0	110.1
Dividend (¢)	110	100
Percentage franked	100	100
Net tangible assets per share ($)	2.79	2.60
Interest cover (times)	–	–
Return on equity (%)	15.1	15.0
Debt-to-equity ratio (%)	–	–
Current ratio	5.2	3.1

Euroz Limited

EZL

<www.euroz.com.au>

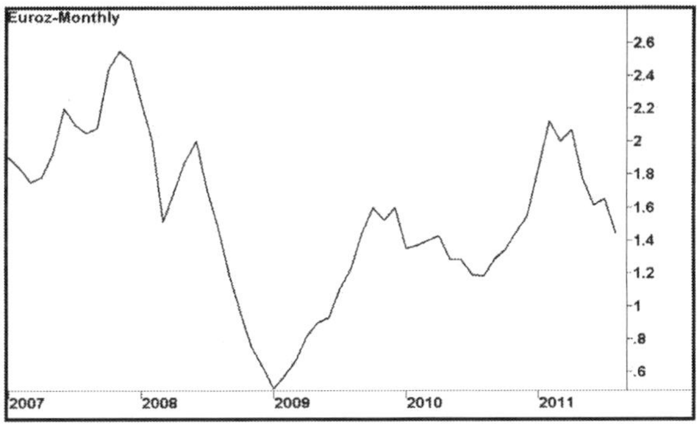

Share price ($)	1.44
12-month high ($)	2.34
12-month low ($)	1.13
Market capitalisation ($mn)	205.9
Price-to-NTA-per-share ratio	1.7
5-year share price return (% p.a.)	10.4
Dividend reinvestment plan	No

Sector: Financials	Company	Sector
Price/earnings ratio (times)	7.4	10.8
Dividend yield (%)	12.5	6.8

Perth-based stockbroker Euroz has its roots in the engineering firm of Treloar Enterprises, established in the early 1960s. It took its present name and form in 2000, and is today a leader in Western Australian investment banking. It is a holding company and operates through two wholly owned subsidiaries. The first is Euroz Securities, which works across four broad areas—institutional dealing, retail dealing, research and corporate finance. The second is Westoz Funds Management, which manages two publicly listed funds, Ozgrowth and Westoz Investment Company. Euroz staff members own much of the company's equity.

Latest business results (June 2011, full year)

In a difficult year for stockbrokers, Euroz managed to squeeze out a modest rise in its profits. Stock-broking revenues actually rose by more than 20 per cent, but profits were down 25 per cent. However, the company's own Principal Trading operation achieved another big jump in profits—up more than seven times—although revenues were down. The Funds Management business saw revenues and profits both down. New capital raisings, mainly in the resources sector, were a particular feature of the year's business, with $1.2 billion raised, compared with $722 million in the previous year. This included $200 million for Aurora Oil & Gas, $164.2 million for Independence Group, $148.5 million for Indophil Resources and $136 million for each of Mineral Deposits and Teranga Gold. At June 2011 Westoz

Funds Management held $286 million in funds under management, slightly down from $295 million a year earlier.

Outlook

Euroz occupies a strong position within the Western Australian financial sector, and its fortunes are tied intimately to trends in the state's economy, which in turn are quite allied to the resources sector. It is highly regarded for its research division, and especially for its specialised knowledge of Western Australian companies. Its institutional dealing division is also well regarded for its in-depth knowledge of Western Australian companies, and is one of the largest teams in Australia with a specialty in the small- and medium-cap end of the market, and an extensive client base of Australian and international investors. Its corporate finance arm has extensive experience in mergers and acquisitions, underwriting and equity capital markets. However, the company's business results are capable of quite sharp fluctuations. Euroz has a strong balance sheet, with no debt and $68 million in cash holdings, and appears to be well able to weather financial market volatility.

Year to 30 June	2010	2011
Revenues ($mn)	76.5	77.8
Stockbroking (%)	53	63
Principal Trading (%)	18	12
Funds Management (%)	13	12
EBIT ($mn)	31.3	31.5

Year to 30 June	2010	2011
EBIT margin (%)	41.0	40.5
Profit before tax ($mn)	33.5	34.4
Profit after tax ($mn)	26.3	26.6
Earnings per share (¢)	20.1	19.4
Cash flow per share (¢)	20.2	20.2
Dividend (¢)	12	18
Percentage franked	100	100
Net tangible assets per share ($)	0.83	0.84
Interest cover (times)	–	–
Return on equity (%)	25.6	23.3
Debt-to-equity ratio (%)	–	–
Current ratio	3.4	2.7

Fantastic Holdings Limited

FAN

<www.fantasticholdings.com.au>

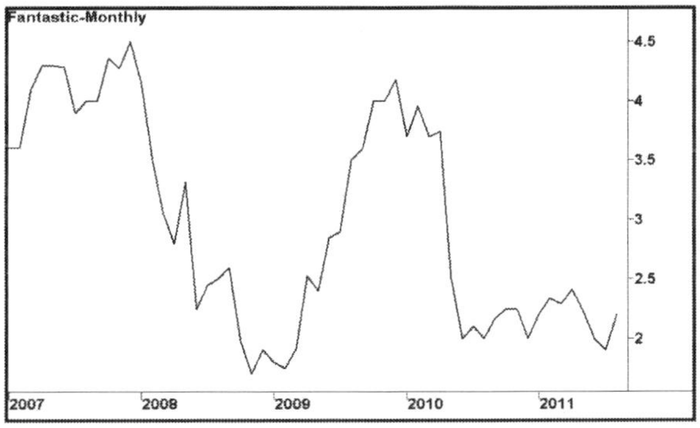

Share price ($)	2.20
12-month high ($)	2.47
12-month low ($)	1.70
Market capitalisation ($mn)	226.4
Price-to-NTA-per-share ratio	2.5
5-year share price return (% p.a.)	−2.7
Dividend reinvestment plan	No

Sector: Consumer discretionary	Company	Sector
Price/earnings ratio (times)	11.6	13.1
Dividend yield (%)	5.0	3.5

Sydney-based furniture manufacturer and retailer Fantastic Holdings evolved from a struggling furniture chain that was acquired in 1996 by a group of partners and relaunched. Today, it is one of Australia's leading budget furniture chains, operating nationwide. It has grown through organic expansion and acquisition, and operates a total of 72 company-owned and franchised Fantastic Furniture outlets, 29 Plush leather goods stores, 14 Original Mattress Factory stores, 11 Dare Gallery stores and two Le Cornu stores.

Latest business results (June 2011, full year)

Fantastic rebounded from the previous year—when profits edged down—with a modest increase, a good result in an environment of sluggish consumer discretionary spending. However, much of the growth came from new store openings. On a same-store basis sales actually dipped 1.1 per cent. The company's two core businesses, Fantastic Furniture and Plush, both delivered solid increases in sales and profits. The Original Mattress Factory brand did slightly better than in the previous year. However, both Dare Gallery and Le Cornu suffered sales and profits declines. During the year the company opened five new Fantastic Furniture stores, as well as three for Plush and two for Dare Gallery. It closed two Fantastic Furniture and two Plush stores.

Outlook

Fantastic has achieved success in the budget furniture sector through a policy of careful planning and strict cost containment. However, despite operating generally at the budget end of the market, it is still not immune to slowing consumer spending trends, though it believes that a weaker economy could help it boost market share. In addition, with continuing cost-cutting initiatives it believes it might be able to boost profits further in the June 2012 year. It is a significant beneficiary of the strength of the dollar. With the Le Cornu and Dare Gallery stores continuing to struggle, the company has announced a strategic review of their futures. It will also now wait a year before deciding whether to expand the Original Mattress Factory concept outside New South Wales and Canberra, hoping first to consolidate this business in those two regions. Fantastic has established a China-based design and product-sourcing office, which it believes will enhance quality, help build partnerships with suppliers and reduce costs, and it says the first product ranges designed and sourced through this office have been received favourably by customers. The company plans 10 new store openings in the June 2012 year.

Year to 30 June	2010	2011
Revenues ($mn)	419.1	436.7
EBIT ($mn)	25.7	28.0
EBIT margin (%)	6.1	6.4

Year to 30 June	2010	2011
Gross margin (%)	45.7	47.5
Profit before tax ($mn)	25.1	27.2
Profit after tax ($mn)	18.5	19.5
Earnings per share (¢)	18.1	19.0
Cash flow per share (¢)	22.4	24.7
Dividend (¢)	10.25	11
Percentage franked	100	100
Net tangible assets per share ($)	0.80	0.89
Interest cover (times)	43.7	35.1
Return on equity (%)	21.8	20.3
Debt-to-equity ratio (%)	23.8	7.7
Current ratio	1.8	2.0

Finbar Group Limited

FRI

<www.finbar.com.au>

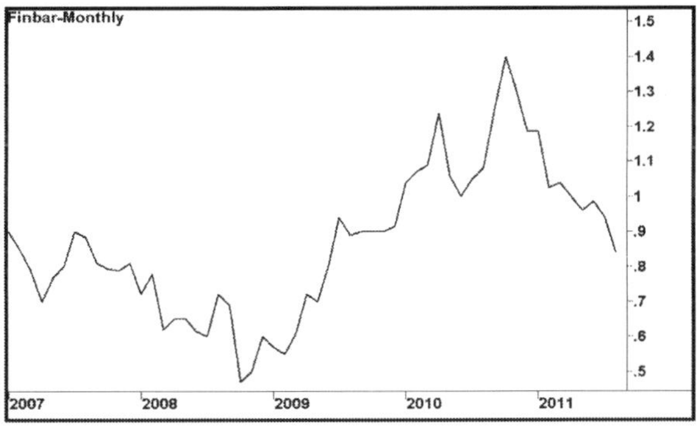

Share price ($)	0.84
12-month high ($)	1.51
12-month low ($)	0.80
Market capitalisation ($mn)	173.6
Price-to-NTA-per-share ratio	1.0
5-year share price return (% p.a.)	9.4
Dividend reinvestment plan	Yes

Sector: Financials	Company	Sector
Price/earnings ratio (times)	6.5	10.8
Dividend yield (%)	10.1	6.8

Perth property developer Finbar has roots that date back to 1984. It specialises in the development of medium- to high-density residential apartments and commercial/retail buildings, primarily in the Perth metropolitan area, although it has also been expanding to the Pilbara mining region. It works either directly or in tandem with joint venture partners. It also maintains a small rental property business through its wholly owned subsidiary Finbar Property Trust.

Latest business results (June 2011, full year)

Profits edged up, despite reduced revenues, reflecting the timing of property settlements. Most of the result came from the completion of two major apartment projects. The larger of these was the Times Two development in East Perth, with 172 of the 202 units settling during the year. The other was The Edge in Victoria Park, with 70 units settling during the year. Other completed projects included Delmar at Mandurah Ocean Marina, The Saint and Code, both in East Perth, and the Gateway Office Building at Victoria Park. This last building is being held by the company as an investment property and has been 93 per cent leased. Commercial property development and rental income comprised about 12 per cent of total company revenues, up from around 4 per cent in the previous year. During the year Finbar made a further modest reduction in its net debt.

Outlook

Finbar is a beneficiary of the strong Western Australian economy and a generally resilient property market. Although its results in part reflect timing issues, it has also achieved noteworthy success in being able to boost its business during the economic downturn. With strong cash flow, good access to finance and carefully selected joint venture partners it has been able to buy new development sites at good prices, and it has a strong pipeline of projects under construction or in the planning stages, and these will provide a base for continued strength in future years. It has no scheduled project completions in the December 2011 half, but it expects good returns from the completion in the June 2012 half of the 28-storey Fairlanes apartment and office project and the 10-storey 18 on Plain apartment development. Finbar has recently ventured to Karratha in the Pilbara region, and has under construction there a nine-storey complex, Pelago West, incorporating apartments, offices and shops. A second development, Pelago East, is also planned.

Year to 30 June	2010	2011
Revenues ($mn)	198.9	97.4
EBIT ($mn)	29.4	32.5
EBIT margin (%)	14.8	33.4
Gross margin (%)	19.6	28.7
Profit before tax ($mn)	32.2	34.9

Year to 30 June	2010	2011
Profit after tax ($mn)	23.6	24.0
Earnings per share (¢)	16.1	13.0
Cash flow per share (¢)	16.1	13.0
Dividend (¢)	7.5	8.5
Percentage franked	100	100
Net tangible assets per share ($)	0.69	0.82
Interest cover (times)	–	–
Return on equity (%)	25.0	17.0
Debt-to-equity ratio (%)	32.0	19.0
Current ratio	2.0	1.6

Fleetwood Corporation Limited

FWD

<www.fleetwood.com.au>

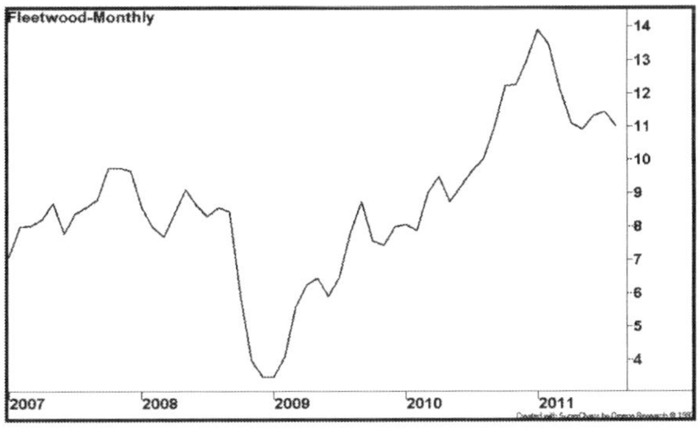

Share price ($)	11.00
12-month high ($)	14.25
12-month low ($)	9.53
Market capitalisation ($mn)	638.8
Price-to-NTA-per-share ratio	3.1
5-year share price return (% p.a.)	19.5
Dividend reinvestment plan	Yes

Sector: Consumer discretionary	Company	Sector
Price/earnings ratio (times)	12.2	13.1
Dividend yield (%)	6.6	3.5

Western Australian company Fleetwood, established in 1964, is a leader in the caravan and portable building businesses. Its Perth-based Coromal Caravans division is the second-largest caravan manufacturer in Australia and its Melbourne-based Windsor Caravans business is the fourth largest. The company also makes caravan spare parts and accessories, along with canopies for utility vehicles. In addition, it is a prominent manufacturer of park homes and portable accommodation for recreational and commercial use, with operations in Western Australia, South Australia, Victoria and the Northern Territory, and it operates an accommodation facility, Searipple Village, for Woodside Petroleum workers in Karratha in Western Australia. With the $56 million, August 2010 acquisition of BRB Modular it is now also involved in the construction of prefabricated modular buildings, for sale and rental to schools and other public sector markets in New South Wales, Queensland and Victoria.

Latest business results (June 2011, full year)

Strong demand for the company's caravans and accommodation units, along with nearly an 11-month contribution from BRB Modular, helped Fleetwood to a big leap in sales revenues and profits. Most of the strong result came from the Manufactured Accommodation division, which incorporates BRB Modular, with revenues more than doubling and EBIT up 48 per cent. During the year the company supplied the units for a 186-room village in Karratha. Fleetwood's own Searipple Village maintained a high level of occupancy. BRB contributed $118.8 million of revenue and $11.3 million of EBIT. The Recreational Vehicles division continued to recover from the slump generated by the global financial crisis, with sales up 12 per cent and EBIT rising nearly 17 per cent.

Outlook

Fleetwood has become a significant beneficiary of the Western Australia resources boom and the consequent demand for portable accommodation to manage the influx of workers. This demand continues to grow, and Fleetwood is involved in the tender process for some large projects. Due to intense competition, it is increasingly using Thai manufacturers as a means of reducing costs. The company has integrated BRB into its operations and is working to introduce its products to west coast markets. It is also installing a production line at BRB's Brisbane facility to provide accommodation units to the Queensland and New South Wales resources sector. The caravan business continues its growth, and Fleetwood is working to boost its dealer network. It is also increasingly seeking to source parts and components from Asian suppliers.

Year to 30 June	2010	2011
Revenues ($mn)	291.1	465.8
Manufactured Accommodation (%)	47	63

Year to 30 June	2010	2011
Recreational Vehicles (%)	53	37
EBIT ($mn)	54.7	74.6
EBIT margin (%)	18.8	16.0
Gross margin (%)	10.4	16.0
Profit before tax ($mn)	54.5	73.6
Profit after tax ($mn)	38.7	51.3
Earnings per share (¢)	72.6	90.0
Cash flow per share (¢)	96.6	114.7
Dividend (¢)	68	73
Percentage franked	100	100
Net tangible assets per share ($)	2.86	3.52
Interest cover (times)	225.2	75.3
Return on equity (%)	25.9	28.2
Debt-to-equity ratio (%)	–	1.6
Current ratio	1.8	1.9

Flight Centre Limited

FLT

<www3.flightcentre.com.au/corporate/>

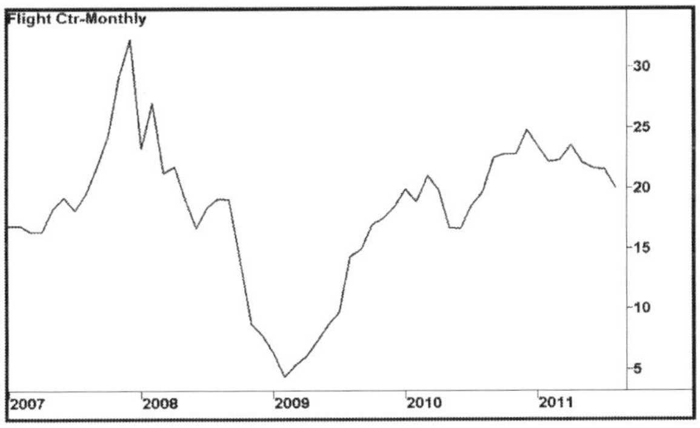

Share price ($)	19.98
12-month high ($)	25.12
12-month low ($)	17.44
Market capitalisation ($mn)	1997.1
Price-to-NTA-per-share ratio	5.1
5-year share price return (% p.a.)	15.4
Dividend reinvestment plan	No

Sector: Consumer discretionary	Company	Sector
Price/earnings ratio (times)	14.3	13.1
Dividend yield (%)	4.2	3.5

Brisbane-based Flight Centre is the largest independent retail travel agency in Australia and New Zealand.

It operates under many brands, including Escape Travel, Student Flights, Travel Associates, Overseas Working Holidays and Infinity Holidays, as well as a growing number of online brands. Its corporate travel management network, FCm Travel Solutions, covers more than 40 countries through strategic licensing agreements with independent travel operators. It has expanded to South Africa, Britain, Canada, the US, India, Singapore, China and Dubai, with around 2240 sales outlets.

Latest business results (June 2011, full year)

Revenues and the pre-tax profit rose, but a large goodwill adjustment on American operations meant after-tax profit was essentially flat on the previous year. In Australia a solid demand for international travel offset continuing weakness in the domestic tourism business. Australia was responsible for about 55 per cent of company revenues but for around 85 per cent of profit. The only other region making a good contribution to profit was the UK, responsible for about 7 per cent of the total. Nevertheless, the company reported that for the first time its activities were profitable at the EBIT level in all 10 countries in which it operates, including initial profit contributions from the US, China and Singapore. Corporate travel was generally firm, as markets recovered from the 2008-09 downturn. During the year the company recorded total transactions of $12.2 billion, up 12 per cent from the previous year. Margins edged down as the company began to put more emphasis on the lower-margin corporate travel market.

Outlook

With $807 million in net cash holdings at June 2011—up from $725 million a year earlier—Flight Centre expects to continue to expand, and is actively seeking further acquisitions. It is also working to boost its existing businesses. However, it has said that for the time being it is not looking to enter new markets. Having achieved a turnaround in its US operations, after two years of significant losses, the company hopes to build profitability in that country, although much depends on economic conditions. It also plans continuing growth in its corporate travel businesses, particularly in the US, and believes it can boost its market share. With the expectation of good business in the large US, UK and Canadian markets, Flight Centre believes June 2012 profits will be around 10 per cent higher than June 2011.

Year to 30 June	2010	2011
Revenues ($mn)	1763.2	1816.9
EBIT ($mn)	203.5	206.9

Year to 30 June	2010	2011
EBIT margin (%)	11.5	11.4
Profit before tax ($mn)	198.5	213.1
Profit after tax ($mn)	139.9	139.8
Earnings per share (¢)	140.3	140.0
Cash flow per share (¢)	194.2	190.1
Dividend (¢)	70	84
Percentage franked	100	100
Net tangible assets per share ($)	3.07	3.95
Interest cover (times)	40.6	–
Return on equity (%)	21.2	19.3
Debt-to-equity ratio (%)	–	–
Current ratio	1.2	1.3

GUD Holdings Limited

GUD

<www.gud.com.au>

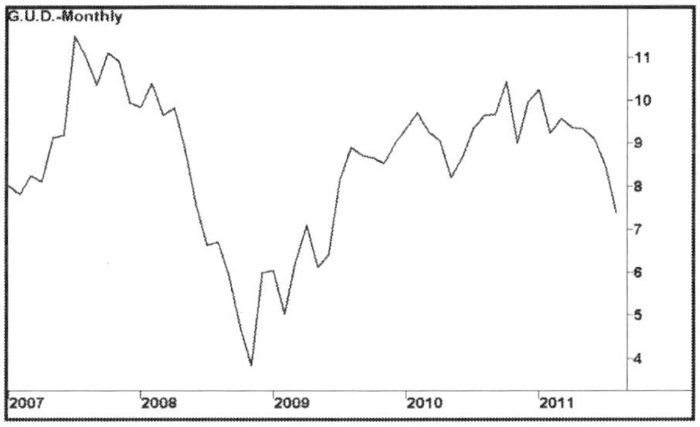

Share price ($)	7.39
12-month high ($)	10.74
12-month low ($)	7.20
Market capitalisation ($mn)	510.6
Price-to-NTA-per-share ratio	5.9
5-year share price return (% p.a.)	8.8
Dividend reinvestment plan	Yes

Sector: Consumer discretionary	Company	Sector
Price/earnings ratio (times)	10.3	13.1
Dividend yield (%)	8.7	3.5

GUD, based in Melbourne and founded in 1940, is a diversified manufacturer and distributor of four broad product lines: Consumer, Automotive, Water and Industrial Products. Consumer Products incorporate Sunbeam electrical appliances and Oates cleaning solutions. Automotive Products include Ryco, Cooper and Wesfil air, oil and fuel filters and Goss replacement fuel pumps. Water products comprise Davey pumps, water pressure systems and spa pool components, Steriflo and Filterpure water treatment systems and Monarch swimming pool products. Industrial Products include Lock Focus locks, Kiroo and Emka hardware for electrical cabinets, Locktech safes and secure filing cabinets and the newly acquired storage products manufacturer Dexion. Through Davey, Dexion and Lock Focus the company enjoys a growing export business.

Latest business results (June 2011, full year)

Sales and profits were up, but this largely reflected a 10-month contribution from the $83 million Dexion acquisition. This new business generated $156.7 million in sales, with EBIT of $4.7 million. There was also an excellent performance from the small but high-margin automotive division, with particularly strong demand for Wesfil products in a competitive market, and additional benefits from the strength of the dollar. The currency helped the company's consumer products business to a 15 per cent profit gain, despite a 6 per cent decline in sales, reflecting the subdued retail environment. Adverse weather caused demand for water products to crash, with sales down 18 per cent and profits plunging 54 per cent. In addition to the figures in the table, the company reported one-off costs of $12.3 million associated with the Dexion acquisition and restructuring initiatives.

Outlook

GUD management have invested heavily in a restructuring of the Dexion business—including factory closures and a major outsourcing program—and believe this will generate significant margin improvement in the June 2012 year. Thanks to the apparent success of this acquisition, the company has now allocated a budget of up to $150 million to buy further underperforming companies. It has also undertaken a restructuring of its Water Products operations, and believes that this division is set for a recovery. Sunbeam products are helped by their involvement with the popular *MasterChef* TV series, and the strong dollar is another bonus. However, continuing weakness in consumer spending will hurt the company, and the strong dollar is a disincentive for GUD's budding export business.

Year to 30 June	2010	2011
Revenues ($mn)	474.7	592.8

Year to 30 June	2010	2011
Consumer Products (%)	52	40
Industrial Products (%)	3	28
Water Products (%)	27	18
Automotive Products (%)	17	14
EBIT ($mn)	71.6	77.1
EBIT margin (%)	15.1	13.0
Gross margin (%)	42.7	39.9
Profit before tax ($mn)	65.2	68.1
Profit after tax ($mn)	46.4	49.0
Earnings per share (¢)	76.5	71.7
Cash flow per share (¢)	94.4	92.0
Dividend (¢)	62	64
Percentage franked	100	100
Net tangible assets per share ($)	1.92	1.25
Interest cover (times)	11.2	8.7
Return on equity (%)	26.6	20.6
Debt-to-equity ratio (%)	7.5	39.6
Current ratio	2.6	1.9

GWA Group Limited

GWA

<www.gwagroup.com.au>

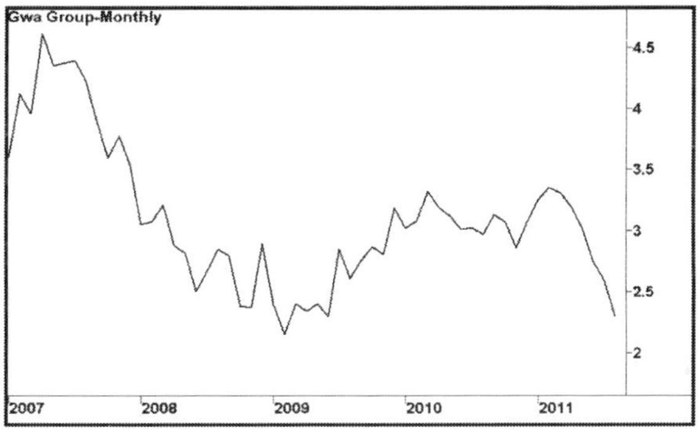

Share price ($)	2.30
12-month high ($)	3.48
12-month low ($)	2.16
Market capitalisation ($mn)	693.5
Price-to-NTA-per-share ratio	16.6
5-year share price return (% p.a.)	0.2
Dividend reinvestment plan	No

Sector: Industrials	Company	Sector
Price/earnings ratio (times)	10.9	11.9
Dividend yield (%)	7.8	5.5

Brisbane-based GWA is a designer, manufacturer, importer and distributor of a wide range of household and commercial products, under numerous brands. GWA Bathrooms and Kitchens specialises in toilets, washbasins, tap ware and other bathroom and kitchen fittings, with brands that include Caroma and Dorf. GWA Heating and Cooling makes hot water and ducted heating and cooling systems. Its brands include Dux and Brivis. GWA Door and Access Systems is a leader in door hardware and fittings, under brands that include Gainsborough, Austral Lock and Gliderol. GWA Commercial Furniture specialises in Sebel-brand commercial furniture and stadium seating.

Latest business results (June 2011, full year)

In a mixed environment for its products, GWA realised an excellent result, with all four of its divisions reporting higher sales and profits. The best result came from the smallest division, Commercial Furniture, with EBIT jumping 56 per cent on just a 3 per cent rise in sales, thanks to supply chain efficiencies. The Door and Access Systems division saw sales up 38 per cent, but this mainly reflected a five-month contribution from the $41 million Gliderol Garage Doors acquisition, and underlying sales growth was a more modest 2.5 per cent. EBIT rose 17 per cent. The Heating and Cooling division benefited from a full-year contribution from the acquisition of Brivis Climate Systems, with sales up 21 per cent and EBIT up 18 per cent. The Bathrooms and Kitchens division was hurt by the strong dollar, with exports down and with the need to reduce some domestic prices to compete with imported products. Sales edged up less than 1 per cent, with EBIT up 5 per cent. Nevertheless, this division, though representing less than half of total turnover, was responsible for 64 per cent of company profit.

Outlook

GWA has undertaken a major restructuring of its operations, resulting in a lower cost base that is helping to boost margins. However, with the dollar remaining high it has determined that further restructuring is necessary, and it plans a reduction in its workforce, the closing of some manufacturing facilities and increased sourcing from overseas manufacturers. With most of its business geared to domestic housing trends it is expecting reduced demand for its products in the near term. In August 2011 it announced the $24 million sale of its Sebel furniture business. It is also seeking further acquisitions.

Year to 30 June	2010	2011
Revenues ($mn)	700.4	726.4
Bathrooms and Kitchens (%)	48	47
Heating and Cooling (%)	23	27
Door and Access Systems (%)	12	16

Year to 30 June	2010	2011
Commercial Furniture (%)	11	10
EBIT ($mn)	95.0	107.2
EBIT margin (%)	13.6	14.8
Gross margin (%)	39.4	35.7
Profit before tax ($mn)	80.0	92.0
Profit after tax ($mn)	55.9	63.4
Earnings per share (¢)	18.6	21
Cash flow per share (¢)	24.7	27.2
Dividend (¢)	18	18
Percentage franked	100	100
Net tangible assets per share ($)	0.21	0.14
Interest cover (times)	6.3	7.1
Return on equity (%)	13	14.5
Debt-to-equity ratio (%)	40.8	45
Current ratio	2.4	2.3

Harvey Norman Holdings Ltd

HVN

<www.harveynormanholdings.com.au>

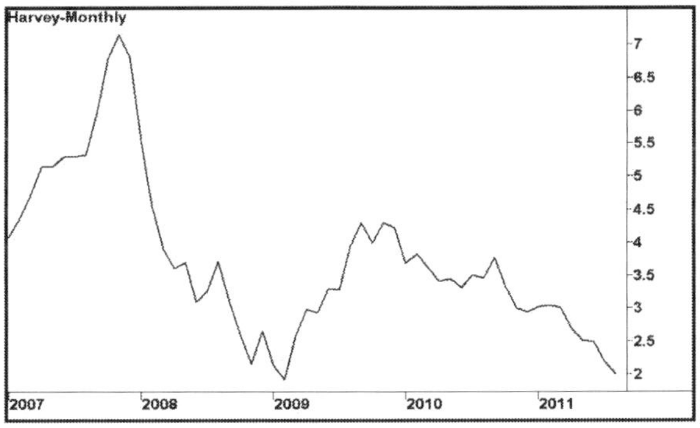

Share price ($)	2.00
12-month high ($)	3.95
12-month low ($)	1.76
Market capitalisation ($mn)	2124.6
Price-to-NTA-per-share ratio	1.0
5-year share price return (% p.a.)	−7.1
Dividend reinvestment plan	No

Sector: Consumer discretionary	Company	Sector
Price/earnings ratio (times)	8.4	13.1
Dividend yield (%)	6.0	3.5

Sydney-based Harvey Norman, established in 1982, operates a chain of nearly 300 retail stores specialising in electrical and electronic goods, home appliances, furniture, flooring, carpets and manchester, throughout Australia, New Zealand, Ireland, Singapore, Malaysia, Slovenia and Croatia, under the Harvey Norman, Domayne, Joyce Mayne, Norman Ross and Space banners. Many of the stores are independently held as part of a franchise operation, from which Harvey Norman receives income for advisory and advertising services. It also receives a considerable amount of income from its $2 billion property portfolio, from its own stores and from the provision of finance to franchisees and customers.

Latest business results (June 2011, full year)

Revenues and profits were up in an environment of sluggish consumer spending. However, much of the rise in revenues came from the company's acquisition in July 2010 of 29 stores from the failed Clive Peeters chain, although this business traded at a big loss. The profit rise derived mainly from a property sale and property revaluations, and the company's underlying profit fell 18 per cent, led by weak business at its domestic franchise stores. Furniture and bedding remained strong, but electrical and electronics business was hurt by price deflation and consumer caution. New Zealand sales were also down, hurt by a GST increase and the Christchurch earthquakes. Slovenian business improved marginally, and

Asia was relatively strong. But Ireland remained in the red.

Outlook

Harvey Norman fears that weakness is set to continue in the domestic retail industry, although it says that it is gaining market share in some categories, and that it is poised to take advantage of an eventual recovery. It is hopeful that the 2011 Rugby World Cup and the 2012 London Olympics will boost sales of electronics products. The company has been converting most of its acquired Clive Peeters and Rick Hart stores to Harvey Norman and Joyce Mayne—although it is also closing some—and believes this will be positive for business. After some years of resistance it is also launching a major e-commerce website, aimed at part in participating in the boom in online purchases among Australians, and it believes this will boost company revenues. It is opening Australia's largest homemaker centre, at Springvale in Melbourne, to be anchored by Ikea and Harvey Norman. It is also opening new stores in Singapore, Slovenia and Croatia. It is working to turn around business in Ireland.

Year to 30 June	2010	2011
Revenues ($mn)	2417.9	2645.4
Franchising Operations (%)	39	35
Retail—New Zealand (%)	25	21

Year to 30 June	2010	2011
Retail—Asia (%)	14	13
Clive Peeters and Rick Hart	0	11
Retail—Ireland and Northern Ireland (%)	9	7
EBIT ($mn)	414.3	409.2
EBIT margin (%)	17.1	15.5
Gross margin (%)	28.0	27.4
Profit before tax ($mn)	386.5	373.9
Profit after tax ($mn)	231.4	252.3
Earnings per share (¢)	21.8	23.7
Cash flow per share (¢)	29.6	32.2
Dividend (¢)	14	12
Percentage franked	100	100
Net tangible assets per share ($)	1.96	2.01
Interest cover (times)	14.9	11.6
Return on equity (%)	11.3	11.7
Debt-to-equity ratio (%)	15.9	21.9
Current ratio	1.6	1.6

Hunter Hall International Limited

HHL

<www.hunterhall.com.au>

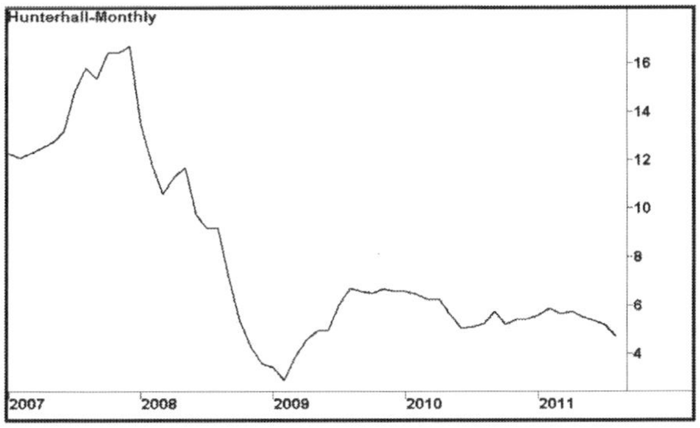

Share price ($)	4.69
12-month high ($)	6.10
12-month low ($)	4.19
Market capitalisation ($mn)	123.0
Price-to-NTA-per-share ratio	5.9
5-year share price return (% p.a.)	–4.5
Dividend reinvestment plan	Yes

Sector: Financials	Company	Sector
Price/earnings ratio (times)	9.9	10.8
Dividend yield (%)	9.6	6.8

Sydney-based Hunter Hall International, founded in 1993, is a funds management company with a specialty in ethical funds. Its main funds are the Value Growth Trust and the Global Ethical Trust. It also operates the Australian Value Trust and the Global Deep Green Trust. It is investment manager for ASX-listed Hunter Hall Global Value Limited, and also for the Hunter Hall Global Opportunities Fund, which is listed on the Dublin Stock Exchange. In February 2011 it launched two new funds: the Global Ethical Trust (Hedged) and the Asian Value Trust. As a matter of policy, Hunter Hall gives 5 per cent of its pre-tax profit to charities that support social or environmental causes, and these are selected by shareholders.

Latest business results (June 2011, full year)

In a volatile market environment the company recorded an increase in its profits. There was a particular contribution from the Global Opportunities Fund, which made a profit of $1.45 million, compared with a loss of $0.75 million in the previous year, and this helped offset a decline in the company's investment management profit, from $17.6 million to $16.2 million. The company did not receive any performance fees. Funds under management dipped 2.6 per cent to $1.77 billion, with net redemptions during the year of $107 million. All the company's funds, apart from the Global Deep Green Trust, recorded positive returns. The Value Growth Trust, the Australian Value Trust and Global Value Limited all outperformed their benchmarks for the year.

Outlook

Hunter Hall has said that its most important objective is to return its funds to their all-time high values. However, it has reported marked weakness in the initial months of the June 2012 year, and has also said it believes the year ahead will be volatile and frightening. It fears that, should market weakness continue, the company's full-year profits could fall 10 per cent to 15 per cent. However, it also believes that the present turmoil is generating cheap valuations on some quality companies, allowing the company to buy stocks that it expects to produce excellent medium-term returns. Its new Asian Value Trust is focused on undervalued small and medium-sized companies in fast-growing Asian economies. Its new Global Ethical Trust (Hedged) is mainly invested in units of the existing Global Ethical Trust, but with the aim of eliminating that trust's foreign currency exposure.

Year to 30 June	2010	2011
Revenues ($mn)	35.5	35.5
EBIT ($mn)	18.6	21.7

Year to 30 June	2010	2011
EBIT margin (%)	52.5	61.1
Profit before tax ($mn)	18.6	21.9
Profit after tax ($mn)	11.7	12.3
Earnings per share (¢)	45.0	47.2
Cash flow per share (¢)	46.1	48.5
Dividend (¢)	45.3	44.9
Percentage franked	100	100
Net tangible assets per share ($)	1.03	0.79
Interest cover (times)	–	–
Return on equity (%)	43.3	51.0
Debt-to-equity ratio (%)	–	–
Current ratio	3.3	2.4

iiNet Limited

IIN

investor.iinet.net.au

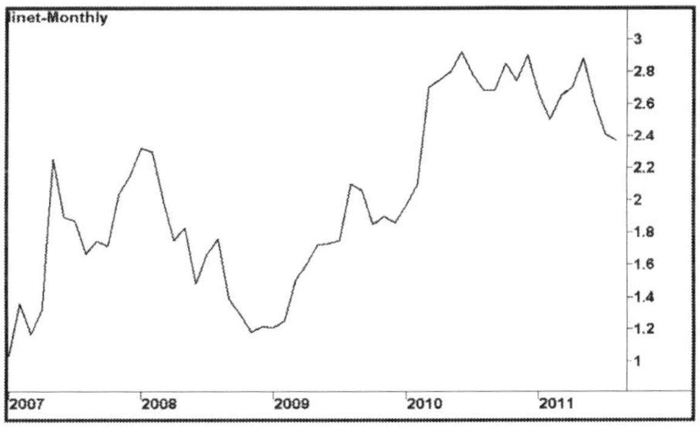

Share price ($)	2.37
12-month high ($)	3.05
12-month low ($)	2.10
Market capitalisation ($mn)	360.4
Price-to-NTA-per-share ratio	–
5-year share price return (% p.a.)	36.1
Dividend reinvestment plan	No

Sector: Telecommunication services	Company	Sector
Price/earnings ratio (times)	9.2	12.5
Dividend yield (%)	5.1	8.7

Perth-based iiNet, founded in a suburban garage in 1993, is a leading internet service provider, with its own broadband network. It also offers phone services, along with a range of other telecommunications services and products, for business and home use. These include web hosting, domain name registry and internet security software. The company's fetchtv service delivers television content via broadband.

Latest business results (June 2011, full year)

A full-year's contribution from the acquisition of Netspace Group and nine months from the acquisition of AAPT's Consumer division lay behind a surge in sales and profits. The company also benefited from some organic growth in the bustling and competitive telecommunications market, including the addition of 7700 customers to its subscriber base and a reduction in customer churn. With the addition of AAPT customers, the company's total number of broadband customers rose 19 per cent to 641000.

Outlook

iiNet is fighting for growth in a mature market where most households are already connected to the internet, and where four companies—Telstra, Optus, iiNet and TPG—now dominate. The result is that the internet service provider industry is consolidating very quickly, with many smaller operators being squeezed out. The company sees only limited scope for gaining much further market share, especially as it has proclaimed its reluctance to chase growth by lowering its prices, and it is instead concentrating on cutting costs and offering new services. The $60 million acquisition from Telecom New Zealand of AAPT's Consumer division is expected to reduce costs by $6 million to $10 million over 18 months as AAPT customers are transferred to iiNet's own network. The company also expects to benefit from the government's planned National Broadband Network, which will help it in regional Australia, where it has been relatively weak. It is also working to cross-sell more of its products to existing customers. At present it is averaging two services per customer. Its aim is to boost this to three services by 2014. It sees significant potential in the small business segment of the internet market, where it has just a 5 per cent share, and it has launched new marketing initiatives to capture more customers. The fetchtv system delivers television programming via the internet, and the company sees this as a key growth initiative as home media devices continue to converge.

Year to 30 June	2010	2011
Revenues ($mn)	473.3	697.2
EBIT ($mn)	41.4	54.7
EBIT margin (%)	8.7	7.8
Gross margin (%)	40.9	37.2

Year to 30 June	2010	2011
Profit before tax ($mn)	39.2	48.2
Profit after tax ($mn)	34.6	39.0
Earnings per share (¢)	22.8	25.7
Cash flow per share (¢)	46.2	54.4
Dividend (¢)	9	12
Percentage franked	100	100
Net tangible assets per share ($)	–	–
Interest cover (times)	18.6	8.4
Return on equity (%)	16.2	16.7
Debt-to-equity ratio (%)	19.8	39.7
Current ratio	0.5	0.6

IMF (Australia) Limited

IMF

<www.imf.com.au>

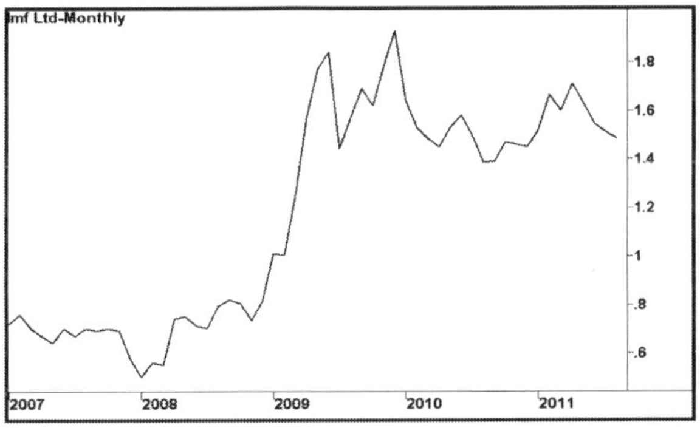

Share price ($)	1.48
12-month high ($)	1.80
12-month low ($)	1.32
Market capitalisation ($mn)	182.3
Price-to-NTA-per-share ratio	6.6
5-year share price return (% p.a.)	28.7
Dividend reinvestment plan	No

Sector: Financials	Company	Sector
Price/earnings ratio (times)	8.0	10.8
Dividend yield (%)	10.1	6.8

Sydney-based IMF is a business that provides funding for legal claims and related services. Most cases involve class actions against corporations with a claim size of over $2 million. IMF generally pays all fees and other costs, and in return takes a commission—usually between 20 per cent and 45 per cent—of any settlement or judgement proceeds. In August 2011 it opened a New York office.

Latest business results (June 2011, full year)

IMF enjoyed an excellent year, with a surge in profits, thanks to the resolution of seven cases during the year, which realised a gross profit of $35.4 million. Two of these cases provided the bulk of the company's income. The first was against the Australian government, in relation to punitive actions it had taken involving Pan Pharmaceuticals, and realised a gross profit for IMF of $18.1 million. The other significant case was against Oz Minerals, and saw a gross profit for IMF of $12.8 million. At June 2011 the company had a portfolio of 33 outstanding cases with an estimated claim value of $1.78 billion. By comparison, in June 2010 it had 33 outstanding cases with an estimated claim value of $1.4 billion.

Outlook

IMF is Australia's largest litigation funding business, although it is facing competition from a growing number of other smaller entrants to this market. In the decade since its public listing it has completed 123 cases, generating revenue to IMF of $273 million from an investment of $86 million. Of these 123 cases, 83 were settled, 25 were withdrawn, 10 were won in a court judgement and five were lost. The ability to pick cases with a strong likelihood of success has been a key factor in IMF's growth. Of its 33 outstanding cases at June 2011, it believed around a dozen, with an estimated claim total of $675 million, could be settled during the June 2012 year. Despite what appears to be booming business for IMF, its income can vary greatly from year to year, depending on the timing of claim resolutions, and this can be a disincentive for the shares. In addition, as the litigation funding business grows in Australia, IMF faces the possibility of new government regulations on its activities. It sees its entry to the huge US litigation market, with a new wholly owned subsidiary, Bentham Capital, as an enormous growth opportunity, given that only a limited number of dedicated litigation finance businesses are operating in that country. It has employed a leading litigation funding expert to run Bentham Capital, and believes that within three years US-sourced business could represent one-third of all IMF's new cases.

Year to 30 June	2010	2011
Revenues ($mn)	21.7	40.6
EBIT ($mn)	15.0	32.1

Year to 30 June	2010	2011
EBIT margin (%)	69.4	79.1
Profit before tax ($mn)	16.8	33.8
Profit after tax ($mn)	11.9	22.9
Earnings per share (¢)	9.8	18.6
Cash flow per share (¢)	9.9	18.7
Dividend (¢)	5	15
Percentage franked	100	100
Net tangible assets per share ($)	0.26	0.22
Interest cover (times)	–	–
Return on equity (%)	17.3	28.6
Debt-to-equity ratio (%)	–	–
Current ratio	6.3	6.9

Incitec Pivot Limited

IPL

<www.incitecpivot.com.au>

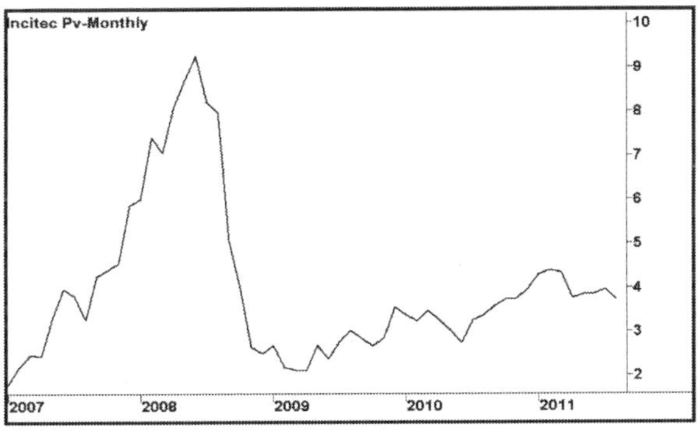

Share price ($)	3.72
12-month high ($)	4.72
12-month low ($)	3.14
Market capitalisation ($mn)	6058.8
Price-to-NTA-per-share ratio	8.3
5-year share price return (% p.a.)	31.0
Dividend reinvestment plan	Yes

Sector: Materials	Company	Sector
Price/earnings ratio (times)	13.6	12.3
Dividend yield (%)	2.1	2.2

Melbourne-based Incitec Pivot was formed in 2003 from the merger of two of Australia's leading fertiliser manufacturers and distributors, Incitec and Pivot, both with histories dating back more than 80 years. In 2006 it acquired Southern Cross Fertilisers, and is today Australia's leading supplier of fertilisers. Following the 2008 acquisition of Dyno Nobel, the company has also become a global force in the mining industry. It is now North America's leading supplier of explosives products and services, the second-largest supplier in Australia and has growing sales in Asia. It operates 20 manufacturing facilities in Australia, the US, Canada, Mexico, Indonesia and Turkey, and with joint venture operations in China, South Africa and Malaysia.

Latest business results (March 2011, half year)

A solid recovery in global fertiliser prices, along with a strongly improved performance from Incitec Pivot's North American explosives business, powered the company to a solid rise in sales and profits and easily offset the adverse impact of the strong dollar. Explosives represented 54 per cent of total revenues, with sales up 12 per cent from the March 2010 half. US sales actually jumped 28 per cent in local currency, reflecting a recovery in the American economy. The company benefited from both higher volumes and some higher prices. However, Asia Pacific explosive sales edged down, due mainly to adverse weather in Queensland, New South Wales and Western Australia that affected mine operations. Fertiliser volumes actually fell by 9 per cent, due especially to flooding on the Australian east coast, but higher prices meant that total sales revenues rose by 19 per cent.

Outlook

Incitec Pivot is enjoying vibrant business as rising global food prices stimulate demand for fertiliser. It has also been benefiting from its exposure to a recovering US economy, with North American explosives sales representing nearly 40 per cent of total company turnover. Nevertheless, fertiliser demand and pricing remain quite volatile, with the weather a key factor, and the company is working to increase its exposure to the more predictable explosives market. Its new $935 million Moranbah ammonia nitrate plant should commence operations in mid 2012, with explosives expected to rise thereafter to around 70 per cent of company sales. There has also been some speculation that Incitec Pivot might choose to spin off its fertiliser operations into a separate company.

Year to 30 September	2009	2010
Revenues ($mn)	3418.9	2931.7
EBIT ($mn)	603.9	648.3

Year to 30 September	2009	2010
EBIT margin (%)	17.7	22.1
Profit before tax ($mn)	488.6	595.3
Profit after tax ($mn)	361.9	442.8
Earnings per share (¢)	23.5	27.3
Cash flow per share (¢)	34.5	35.8
Dividend (¢)	4.4	7.8
Percentage franked	48	0
Interest cover (times)	5.2	12.2
Return on equity (%)	11.1	12.7

Half year to 31 March	2010	2011
Revenues ($mn)	1236.4	1424.4
Profit before tax ($mn)	198.9	244.0
Profit after tax ($mn)	146.5	178.6
Earnings per share (¢)	8.5	10.2
Dividend (¢)	1.8	3.3
Percentage franked	0	0
Net tangible assets per share ($)	0.27	0.45
Debt-to-equity ratio (%)	37.7	38.1
Current ratio	1.1	1.4

Industrea Limited

IDL

<www.industrea.com.au>

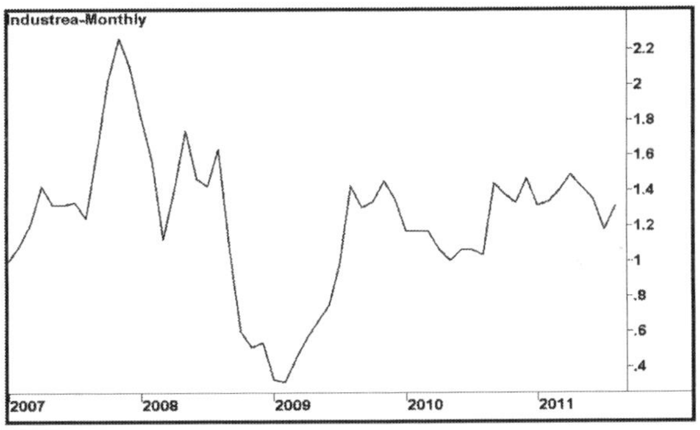

Share price ($)	1.31
12-month high ($)	1.60
12-month low ($)	0.96
Market capitalisation ($mn)	478.4
Price-to-NTA-per-share ratio	4.1
5-year share price return (% p.a.)	27.4
Dividend reinvestment plan	Yes

Sector: Industrials	Company	Sector
Price/earnings ratio (times)	9.6	11.9
Dividend yield (%)	3.1	5.5

Brisbane-based Industrea, with a history dating back to 1987, is involved in the provision of specialised mining products and services, with an emphasis on enhancing the safety and productivity of mining operations. In mining services it is a leader in open-cut contract mining services, equipment hire and civil contracting services. It operates three diesel equipment manufacturing businesses, with a focus on the underground mining sector. Its technology operation specialises in the manufacture of state-of-the-art mine safety equipment. The company also maintains an international division that is particularly involved in supplying the Chinese mining industry, and it is increasingly active in many other countries.

Latest business results (June 2011, full year)

Industrea is strongly geared to the mining boom, and it posted a strong rise in revenues and pre-tax profit. However, a tax benefit in the previous year meant that in the latest results the after-tax profit declined. The Mining Technology division enjoyed an excellent performance, with sales up 62 per cent and profits nearly doubling, with strong sales worldwide for the company's collision avoidance systems and growing Chinese demand for gas drainage and directional drilling systems. The Mining Services division, which mainly performs work for Australian mining operations, also enjoyed a good year. But a slowing of diesel equipment sales to China led to revenues and profits tumbling in the Mining Equipment division.

Consequently the company's total sales to China fell 27 per cent to $93.7 million, about a quarter of total turnover.

Outlook

Industrea has a focus on products that boost mine safety and productivity, and these are an investment priority for mining companies around the world. Such is demand that the company is forecasting revenue growth of at least 20 per cent in the June 2012 year. Though Australia remains the centre of its operations, it has been working hard to penetrate overseas markets, and has been achieving particular success in China. It has been seeing a solid recovery in Chinese demand for diesel equipment, and the launch of its first Chinese-manufactured diesel vehicle in October 2011 is expected to boost sales further. It is now expanding to other markets such as Russia and Indonesia, with sales starting to rise strongly. The March 2011 acquisition of the AJ Lucas underground in-seam gas service business provides Industrea with a new business in the provision of gas management services to underground longwall coal mines.

Year to 30 June	2010	2011
Revenues ($mn)	312.6	356.6
Mining Services (%)	41	47
Mining Technology (%)	23	32
Mining Equipment (%)	36	21
EBIT ($mn)	70.1	83.0
EBIT margin (%)	22.4	23.3

Year to 30 June	2010	2011
Profit before tax ($mn)	53.6	67.2
Profit after tax ($mn)	57.4	47.9
Earnings per share (¢)	18.5	13.7
Cash flow per share (¢)	30.5	24.1
Dividend (¢)	3.9	4
Percentage franked	100	100
Net tangible assets per share ($)	0.20	0.32
Interest cover (times)	4.3	5.2
Return on equity (%)	28.8	17.2
Debt-to-equity ratio (%)	75.1	50.1
Current ratio	0.9	1.7

Infomedia Limited

IFM

<www.infomedia.com.au>

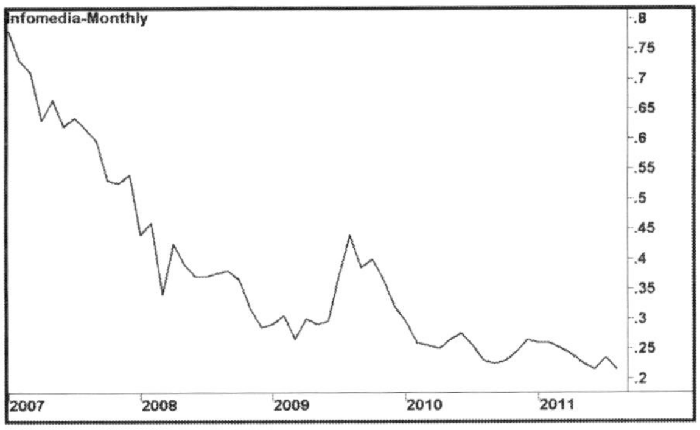

Share price ($)	0.22
12-month high ($)	0.27
12-month low ($)	0.18
Market capitalisation ($mn)	66.7
Price-to-NTA-per-share ratio	9.8
5-year share price return (% p.a.)	−13.5
Dividend reinvestment plan	No

Sector: Information technology	Company	Sector
Price/earnings ratio (times)	6.7	18.2
Dividend yield (%)	10.9	3.9

Sydney electronic data company Infomedia was formed in 1990, and has grown into a world leader in the development of specialised electronic catalogues. Its main product, Microcat, is an electronic parts catalogue (EPC) for the automotive industry—with versions for many leading car companies—which is shipped to customers in over 160 countries, in 34 languages. It operates from disc and the internet, and enables service personnel in a motor dealership to identify the correct replacement parts for a vehicle. The company also produces the Superservice Menus data management product, which provides automotive dealers with a range of service, repair and warranty management tools, and it is developing a range of similar products.

Latest business results (June 2011, full year)

With most of its sales abroad, Infomedia was another victim of the strong dollar, with sales and profits down. On a constant-currency basis business actually improved in all regions. Europe, about 45 per cent of company turnover, and North America, about 23 per cent, both saw sales and profits down. But Asia-Pacific, also about 23 per cent, achieved double-digit sales and profit rises. The company also made a currency hedging gain of $4.8 million, down from $5.2 million in the previous year. There was continuing strong demand for the company's Supersize Menus product, with revenues up $1.9 million on a constant-currency basis. The company reported that an emphasis on cost efficiencies led to the renegotiation of some technology and services supply agreements, with consequent reductions in its expenses.

Outlook

With the bulk of its sales overseas, Infomedia's results are greatly affected by exchange rate movements, and also by the company's own quite extensive hedging policies. In a major strategic move, it is working to move as much as possible of its EPC business online, with a new product called Microcat LIVE. This has been successfully launched for Toyota and Ford dealers in the US, and the company believes that by mid or late 2012 all OEM customers will have been converted to the new system. It is seeing a stream of new business for Superservice Menus, and is set to launch it in the US for General Motors and Toyota dealers. It is also experiencing growing demand for its Auto PartsBridge product, launched in 2009, which streamlines the parts ordering process for the collision repair industry.

Year to 30 June	2010	2011
Revenues ($mn)	50.5	48.9
EBIT ($mn)	14.4	13.2
EBIT margin (%)	28.6	26.9

Year to 30 June	2010	2011
Gross margin (%)	51.7	55.2
Profit before tax ($mn)	14.5	13.4
Profit after tax ($mn)	11.3	10.0
Earnings per share (¢)	3.7	3.3
Cash flow per share (¢)	4.9	5.2
Dividend (¢)	2.4	2.4
Percentage franked	0	100
Net tangible assets per share ($)	0.02	0.02
Interest cover (times)	–	–
Return on equity (%)	32.7	28.9
Debt-to-equity ratio (%)	–	–
Current ratio	2.3	2.8

IOOF Holdings Limited

IFL

<www.ioof.com.au>

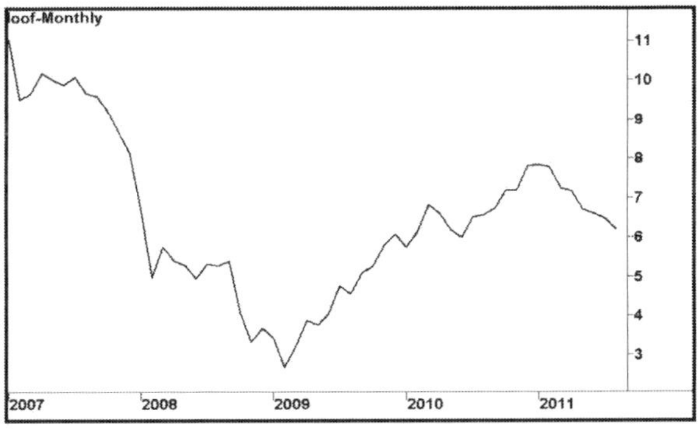

Share price ($)	6.20
12-month high ($)	8.14
12-month low ($)	4.96
Market capitalisation ($mn)	1437.8
Price-to-NTA-per-share ratio	10.7
5-year share price return (% p.a.)	−2.0
Dividend reinvestment plan	No

Sector: Financials	Company	Sector
Price/earnings ratio (times)	14.4	10.8
Dividend yield (%)	6.9	6.8

IOOF, with its headquarters in Melbourne, dates back to its formation as a friendly society—the Independent Order of Odd Fellows—in 1846. Today it is a fully integrated financial services company offering a wide range of financial advice and distribution services, platform management and administration services, trustee services and managed investment products. Its brands include Bridges Financial Services, Consultum Financial Advisers, Perennial Investment Partners, Australian Executor Trustees, Spectrum Super, Pursuit and Ord Minnett. In 2011 it made a takeover bid for the publicly listed financial services provider DKN Financial Group.

Latest business results (June 2011, full year)

In a weak market environment for the wealth management sector, IOOF recorded an excellent result, with a strong rise in its profits. A major factor was a decline in the company's cost base, a result of a big restructuring at the company, which involved consolidating its eight investment platforms down to five, as well as a rationalisation of many of its operations. Net inflows to the company's platforms were $650 million. The company said its annualised inflow growth of 6 per cent was significantly ahead of the industry average of 2 per cent. Thanks to the significant decline in its costs, the core Platform Management and Administration division saw profits jump 27 per cent on just a small increase in revenues. The Investment Management division, the other main contributor to company profits, achieved an earnings increase of nearly 20 per cent, again on just a small rise in revenues. At June 2011 the company had funds under management, administration, advice and supervision totalling $106.2 billion, up 7.2 per cent from a year earlier.

Outlook

The wealth management sector has become increasingly attractive, thanks to an ageing population and growing superannuation fund inflows, and IOOF has become one of the mid-tier leaders. It has grown rapidly through some 30 mergers and acquisitions over 10 years, most notably the $540 million merger with Australian Wealth Management in 2008, which helped deliver significant cost benefits. Its expected $94 million takeover of DKN Financial Group will hand it new products and platforms for financial advisers. However, with financial markets remaining volatile, the company has been reluctant to provide a forecast for the new financial year. IOOF continues to seek out further acquisitions, though is also itself increasingly spoken of as a takeover target.

Year to 30 June	2010	2011
Revenues ($mn)	626.7	642.6
Platform Management and Admin. (%)	63	62

Year to 30 June	2010	2011
Investment Management (%)	23	24
Financial Advice and Distribution (%)	10	11
Estate and Trustee Services (%)	3	3
EBIT ($mn)	99.9	143.9
EBIT margin (%)	15.9	22.4
Profit before tax ($mn)	105.7	151.9
Profit after tax ($mn)	77.4	99.5
Earnings per share (¢)	33.7	43.1
Cash flow per share (¢)	43.6	52.5
Dividend (¢)	35	43
Percentage franked	100	100
Net tangible assets per share ($)	0.44	0.58
Interest cover (times)	–	–
Return on equity (%)	8.9	11.3
Debt-to-equity ratio (%)	–	–

IRESS Market Technology Limited

IRE

<www.iress.com.au>

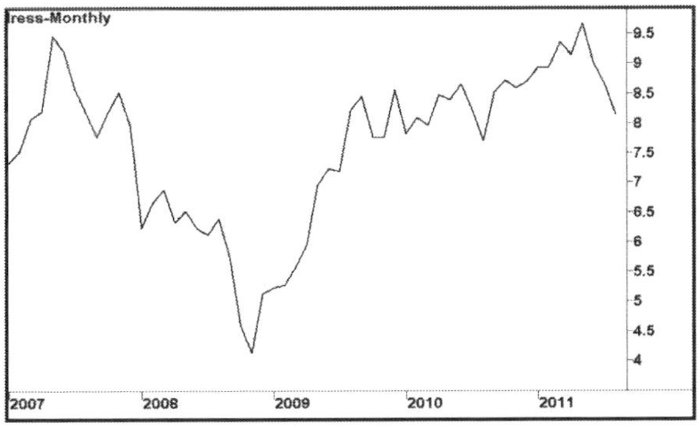

Share price ($)	8.15
12-month high ($)	9.68
12-month low ($)	7.25
Market capitalisation ($mn)	1034.4
Price-to-NTA-per-share ratio	13.4
5-year share price return (% p.a.)	11.5
Dividend reinvestment plan	No

Sector: Information technology	Company	Sector
Price/earnings ratio (times)	20.2	18.2
Dividend yield (%)	4.7	3.9

Melbourne-based IRESS was founded in 1993. It produces the prominent IRESS (Integrated Real-time Equity System) sharemarket information system, used widely throughout the Australian investment community. Within the IRESS system it offers a portfolio of information and trading products with numerous applications, for stockbrokers, fund managers and other financial professionals. It is also active in wealth management services, with its Xplan financial planning software. It has expanded its operations to New Zealand, Canada, Singapore, Hong Kong, Taiwan and South Africa. ASX owns about 19 per cent of IRESS's equity.

Latest business results (June 2011, half year)

Revenues grew as the company expanded its fields of operations, but profits were hit by volatile markets, the strong dollar and rising costs. Excluding the impact of all these, the company reported that the after-tax profit rose 6 per cent from the June 2010 half. IRESS segments its operations into two divisions: Financial Markets, which represents about three-quarters of turnover, and Wealth Management. The former business saw revenues rise in Australia and Canada, and an initial contribution from the January 2011, $56 million acquisition of South

African technology services provider Peresys. The Wealth Management division achieved some solid growth domestically, but in South Africa, its other main sphere of operations, revenues and profits were down, as client numbers declined. The company's Asian businesses fell more deeply into the red.

Outlook

IRESS is heavily geared to levels of stock market activity, which has fuelled some strong growth, but has also led more recently to a degree of business volatility. It says that all the top 20 Australian stockbroking houses, and many others, use IRESS as their primary ASX market data source, and it reports high levels of customer loyalty. The Peresys acquisition is seen as a major step towards building a presence in South Africa, and IRESS is introducing a range of new products. It continues to invest in Asia, despite businesses there remaining in the red. It is also working towards entry into the big UK market. The planned introduction of the new Chi-X securities exchange in Australia could boost demand, with IRESS launching new products in response. With no debt and more than $44 million in cash, IRESS is looking for further acquisitions. There has been speculation that the ASX may launch a full takeover bid for IRESS shares.

Year to 31 December	2009	2010
Revenues ($mn)	169.5	179.8
EBIT ($mn)	54.2	64.4
EBIT margin (%)	32.0	35.8
Profit before tax ($mn)	55.9	67.8
Profit after tax ($mn)	42.8	50.5
Earnings per share (¢)	34.8	40.3
Cash flow per share (¢)	51.9	52.4
Dividend (¢)	34	38
Percentage franked	100	79
Interest cover (times)	–	–
Return on equity (%)	35.6	38.6

Half year to 30 June	2010	2011
Revenues ($mn)	89.7	101.1
Profit before tax ($mn)	32.1	30.4
Profit after tax ($mn)	26.9	21.7
Earnings per share (¢)	21.6	17.2
Dividend (¢)	14	14
Percentage franked	100	90
Net tangible assets per share ($)	0.75	0.61
Debt-to-equity ratio (%)	–	–
Current ratio	3.9	1.9

Lend Lease Group

LLC

<www.lendlease.com.au>

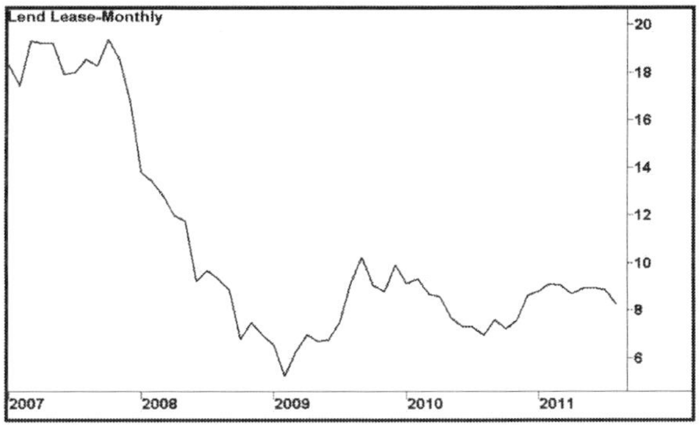

Share price ($)	8.25
12-month high ($)	9.28
12-month low ($)	6.93
Market capitalisation ($mn)	4709.9
Price-to-NTA-per-share ratio	2.1
5-year share price return (% p.a.)	−8.2
Dividend reinvestment plan	Yes

Sector: Financials	Company	Sector
Price/earnings ratio (times)	9.0	10.8
Dividend yield (%)	4.2	6.8

Sydney-based Lend Lease, founded in 1958, is a global property developer and investment manager, involved in numerous large-scale projects. It classifies its many diverse activities into four broad areas. The Development business is involved in the development of master-planned urban communities, inner-city mixed-use developments, apartments, retail projects and the senior living sector. The Construction business provides project management, engineering and construction services. The Investment Management business provides real estate investment management, retail property management and asset management services. The Infrastructure Development business manages and invests in large public-private partnership projects.

Latest business results (June 2011, full year)

Lend Lease reported an excellent result, with profits surging despite a decline in revenues. Much of the strength in profits—around 40 per cent—came from asset sales. These included the company's 50 per cent stake in the King of Prussia shopping mall in the US, which contributed more than $100 million to the after-tax profit. All regions experienced profit growth, with the Americas the best, reporting a fivefold surge, thanks especially to the shopping mall sale. Australian profits rose 14 per cent, partly due to an infrastructure acquisition, but also reflecting continuing strength in housing developments and the company's aged care businesses. European and Asian businesses benefited from asset sales, but otherwise were generally weak.

Outlook

Lend Lease has an enormous pipeline of projects around the world, and company profits can fluctuate quite strongly, depending on when particular major developments reach completion. The company itself has expressed optimism about the outlook, with Australian infrastructure a particular bright spot, thanks especially to the company's March 2011 acquisition of the contracting business Valemus Australia for $960 million. At the end of July 2011 Lend Lease had a domestic infrastructure backlog of $6 billion, and was expecting new contracts worth more than $1.5 billion. It has much riding on the massive Barangaroo Sydney CBD project, with the start of construction of the first commercial tower due to commence by the end of 2011. New domestic projects include the $900 million Queensland Children's Hospital and more than $200 million worth of rail and road developments. However, the company's heavy exposure to Europe and America—47 per cent of June 2011 revenues—makes it vulnerable to sluggish economies in those regions. Asia remains a small part of business, although the company believes prospects there are excellent.

Year to 30 June	2010	2011
Revenues ($mn)	10359.2	8926.7
EBIT ($mn)	476.4	669.3

Year to 30 June	2010	2011
EBIT margin (%)	4.6	7.5
Profit before tax ($mn)	450.8	631.5
Profit after tax ($mn)	345.6	492.8
Earnings per share (¢)	72.9	91.7
Cash flow per share (¢)	81.3	101.4
Dividend (¢)	32.1	35
Percentage franked	100	29
Net tangible assets per share ($)	4.69	3.99
Interest cover (times)	18.6	17.7
Return on equity (%)	12.0	14.2
Debt-to-equity ratio (%)	–	17.8
Current ratio	0.8	0.7

Little World Beverages Limited

LWB

<www.littleworldbeverages.com>

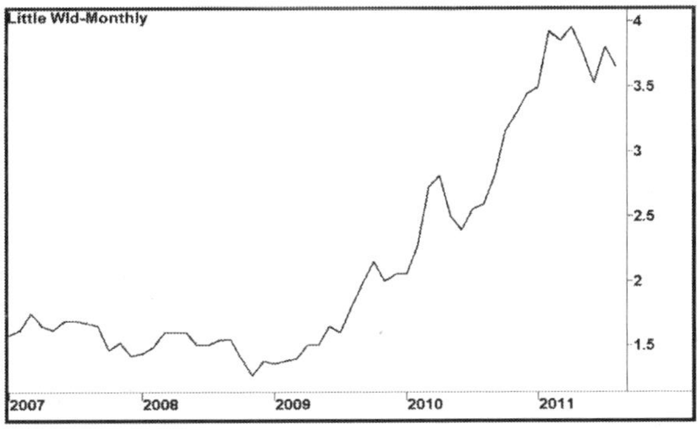

Share price ($)	3.65
12-month high ($)	4.02
12-month low ($)	2.59
Market capitalisation ($mn)	238.1
Price-to-NTA-per-share ratio	5.8
5-year share price return (% p.a.)	27.5
Dividend reinvestment plan	No

Sector: Consumer staples	Company	Sector
Price/earnings ratio (times)	25.3	16.5
Dividend yield (%)	2.7	4.8

Fremantle brewer Little World Beverages was founded in 2000. Its Little Creatures Brewing makes a small range of beers and one cider from its brewery in Fremantle. In 2009 it launched a second brewery, White Rabbit, in Healesville, Victoria. It plans a third brewery at a site in Geelong, Victoria. It also operates hospitality facilities in Fremantle and Victoria. It has taken a 20 per cent equity stake in the Byron Bay boutique brewer Stone & Wood Brewing Company. The giant Japanese-owned brewing house Lion Nathan owns approximately 40 per cent of the equity of Little World.

Latest business results (June 2011, full year)

In an environment of weak consumer spending, including sluggish beer demand, Little World once again achieved an excellent gain in sales and profits. The continuing strong growth in profits—ahead of sales growth—showed the company's success in holding down costs and boosting margins. This partly reflected the success of the new White Rabbit brewery and its beers, with growing economies of scale leading to margin expansion. There was also a solid contribution from the company's expanded marketing effort and a consequent increase in distribution, with strong demand from east coast markets for the company's Fremantle-brewed Little Creatures beers.

Outlook

Little World has been achieving great success as part of the new wave of boutique breweries around Australia that have been enjoying a boom in popularity. Its beers have been highly rated in numerous competitions, and in a relatively short time have acquired an excellent reputation. Some of the success has been due to strong corporate backing for the company, which has meant a clear business plan for growth, and access to the necessary finance. In a key strategic move, the company has expanded from its Fremantle roots to launch itself into the sophisticated food and drink culture of Melbourne, and in a short time has achieved great popularity. It has shown great prescience in launching its new White Rabbit brewery and pub at a central location in Healesville, the main town in the wine-growing region of Yarra Valley, and rapidly becoming a centre of food tourism. It expects its new brewery at Valley Mill in Geelong to begin production in 2012. Little World shares have at times been strong on speculation that Lion Nathan will attempt a complete takeover of the company.

Year to 30 June	2010	2011
Revenues ($mn)	55.3	68.8
EBIT ($mn)	10.5	14.0
EBIT margin (%)	19.0	20.4
Gross margin (%)	65.7	65.7

Year to 30 June	2010	2011
Profit before tax ($mn)	9.4	13.2
Profit after tax ($mn)	6.8	9.2
Earnings per share (¢)	11.5	14.4
Cash flow per share (¢)	15.5	18.4
Dividend (¢)	9.5	10
Percentage franked	100	100
Net tangible assets per share ($)	0.55	0.63
Interest cover (times)	9.1	17.8
Return on equity (%)	21.3	24.4
Debt-to-equity ratio (%)	45.8	36.8
Current ratio	1.5	0.4

Lycopodium Limited

LYL

<www.lycopodium.com.au>

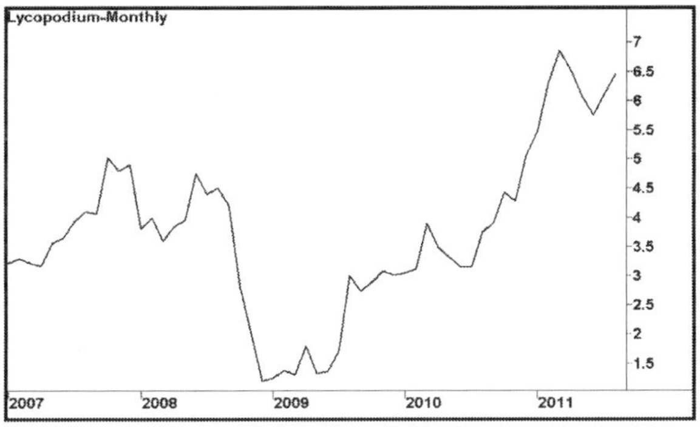

Share price ($)	6.45
12-month high ($)	7.42
12-month low ($)	3.67
Market capitalisation ($mn)	249.3
Price-to-NTA-per-share ratio	5.7
5-year share price return (% p.a.)	24.2
Dividend reinvestment plan	No

Sector: Industrials	Company	Sector
Price/earnings ratio (times)	14.6	11.9
Dividend yield (%)	4.7	5.5

Founded in 1992, Perth-based Lycopodium is an engineering and project management company. It works through five wholly owned domestic subsidiaries and one abroad. Lycopodium Minerals, Lycopodium Minerals QLD and Orway Mineral Consultants (WA) all provide services to the minerals processing industry. Lycopodium Process Industries provides services to a wide range of manufacturing industries, including chemical, pharmaceutical, food, automotive and bio-fuels. Sherwood Utilities provides specialist maintenance and reliability engineering services to the minerals processing, mining, oil, gas and petrochemical industries. Lycopodium Minerals Canada is working to obtain contracts in North American markets. The company has offices in Perth, Brisbane, Melbourne, Sydney and Gladstone in Australia, and in Canada, Ghana and the Philippines. Around 40 per cent of sales revenues derive from overseas projects.

Latest business results (June 2011, full year)

Revenues and profits rose pleasingly after the disappointing result of the previous year. During the year the company completed an exceptionally large number of feasibility studies, with many of these leading to engineering, procurement and construction management (EPCM) contracts, and this latter business rose sharply, with revenues up nearly threefold and profits nearly doubling.

By contrast, the Project Services business, which helps companies deliver projects, and which had seen two straight years of strong growth, this time faltered, with revenues tumbling 40 per cent and profits down 37 per cent. The Study Services business, which is involved in project planning activities, saw revenues up 7 per cent, but profits fell 12 per cent. A very small fourth business segment, design and construct, which delivers turnkey projects, reversed the previous year's strong result, with sales down 60 per cent and profits down 33 per cent.

Outlook

Lycopodium continues to reap some important EPCM contracts from all its feasibility studies, and, based on orders in hand, it forecasts that June 2012 revenues will rise to $188 million, with an after-tax profit of $18.5 million. In April 2011 it won a major EPCM contract from Rio Tinto for the Marandoo Mine Phase 2 project in the Pilbara. Lycopodium will provide services in relation to the plant upgrade and associated project infrastructure, with expected revenues of $105 million over two to three years. It has also won a big EPCM contract from Newmont Mining for the Akyem gold mining project in Ghana. The company has declared that skill shortages are a constraint on its business.

Year to 30 June	2010	2011
Revenues ($mn)	119.6	168.5
EPCM (%)	29	61
Study Services (%)	27	20
Project Services (%)	41	17
EBIT ($mn)	18.8	23.9
EBIT margin (%)	15.7	14.2
Profit before tax ($mn)	18.7	24.9
Profit after tax ($mn)	16.1	17.1
Earnings per share (¢)	41.6	44.3
Cash flow per share (¢)	45.7	47.6
Dividend (¢)	27	30
Percentage franked	100	100
Net tangible assets per share ($)	1.00	1.13
Interest cover (times)	272.2	–
Return on equity (%)	38.3	36.2
Debt-to-equity ratio (%)	–	–
Current ratio	2.7	2.1

M2 Telecom. Group Limited

MTU

<m2.com.au>

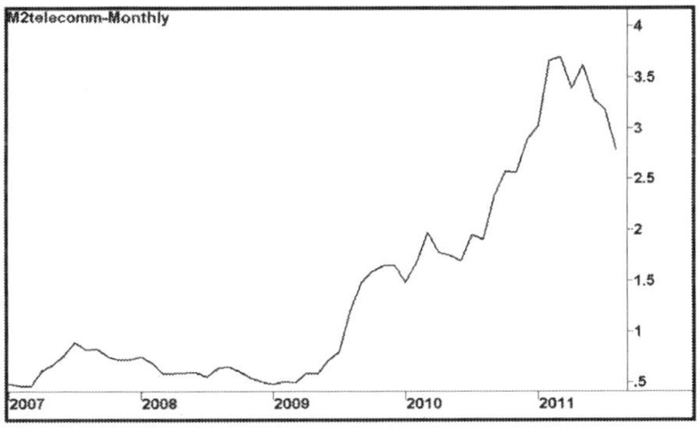

Share price ($)	2.78
12-month high ($)	4.08
12-month low ($)	1.75
Market capitalisation ($mn)	343.7
Price-to-NTA-per-share ratio	–
5-year share price return (% p.a.)	63.5
Dividend reinvestment plan	Yes

Sector: Telecommunication services	Company	Sector
Price/earnings ratio (times)	12.3	12.5
Dividend yield (%)	5.8	8.7

Established in 1999, Melbourne-based M2 provides fixed-line, mobile and data telecommunications services to small and medium-sized businesses. It has grown rapidly through acquisition. Its retail division offers a suite of bundled telecommunications services through the Commander, People Telecom, M2 Telecom, Southern Cross Telco and Clear Telecoms businesses. Its other core activity, M2 Wholesale, was established as an aggregator and enabler of Optus mobile services. It has offices throughout Australia, and the company claims an approximate 1 per cent share of the Australian telecommunications market. It also provides fixed-line, 3G mobile and broadband services in New Zealand.

Latest business results (June 2011, full year)

M2 enjoyed another superb result, with profits surging on just a modest increase in revenues. The main contribution came from improvements in the efficiency of the company's operations as it continued to grow, with a significant improvement in its wholesale purchasing arrangements, some reduced costs and organic customer growth. Three acquisitions were made during the year—the business assets of Clear Telecoms and the customers of Austar Mobile and Edirect. These made a relatively small contribution to the results, although the latter two companies have substantially boosted the company's residential customer base. During the year the company's staff numbers grew 14 per cent to 488.

Outlook

M2 has enjoyed some dynamic growth, and it is forecasting after-tax profit growth of around 15 per cent in the June 2012 year. It is also forecasting higher profit margins as it eliminates some $55 million worth of low-margin business, which means that revenues are expected to drop. From September 2011 it is rolling out over 18 months its new Ninja business support system, based on advanced technology from UK telecom support specialist Cerillion. This will replace the company's current billing and customer support systems, and is expected to deliver significant cost efficiencies. M2 believes the advent of the planned National Broadband Network offers it many opportunities as it plays to the company's strengths as a reseller of fixed services. M2 lays particular emphasis on a high level of marketing ability, and it sees sales skills and customer service as key capabilities that will help determine the winners from the NBN. It is working to move into hosted solutions and cloud products. It is also looking to make further acquisitions, in both Australia and New Zealand.

Year to 30 June	2010	2011
Revenues ($mn)	406.1	426.8
Retail (%)	62	60
Wholesale (%)	38	40
EBIT ($mn)	26.2	41.2
EBIT margin (%)	6.4	9.7
Gross margin (%)	21.9	24.5

Year to 30 June	2010	2011
Profit before tax ($mn)	24.2	40.4
Profit after tax ($mn)	16.2	27.7
Earnings per share (¢)	14.6	22.6
Cash flow per share (¢)	19.1	27.5
Dividend (¢)	10	16
Percentage franked	100	100
Net tangible assets per share ($)	0.05	–
Interest cover (times)	13.2	52.3
Return on equity (%)	25.8	32.4
Debt-to-equity ratio (%)	2.0	18.3
Current ratio	1.2	0.9

Macarthur Coal Limited

MCC

<www.macarthurcoal.com.au>

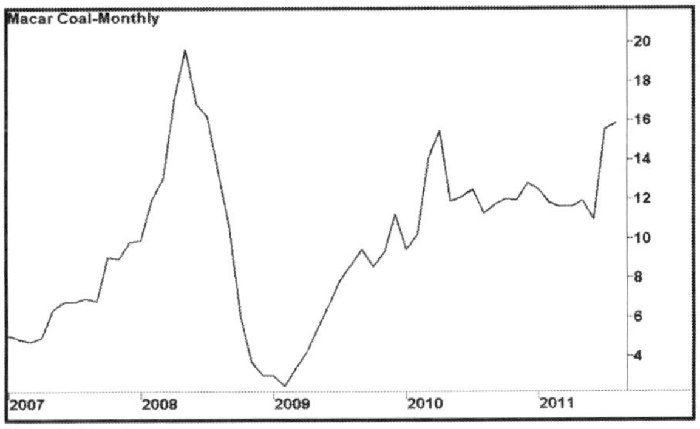

Share price ($)	15.86
12-month high ($)	15.94
12-month low ($)	10.09
Market capitalisation ($mn)	4791.2
Price-to-NTA-per-share ratio	2.7
5-year share price return (% p.a.)	29.6
Dividend reinvestment plan	No

Sector: Materials	Company	Sector
Price/earnings ratio (times)	19.2	12.3
Dividend yield (%)	2.5	2.2

Brisbane-based Macarthur Coal is involved in coal exploration and development, as well as mine management. Its activities are centred on Queensland's Bowen Basin, where it holds 73.3 per cent of the Coppabella and the Moorvale mines, which are responsible for around one-third of Australian exports of low volatile pulverised coal injection coal (PCI coal). The company is a key supplier to the steel mills of Asia, Europe and Brazil. It also produces some thermal and coking coal. In addition, it owns 50 per cent of the Middlemount mine, and through a series of joint ventures the company has a large number of prospective exploration tenement holdings. In July 2011 a consortium of America's Peabody Energy and Luxemburg-based ArcelorMittal launched a $4.7 billion takeover bid for Macarthur.

Latest business results (June 2011, full year)

Profits soared. However, this largely reflected the selling down of some of Macarthur's interests in its Middlemount and Codrilla operations. Otherwise, in what was a difficult year for the company, profits just edged up, thanks to higher prices for metallurgical coal in the fourth quarter, following severe disruption caused by heavy rains and flooding. The company reported that its underlying profit after tax was $142.4 million, up from $139.1 million in the previous year. Because of the floods it shipped just 3.9 million tonnes, down from 5.3 million tonnes a year earlier.

Outlook

Much of Macarthur's future depends on the outcome of the takeover bid. The company itself has advised its shareholders not to take any action, and has said that it is in discussions with other interested parties concerning possible alternative proposals. Meanwhile, Macarthur is working towards its goal of boosting annual sales to 9.2 million tonnes by 2014. Its Middlemount mine has reached the final stage of development and is on the verge of initial production. The company is also working to develop its Codrilla holding as a fourth mine. However, in the near term it expects to continue to be affected by the after-effects of the floods. Restrictions on permitted water discharge volumes mean that water has been retained in its mines, hampering operations. The company is also facing problems of labour shortages and escalating costs in many areas of its operations. Nevertheless, with the addition of the new Middlemount mine, it believes it can ship 5.0 million to 5.3 million tonnes of coal in the June 2012 year.

Year to 30 June	2010	2011
Revenues ($mn)	670.5	687.3
EBIT ($mn)	170.8	309.0
EBIT margin (%)	25.5	45.0
Gross margin (%)	40.7	39.1
Profit before tax ($mn)	172.8	325.8
Profit after tax ($mn)	125.1	241.4
Earnings per share (¢)	49.3	82.8
Cash flow per share (¢)	61.6	93.0

Year to 30 June	2010	2011
Dividend (¢)	23	40
Percentage franked	100	100
Net tangible assets per share ($)	4.34	5.94
Interest cover (times)	–	–
Return on equity (%)	11.7	16.5
Debt-to-equity ratio (%)	–	–
Current ratio	3.7	9.1

Melbourne IT Limited

MLB

<www.melboumeitinfo>

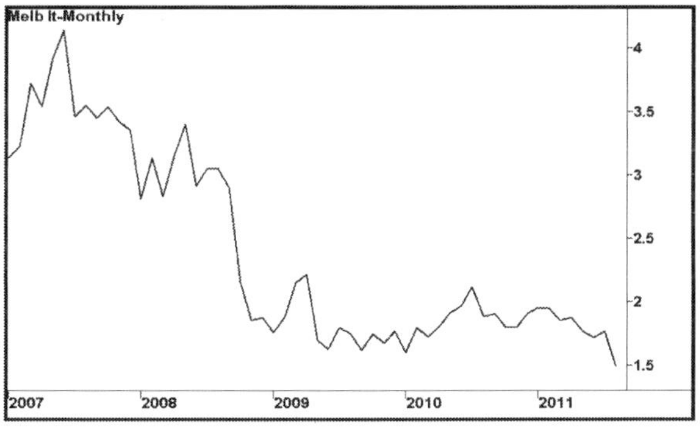

Share price ($)	1.49
12-month high ($)	2.06
12-month low ($)	1.32
Market capitalisation ($mn)	119.6
Price-to-NTA-per-share ratio	–
5-year share price return (% p.a.)	−1.5
Dividend reinvestment plan	Yes

Sector: Information technology	Company	Sector
Price/earnings ratio (times)	7.4	18.2
Dividend yield (%)	10.1	3.9

Internet domain name registry Melbourne IT started in 1996. It initially registered <.com.au> domain names, but in 1999 was accredited by the Internet Corporation for Assigned Names and Numbers to provide register services for the .com, .net and .org domain spaces. Today it operates on a global basis supplying more than 40 different domain name types. It has also diversified into other businesses, including web hosting, corporate branding, website strategy services and courtroom recording systems.

Latest business results (June 2011, half year)

Sales and profits fell, with the strong dollar and weak economies in Europe and America hurting business. All five of the company's divisions recorded lower revenues, with the small Enterprise Services division posting a particularly bad result, with revenues down 24 per cent to $13.2 million and EBIT plunging 75 per cent, in part a reflection of an absence of larger contracts. The company's largest division, Global Partner Solutions, responsible for nearly 30 per cent of company turnover, saw revenues down 11 per cent, due especially to the strong dollar and intense competition in the domain name and web hosting markets, with EBIT falling 9 per cent. The Digital Brand Services division, which manages companies' online brand presence, recorded a 5 per cent drop in revenues, due to the strong dollar, but with EBIT rising 5 per cent and the addition of 121 new customers.

Outlook

With about 60 per cent of its business overseas, Melbourne IT is a victim not only of currency volatility but also of weak economies in Europe and America. It is also being hurt as domain name and web hosting increasingly become commodity-type businesses, subject to strong competition and low margins. In partial response, it has begun a pilot program of outsourcing some services to a new low-cost business centre in the Philippines. It is also introducing a new series of top-level domain names—such as .bank, .hotel and .airline—that will appeal to commercial customers. It has also been installing new IT systems for its operations that it expects to bring significant cost benefits. Software house Reckon has taken a 5 per cent equity stake in Melbourne IT, and the companies expect to work together on software sales through jointly developed online platforms. There has also been growing speculation that Reckon or another IT company might make a takeover bid for Melbourne IT.

Year to 31 December	2009	2010
Revenues ($mn)	199.0	189.2
EBIT ($mn)	23.4	21.2
EBIT margin (%)	11.8	11.2

Year to 31 December	2009	2010
Profit before tax ($mn)	22.1	20.1
Profit after tax ($mn)	16.8	16.1
Earnings per share (¢)	21.4	20.2
Cash flow per share (¢)	32.7	29.5
Dividend (¢)	15	15
Percentage franked	100	100
Interest cover (times)	–	–
Return on equity (%)	19.6	17.9

Half year to 30 June	2010	2011
Revenues ($mn)	97.9	87.3
Profit before tax ($mn)	9.4	6.6
Profit after tax ($mn)	7.0	4.9
Earnings per share (¢)	8.8	6.2
Dividend (¢)	7	7
Percentage franked	100	100
Net tangible assets per share ($)	–	–
Debt-to-equity ratio (%)	32.9	23.8
Current ratio	1.0	1.0

Mermaid Marine Australia Ltd

MRM

<www.mma.com.au>

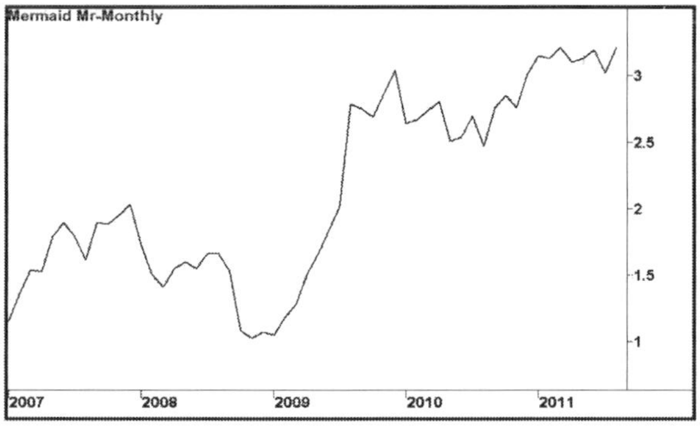

Share price ($)	3.21
12-month high ($)	3.44
12-month low ($)	2.43
Market capitalisation ($mn)	691.4
Price-to-NTA-per-share ratio	2.6
5-year share price return (% p.a.)	41.2
Dividend reinvestment plan	Yes

Sector: Industrials	Company	Sector
Price/earnings ratio (times)	15.2	11.9
Dividend yield (%)	2.8	5.5

Based in Fremantle, and established in 1984, Mermaid Marine is a leading supplier of marine logistics services to the offshore oil and gas industry. It owns and operates around 30 vessels that are available for a range of uses, including harbour tugs, survey vessels, fast-response crew vessels, platform support vessels, supply vessels and accommodation vessels. It manages the Dampier Supply Base, a multi-user facility able to service the range of operators working in the North West Shelf region. A specialised slipway, capable of docking vessels over 2000 tonnes in displacement, provides a range of marine maintenance services. In a joint venture with Toll Holdings, the company also operates a second facility at Broome, for servicing projects in the Browse Basin. In addition, it works internationally in the supply of vessels for specialist marine services.

Latest business results (June 2011, full year)

Continuing strong oil and gas activity in the North West Shelf region and work on the $43 billion Gorgon gas project helped generate very healthy increases in revenues and profits for Mermaid. The company's major activity is Vessel operations, and profits for this business rose 15 per cent, with continuing high fleet utilisation of an average 81 per cent. Two major new long-term contracts with Woodside underpinned the result. The smaller Supply Base business recorded strong demand throughout the year, with high utilisation rates, and profits leapt 52 per cent. The Slipway business, just a small part of operations, enjoyed an excellent year, with profits nearly trebling.

Outlook

Mermaid Marine is a significant beneficiary of the dynamic Western Australia oil and gas industry, with an estimated $170 billion expected to be spent on major new projects between 2011 and 2017. A new three-year contract with Chevron to transport fuel to Barrow Island will generate revenues of more than $80 million over three years. The company is also seeking new high-value international contracts, with this business responsible for about 8 per cent of June 2011 revenues. It has expanded into a new market with the purchase in mid 2011 of a 75-metre platform supply vessel, and it has already won a major contract for this. However, Mermaid will be hurt by growing competition in many of its markets, which could place pressure on margins. It is also seeing its costs rise, with sharply escalating wage claims a particular threat.

Year to 30 June	2010	2011
Revenues ($mn)	193.8	285.3
Vessels (%)	77	74

Year to 30 June	2010	2011
Supply Base (%)	20	20
Slipway (%)	3	5
EBIT ($mn)	50.8	67.3
EBIT margin (%)	26.2	23.6
Profit before tax ($mn)	41.8	58.2
Profit after tax ($mn)	37.9	43.2
Earnings per share (¢)	20.4	21.1
Cash flow per share (¢)	28.2	31.0
Dividend (¢)	8	9
Percentage franked	100	100
Net tangible assets per share ($)	1.05	1.25
Interest cover (times)	5.7	7.4
Return on equity (%)	20.7	18.5
Debt-to-equity ratio (%)	66.7	29.4
Current ratio	1.7	1.5

Metcash Limited

MTS

<www.metcash.com>

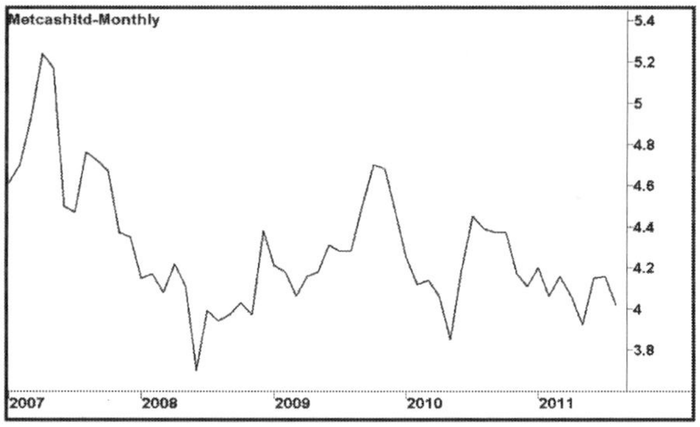

Share price ($)	4.02
12-month high ($)	4.57
12-month low ($)	3.62
Market capitalisation ($mn)	3090.8
Price-to-NTA-per-share ratio	36.8
5-year share price return (% p.a.)	4.3
Dividend reinvestment plan	No

Sector: Consumer staples	Company	Sector
Price/earnings ratio (times)	12.8	16.5
Dividend yield (%)	6.7	4.8

Sydney-based Metcash, with a history dating back to the 1920s, is Australia's third-largest grocery retail and wholesale company. Its principal business is IGA Distribution, which operates from six major distribution centres and supplies more than 2500 independent grocery stores in most states, with about 2000 of these IGA or FoodWorks stores. Its Australian Liquor Marketers division supplies liquor to more than 15000 outlets throughout Australia and New Zealand, from 18 distribution centres, with four national independent retail brands—Cellarbrations, IGA Liquor, Bottle-O and Bottle-O Neighbourhood. The Campbells Wholesale business operates from more than 35 warehouses, and supplies groceries to convenience stores, petrol stations and other smaller outlets. In 2010 Metcash acquired a 50.1 per cent stake in the Mitre 10 hardware wholesaler.

Latest business results (April 2011, full year)

Metcash reported a solid single-digit increase in sales and profits. Both the IGA and the Campbells Wholesale operations saw sales and profits up, despite a challenging retail environment that included some price deflation and growing competition from a series of rival operations. The IGA business achieved sales growth of 6 per cent. Excluding the impact of new store openings during the year the increase was 4.5 per cent. However, some cost pressures meant that profit margins fell a little. The Campbells Wholesale growth followed a restructuring of the business that included the closure of eight underperforming warehouses. The liquor business was hit by a subdued Australian liquor market and a large contract loss, and sales and profits were down. There was a strong full-year contribution from the new Mitre 10 acquisition.

Outlook

Metcash-supplied stores now hold around 19 per cent of the national grocery market, and an estimated 35 per cent of the convenience sector. The company continues to grow modestly despite intense competition from rivals that include not only the two majors, Coles and Woolworths, but also entrants from abroad such as Aldi and Costco. It has made a $215 million bid to buy the Franklins grocery chain, and has provisionally won the required regulatory approval for this. It could move to full ownership of Mitre 10 in 2012 or 2013, and it sees great potential from this business. It intends to launch a program of new store openings, and it is refurbishing existing stores and expanding the product range. It is also working to establish a new national distribution centre.

Year to 30 April	2010	2011
Revenues ($mn)	11517.4	12364.0
Food Distribution (%)	62	61
Liquor Distribution (%)	23	19
Cash and Carry Distribution (%)	14	14

Year to 30 April	2010	2011
Hardware Distribution (%)	1	6
EBIT ($mn)	393.5	423.2
EBIT margin (%)	3.4	3.4
Gross margin (%)	9.4	9.5
Profit before tax ($mn)	330.0	356.9
Profit after tax ($mn)	227.6	241.4
Earnings per share (¢)	29.7	31.4
Cash flow per share (¢)	35.8	38.4
Dividend (¢)	26	27
Percentage franked	100	100
Net tangible assets per share ($)	0.05	0.11
Interest cover (times)	6.2	6.4
Return on equity (%)	17.5	17.9
Debt-to-equity ratio (%)	39.7	47.3
Current ratio	1.4	1.4

Mineral Resources Limited

MIN

<www.mineralresources.com.au>

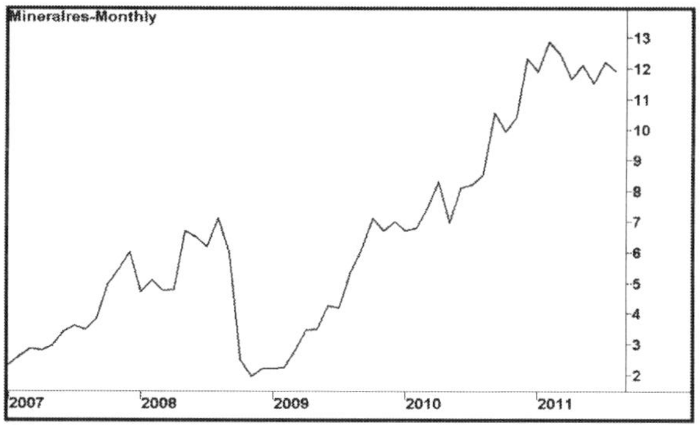

Share price ($)	11.92
12-month high ($)	13.63
12-month low ($)	8.39
Market capitalisation ($mn)	2190.5
Price-to-NTA-per-share ratio	3.6
5-year share price return (% p.a.)	60.0
Dividend reinvestment plan	Yes

Sector: Industrials	Company	Sector
Price/earnings ratio (times)	13.2	11.9
Dividend yield (%)	3.5	5.5

Mineral Resources, based in Perth, was founded in 1993, and is a mining and mining support company.

It operates through five subsidiaries. PIHA is a leader in specialist pipeline engineering and construction, with operations in Australia and Asia. Crushing Services International provides contract crushing, screening and processing services to the resources sector in Australia and overseas, as well as other specialist mining services. Process Minerals International is a minerals processor and exporter, with a specialty in bringing new mines into production on behalf of owners. Polaris Metals is an iron ore producer, with a series of projects in Western Australia. Mesa Minerals (64 per cent owned) is an emerging manganese producer and a provider of manganese production technology.

Latest business results (June 2011, full year)

Mineral Resources delivered an excellent result, with revenues and profits soaring on the back of a growing number of projects. Revenues from the sale of goods and equipment jumped 145 per cent to $376.1 million. Contract and operational revenues rose 50 per cent to $232.6 million. Chinese revenues were up 90 per cent from the previous year, and represented about a quarter of total company turnover. The company exported 2.26 million tonnes of iron ore from Port

Hedland, a 158 per cent increase on the previous year.

Outlook

With more than $78 million in net cash holdings, Mineral Resources plans to continue to expand quite aggressively in order to reap the benefits of what it forecasts will be five more years of high iron ore prices. It sees great potential in its Carina mine, which it acquired in the takeover of Polaris Metals in 2010, with iron ore production due to start in the December 2011 quarter. It has been working on a $44 million project to upgrade facilities at Kwinana bulk terminal, south of Perth, to handle the Carina output. In March 2011 it completed construction of a crushing and processing plant at the Christmas Creek iron ore mine in the Pilbara, under a 10-year build, own and operate contract with Fortescue Metals, with an initial capacity of 19 million tonnes per year. This is to be expanded to 44 million tonnes during 2012. Mineral Resources has acquired the unlisted company Auvex Resources, which will enable it to proceed with its stalled Ant Hill/Sunday Hill manganese project in Western Australia.

Year to 30 June	2010	2011
Revenues ($mn)	312.6	609.5
EBIT ($mn)	84.4	209.3

Year to 30 June	2010	2011
EBIT margin (%)	27.0	34.3
Profit before tax ($mn)	81.7	208.9
Profit after tax ($mn)	62.5	151.0
Earnings per share (¢)	44.0	90.0
Cash flow per share (¢)	57.6	105.6
Dividend (¢)	20	42
Percentage franked	100	100
Net tangible assets per share ($)	2.59	3.33
Interest cover (times)	31.1	562.6
Return on equity (%)	20.7	28.3
Debt-to-equity ratio (%)	–	–
Current ratio	1.5	1.6

Monadelphous Group Limited

MND

<www.monadelphous.com.au>

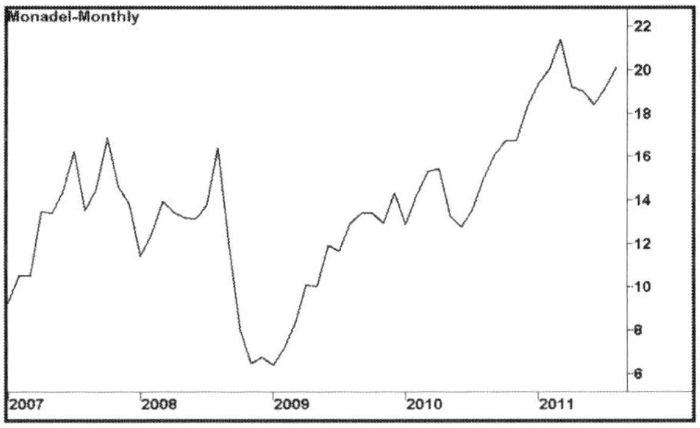

Share price ($)	20.10
12-month high ($)	22.40
12-month low ($)	14.64
Market capitalisation ($mn)	1760.3
Price-to-NTA-per-share ratio	9.4
5-year share price return (% p.a.)	31.3
Dividend reinvestment plan	No

Sector: Industrials	Company	Sector
Price/earnings ratio (times)	18.5	11.9
Dividend yield (%)	4.7	5.5

Perth-based Monadelphous, established in the early 1970s, is an engineering company that provides a wide range of construction, maintenance, project management and support services to the minerals, energy and infrastructure industries. It operates from branches throughout Australia, with a client base that includes most of the country's resource majors. A subsidiary, MIE, provides specialist instrumentation and electrical services. Monadelphous also operates Skystar Airport Services, a company that provides airport ground handling services.

Latest business results (June 2011, full year)

Monadelphous enjoyed another excellent result, with its 10th consecutive year of higher profits. Solid growth was achieved across the company's operations and in all three key markets of resources, energy and infrastructure. The Engineering Construction division, responsible for more than 60 per cent of company turnover, achieved a 10 per cent increase in sales, with a particularly strong contribution from the company's work on Woodside Petroleum's Pluto LNG project. This division has also been active in the Queensland coal industry. The Maintenance and Industrial Services division boosted sales by nearly 7 per cent. The company's new Infrastructure division saw sales up by 167 per cent, with a series of projects in the water and sewage sectors. The resources sector was responsible for just 56 per cent of the company's business, down from 93 per cent four years earlier, as Monadelphous increasingly moved into the energy and infrastructure markets. During the year the company was awarded approximately $650 million in new contracts and contract extensions, roughly in line with the previous year.

Outlook

Monadelphous has become a key provider for the Pluto LNG project, and believes it has now established a platform for sustained growth as a major participant in the construction and commissioning of further large-scale LNG projects. Meanwhile, its Maintenance and Industrial Services division continues to grow, with a series of long-term contracts delivering a degree of recurring income. The new Infrastructure division is rapidly providing the company with a third leg of growth, particularly in the water and sewage treatment sectors, and it has made a significant investment in specialised pipeline equipment to support future expansion. Skill shortages and rising wage demands remain a constraint for the company, but, with its involvement in what it describes as an unprecedented level of tendering activity, the prospects are excellent for further strong growth.

Year to 30 June	2010	2011
Revenues ($mn)	1275.4	1443.9
Engineering Construction (%)	66	62
Maintenance and Industrial Serv. (%)	29	27

Year to 30 June	2010	2011
Infrastructure (%)	5	11
EBIT ($mn)	112.6	128.9
EBIT margin (%)	8.8	8.9
Gross margin (%)	11.7	12.2
Profit before tax ($mn)	115.1	131.6
Profit after tax ($mn)	83.2	95.1
Earnings per share (¢)	96.9	108.8
Cash flow per share (¢)	116.4	136.8
Dividend (¢)	83	95
Percentage franked	100	100
Net tangible assets per share ($)	1.65	2.15
Interest cover (times)	–	–
Return on equity (%)	62.4	56.3
Debt-to-equity ratio (%)	–	–
Current ratio	1.2	1.2

Mortgage Choice Limited

MOC

<www.mortgagechoice.com.au>

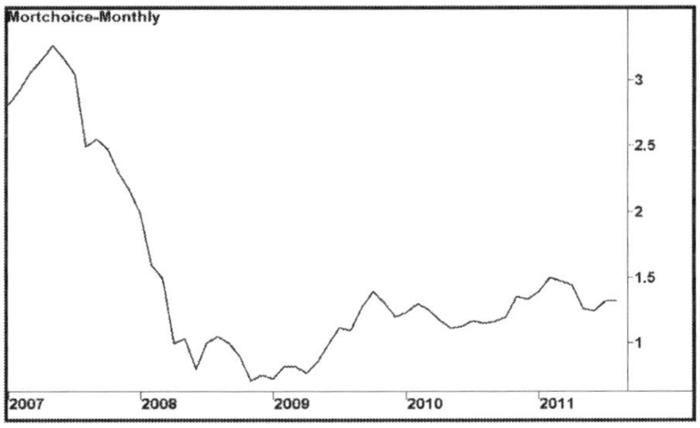

Share price ($)	1.32
12-month high ($)	1.61
12-month low ($)	1.05
Market capitalisation ($mn)	156.3
Price-to-NTA-per-share ratio	1.8
5-year share price return (% p.a.)	–4.5
Dividend reinvestment plan	No

Sector: Financials	Company	Sector
Price/earnings ratio (times)	5.8	10.8
Dividend yield (%)	9.8	6.8

Sydney company Mortgage Choice was established in 1992 and is today one of the country's largest mortgage brokers. It works through a national network of hundreds of franchises and loan consultants, supported by its own offices, and providing advice on mortgages, personal loans, commercial loans, equipment finance and insurance products. Its LoanKit business is a mortgage aggregator. In October 2010 it acquired the HelpMeChoose.com.au insurance and mortgage comparison website. Count Financial owns 17.3 per cent of the Mortgage Choice equity.

Latest business results (June 2011, full year)

Profits rose strongly, although this good result incorporated some accounting adjustments. On a cash basis, stripping out these adjustments, Mortgage Choice's after-tax profit rose 7.4 per cent to $15.9 million. During the year the company generated housing loan approvals of $9.9 billion, down from $10.1 billion in the June 2010 year. Origination commission income from new mortgages fell 6 per cent to $49.1 million. However, trailing commission revenue on existing loans rose 1 per cent to $83.8 million. At June 2011 the company's loan book stood at $42.4 billion, up 6 per cent from a year earlier. Mortgage Choice claimed a rise from 3.8 per cent to 4.1 per cent in its market share for all new home loans in Australia.

Outlook

Mortgage Choice is well established throughout Australia with a good reputation. Market surveys reveal that more than 40 per cent of new home loans in Australia are sourced through mortgage brokers. The company has achieved a name for independence, as it does not sell products of its own, and also because it pays franchisees the same rate for the home loan they write, regardless of the fee paid by the lender that the customer selects. However, with volatile economies around the world and a weakening domestic housing environment, it remains to be seen whether Mortgage Choice can maintain growth. The company itself expresses optimism that a combination of a housing price correction, a growing population and the possibility of lower interest rates suggests the housing market will remain strong. It also sees sharemarket volatility as enhancing the appeal of housing as an investment. It has been working to diversify its revenue streams, and in the June 2011 year it derived $2.4 million in revenue from risk insurance and commercial loan services, up from $2.1 million in the previous year.

Year to 30 June	2010	2011
Revenues ($mn)	170.5	169.0
EBIT ($mn)	33.1	38.7
EBIT margin (%)	19.4	22.9
Profit before tax ($mn)	33.5	39.3

Year to 30 June	2010	2011
Profit after tax ($mn)	23.5	27.5
Earnings per share (¢)	19.7	22.9
Cash flow per share (¢)	20.6	24.2
Dividend (¢)	12	13
Percentage franked	100	100
Net tangible assets per share ($)	0.62	0.74
Interest cover (times)	–	–
Return on equity (%)	32.7	32.8
Debt-to-equity ratio (%)	–	–
Current ratio	1.5	1.6

National Australia Bank Limited

NAB

<www.nabgroup.com>

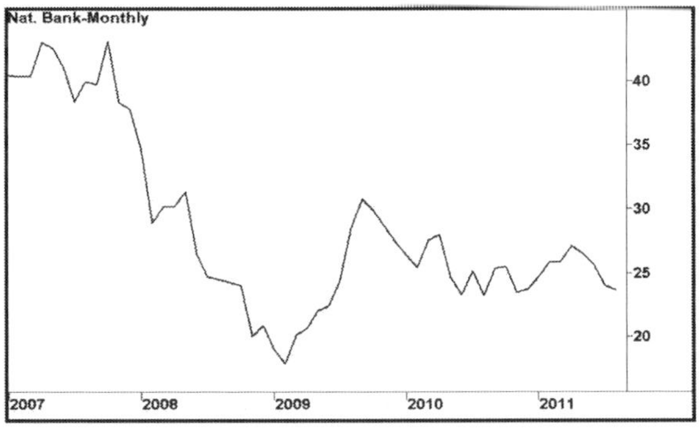

Share price ($)	23.66
12-month high ($)	28.18
12-month low ($)	19.64
Market capitalisation ($mn)	52078.3
Price-to-NTA-per-share ratio	1.8
5-year share price return (% p.a.)	−2.6
Dividend reinvestment plan	Yes

Sector: Financials	Company	Sector
Price/earnings ratio (times)	11.6	10.8
Dividend yield (%)	6.4	6.8

The National Australia Bank, based in Melbourne, has a history dating back to the establishment of the National Bank of Australasia in 1858. It is one of Australia's largest banks, with a wide spread of financial activities. It owns the Clydesdale Bank and Yorkshire Bank in Britain, Great Western Bank, based in South Dakota in the US, and the Bank of New Zealand. It also operates offices in several countries in Asia. Its MLC and NAB Wealth businesses are leading Australian funds management and financial advisory operations. Its nabInvest business is a direct asset management operation.

Latest business results (March 2011, half year)

NAB enjoyed a solid rise in profits, thanks to some market share gains, good growth in home lending and firm cost containment measures. There was a particularly strong contribution from the bank's personal banking business, thanks to gains in market share for both home lending and household deposits, along with a reduced charge for bad and doubtful debts. Business banking was also strong, with the bank retaining its leading market share in business lending. MLC and NAB Wealth saw some modest profit growth, with funds under management up nearly 7 per cent. Wholesale banking profits edged down, due especially to subdued activity in overseas operations. NAB's banking businesses in Britain, New Zealand and the

United States all enjoyed double-digit profit rises in local currencies, as those countries continued their slow economic recovery. The bank's Specialised Group Assets business, which involves the management of much high-yield debt, posted a sharp recovery in profits.

Outlook

NAB's domestic strengths helped shield it from the worst effects of the financial crisis. Now, thanks to its strengths in business banking, and especially in the small and mid-sized sectors, it will be a beneficiary of any recovery in demand for business credit. NAB also has a strong wealth management business, and this too will benefit from any market recovery. However, due to its portfolio of overseas banks NAB remains exposed more than its domestic rivals to the economic and banking woes of Britain, the United States and New Zealand, though it was benefiting as those countries' economies appeared to be slowly recovering. There has been speculation that NAB is interested in buying some of the more than 600 bank branches that Britain's Lloyds Banking Group has offered for sale.

Year to 30 September	2009	2010
Operating income ($mn)	16777.0	17008.0
Net interest income ($mn)	12068.0	12256.0
Operating expenses ($mn)	7979.0	8541.0

Year to 30 September	2009	2010
Profit before tax ($mn)	4983.0	5676.0
Profit after tax ($mn)	2589.0	4224.0
Earnings per share (¢)	137.9	204.0
Dividend (¢)	146	152
Percentage franked	100	100
Non-interest income to total income (%)	28.1	27.9
Cost-to-income ratio (%)	47.6	50.2
Return on equity (%)	7.3	11.0
Return on assets (%)	0.4	0.6

Half year to 31 March	2010	2011
Operating income ($mn)	8682.0	8287.0
Profit before tax ($mn)	2840.0	3247.0
Profit after tax ($mn)	2095.0	2428.0
Earnings per share (¢)	98.4	111.9
Dividend (¢)	74	84
Percentage franked	100	100
Net tangible assets per share ($)	12.41	12.80

Navitas Limited

NVT

<www.navitas.com>

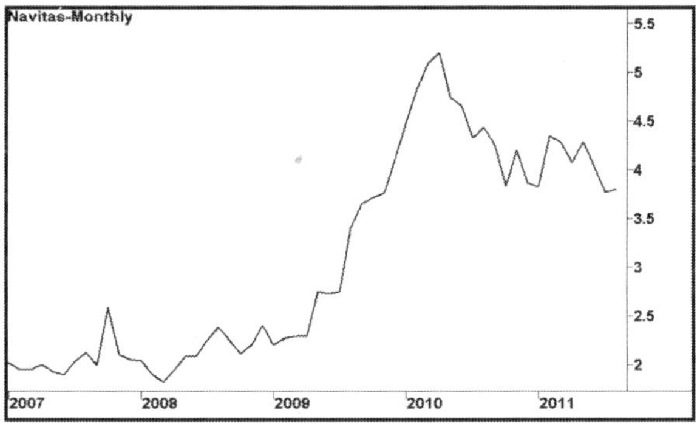

Share price ($)	3.80
12-month high ($)	4.69
12-month low ($)	3.37
Market capitalisation ($mn)	1426.6
Price-to-NTA-per-share ratio	–
5-year share price return (% p.a.)	20.9
Dividend reinvestment plan	No

Sector: Consumer discretionary	Company	Sector
Price/earnings ratio (times)	17.5	13.1
Dividend yield (%)	5.4	3.5

Perth-based Navitas, a prominent provider of education services, has evolved from colleges established in Western Australia in the 1990s. Today it operates through five divisions. The core division, University Programs, provides university pathway and managed campus programs for students from many countries, at colleges in Australia, Britain, Canada, the US, Singapore and Sri Lanka. The English division provides programs in English as a second language, for students and migrants. Of two much smaller businesses, Workforce delivers employee educational and professional development services, and the Student Recruitment division recruits students in India and China for educational institutions in Australia, Canada, the US and Britain. In February 2011 Navitas acquired a fifth business, SAE Group, a prominent international provider of tertiary-level media technology courses.

Latest business results (June 2011, full year)

Revenues and profits again rose, but not at the pace of previous years, and much of the growth came from the contribution of SAE, acquired for $294.3 million. The core University Programs division saw profits up 9 per cent, well down from gains of more than 30 per cent in the previous two years. The strong dollar, visa requirement changes and publicity given to attacks on foreign students in Australia all hurt the company, although these issues were offset by strong enrolments in Canada and Singapore. The English division was especially hit by the strong dollar and a decline in refugee and humanitarian migrants to Australia, with revenues down and profits halving. The Workforce division achieved higher revenues and profits, and the Student Recruitment division moved from loss to profit.

Outlook

Navitas is facing the prospect of subdued growth while the dollar remains high and tougher visa requirements limit foreign student numbers in Australia. It is also experiencing slower expansion than expected in the British market. As a result it expects just minimal growth from its University Programs business in the June 2012 year, although longer term it expects significant business in the huge US market, where it has been investing heavily and rapidly expanding. In the near term at least, much of the company's growth is likely to derive from SAE, which is one of the world's largest media technology institutes, with operations at 53 campuses in 19 countries. New government contracts should help the English division recover, although the strong dollar will continue to hurt this business.

Year to 30 June	2010	2011
Revenues ($mn)	555.4	641.8
University Programs (%)	62	58
English (%)	25	20
SAE (%)	0	10
EBIT ($mn)	89.1	106.8

Year to 30 June	2010	2011
EBIT margin (%)	16.0	16.6
Profit before tax ($mn)	90.3	105.2
Profit after tax ($mn)	64.3	77.4
Earnings per share (¢)	18.8	21.7
Cash flow per share (¢)	21.0	24.8
Dividend (¢)	18.8	20.7
Percentage franked	100	100
Net tangible assets per share ($)	–	–
Interest cover (times)	–	65.8
Return on equity (%)	63.0	44.7
Debt-to-equity ratio (%)	–	43.0
Current ratio	0.5	0.5

Newcrest Mining Limited

NCM

<www.newcrest.com.au>

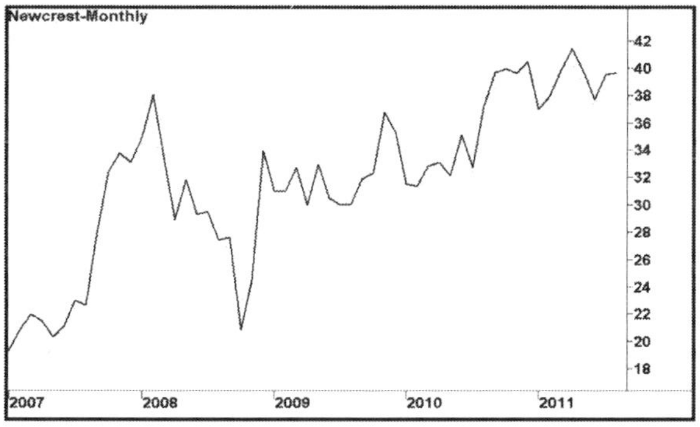

Share price ($)	39.68
12-month high ($)	43.71
12-month low ($)	35.15
Market capitalisation ($mn)	30354.2
Price-to-NTA-per-share ratio	3.0
5-year share price return (% p.a.)	17.7
Dividend reinvestment plan	Yes

Sector: Materials	Company	Sector
Price/earnings ratio (times)	26.9	12.3
Dividend yield (%)	0.8	2.2

Melbourne-based Newcrest, Australia's leading gold producer and one of the largest in the world, was established in 1966 as a subsidiary of the American company Newmont Mining. It was later listed on the ASX. Following the August 2010 acquisition of Lihir Gold, for $9.5 billion, the company operates 10 mines in four countries. It also possesses an extensive portfolio of advanced exploration projects.

Latest business results (June 2011, full year)

Revenues and profits soared, reflecting a 10-month contribution from the Lihir Gold acquisition, and comparisons with the previous year have only limited relevance. Gold production of 2.53 million ounces was 43 per cent higher than in the previous year, mainly as a result of the Lihir acquisition, but also due to a full year's contribution from newly commissioned operations in Papua New Guinea. Copper production fell 13 per cent to 75631 tonnes, with Australian east coast operations hurt by heavy rains. The average gold price received by the company during the year rose 10.1 per cent to $1378 per ounce, with the average copper price up 15.5 per cent to $3.93 per pound. Mine production costs were up 7.4 per cent, with higher energy costs and wages a particular contributing factor. The company reported that by June 2011 some $63 million in annual recurring synergies had been realised from the Lihir takeover.

Outlook

Newcrest continues to be transformed by its takeover of Lihir, and says its target of $85 million in annual recurring synergies will be exceeded. It is restructuring many of its operations, aiming to lay a foundation for sustained growth. It plans to sell two Queensland mines—Mt Rawdon and the 70 per cent-owned Cracow—to a new company formed from the merger of Catalpa Resources and Conquest Mining. Newcrest will eventually hold 33 per cent of the equity of this new company. It expects to spend up to $9 billion on capital projects in the coming five years, with a goal of lifting annual production to four million ounces of gold and 150000 tonnes of copper, with a particular focus on the Cadia Valley operations in New South Wales and the Lihir Island operation in PNG. The company has pledged to return more of its capital to shareholders, in part to address the problem of the disconnect between the gold price and the performance of gold company equities. The company has described the new carbon tax as a significant negative.

Year to 30 June	2010	2011
Revenues ($mn)	2801.8	4102.0
EBIT ($mn)	832.0	1544.0

Year to 30 June	2010	2011
EBIT margin (%)	29.7	37.6
Gross margin (%)	44.0	41.5
Profit before tax ($mn)	811.0	1508.0
Profit after tax ($mn)	556.9	1058.0
Earnings per share (¢)	115.2	147.3
Cash flow per share (¢)	179.0	219.1
Dividend (¢)	25	30
Percentage franked	0	0
Net tangible assets per share ($)	10.19	13.32
Interest cover (times)	39.6	42.9
Return on equity (%)	12.0	11.3
Debt-to-equity ratio (%)	–	4.4
Current ratio	4.3	1.9

Nick Scali Limited

NCK

<www.nickscali.com.au>

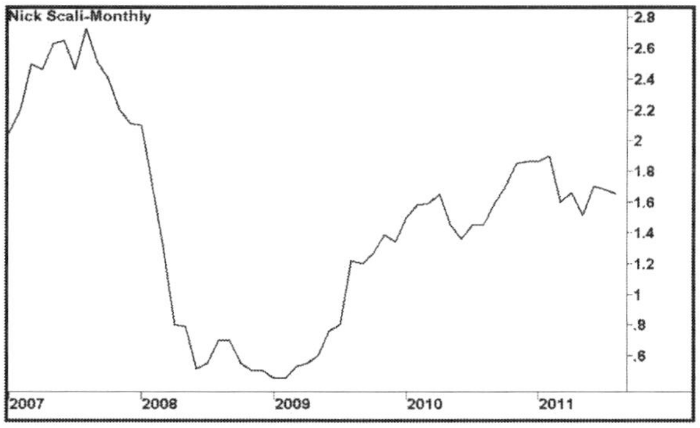

Share price ($)	1.65
12-month high ($)	2.00
12-month low ($)	1.45
Market capitalisation ($mn)	133.7
Price-to-NTA-per-share ratio	5.7
5-year share price return (% p.a.)	7.4
Dividend reinvestment plan	No

Sector: Consumer discretionary	Company	Sector
Price/earnings ratio (times)	11.5	13.1
Dividend yield (%)	5.5	3.5

Sydney-based Nick Scali, with a history dating back more than 45 years, is one of Australia's largest furniture importers and retailers. It specialises in leather and fabric lounge suites along with dining room and bedroom furniture. It has four distribution centres and more than 30 stores in New South Wales, Victoria, Queensland and South Australia. In 2011 it launched two new store brands, Sofas2Go and Chateau d'Ax.

Latest business results (June 2011, full year)

In a weak environment for consumer spending Nick Scali managed to achieve an increase in sales and profits. However, this reflected the company's continuing drive to open new stores. On a same-store basis, revenues dipped 1.6 per cent, though with a pick-up in the second half. Despite aggressive discounting from rivals, the company successfully maintained its profit margins. During the year the company opened two new Nick Scali stores, in New South Wales and Queensland. It also launched its new Sofas2Go brand, with the first two stores in New South Wales, and in June 2011 it opened its first Chateau d'Ax premium furniture store.

Outlook

Nick Scali is directly affected by trends in consumer spending, and is wary about the near-term outlook. Nevertheless, it is pushing ahead with its plans for expansion, with two new Nick Scali stores and three new Sofas2Go stores scheduled to open in the July to December 2011 half. For the longer term the company is targeting a network throughout Australia and New Zealand of 125 Sofas2Go stores, 75 Nick Scali stores and 21 Chateau d'Ax stores. The company's new Sofas2Go brand is aimed at entry-level consumers and first-home buyers. It offers basic products at low cost, leveraging the company's existing purchasing, distribution and support infrastructure. These stores will use a smaller layout than most furniture stores, providing greater site availability and the opportunity for faster store rollout. They will also offer a facility for online ordering. The company has secured the Australasian rights for the premium Italian furniture brand Chateau d'Ax, which is aimed at the top end of the market and is sold at 300 stores in 30 countries. The company's aim is to build this brand slowly throughout Australia, with stores in areas with the appropriate demographics. At June 2011 Nick Scali had a strong balance sheet with net cash holdings of more than $14 million that it can employ for its expansion plans.

Year to 30 June	2010	2011
Revenues ($mn)	96.4	100.0
EBIT ($mn)	15.4	16.1
EBIT margin (%)	16.0	16.1
Gross margin (%)	62.7	62.7

Year to 30 June	2010	2011
Profit before tax ($mn)	16.1	16.8
Profit after tax ($mn)	11.3	11.6
Earnings per share (¢)	13.9	14.3
Cash flow per share (¢)	15.0	15.6
Dividend (¢)	9	9
Percentage franked	100	100
Net tangible assets per share ($)	0.24	0.29
Interest cover (times)	–	–
Return on equity (%)	56.5	49.3
Debt-to-equity ratio (%)	–	–
Current ratio	1.7	1.6

Oakton Limited

OKN

<www.oakton.com.au>

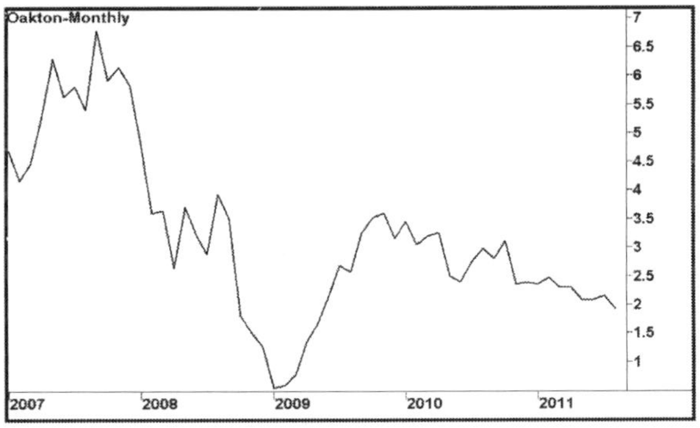

Share price ($)	1.92
12-month high ($)	3.20
12-month low ($)	1.60
Market capitalisation ($mn)	180.1
Price-to-NTA-per-share ratio	6.8
5-year share price return (% p.a.)	−9.2
Dividend reinvestment plan	No

Sector: Information technology	Company	Sector
Price/earnings ratio (times)	10.7	18.2
Dividend yield (%)	4.4	3.9

Melbourne-based technology consultant Oakton was established in 1988. It has grown rapidly through acquisition, and now serves a wide variety of blue-chip corporate and government clients. Working in partnership with leading business system product vendors, it provides guidance on IT requirements, covering the full life cycle of planning and design, custom software development, packaged software implementation, information management and system integration processes. It has an office in India.

Latest business results (June 2011, full year)

Profits fell in a disappointing result that the company blamed on significant and continuing difficulties in its home state of Victoria. Consequently, the proportion of revenues derived from Victoria dropped from 40 per cent in the previous year to 36 per cent. By contrast, the company reported market share gains in New South Wales, which contributed 37 per cent of turnover. The company also enjoyed a resurgence in government contracts, which had slumped in the previous year, and Canberra-derived revenues rose from 20 per cent to 23 per cent of the total. In addition to the figures in the table, the company incurred net costs of $5.2 million in relation to the settlement of a long-running dispute with one of its customers, Tenix Solutions.

Outlook

Oakton management have expressed confidence about the outlook, thanks especially to a turnaround in Victorian operations during the April to June 2011 quarter. The company is also optimistic about a wave of new government work, particularly in IT services. Federal and state government business has in past years provided around a third of Oakton's turnover. Queensland currently provides just 4 per cent of total business, but, with the opening of a new Brisbane office at the end of 2010, the company believes it is now in a position to gain market share in the state. Oakton's strategy is also to invest significant resources in building up its Indian presence, as a means of gaining access to a high level of skills at a lower cost than prevailing in Australia. In May 2011 it opened a new office at Hyderabad, with capacity for around 400 employees, and staff numbers are growing rapidly. However, the IT consultancy business is highly vulnerable to economic conditions, with companies quick to postpone IT spending when the economy deteriorates. It remains to be seen how Oakton will cope with any downturn in domestic corporate spending.

Year to 30 June	2010	2011
Revenues ($mn)	186.4	181.3
EBIT ($mn)	30.0	23.7
EBIT margin (%)	16.1	13.1
Profit before tax ($mn)	28.1	22.6

Year to 30 June	2010	2011
Profit after tax ($mn)	20.2	16.8
Earnings per share (¢)	22.1	18.0
Cash flow per share (¢)	24.7	20.7
Dividend (¢)	6.5	8.5
Percentage franked	100	100
Net tangible assets per share ($)	0.18	0.28
Interest cover (times)	16.0	22.8
Return on equity (%)	23.7	16.5
Debt-to-equity ratio (%)	9.4	4.2
Current ratio	1.5	1.7

Orica Limited

ORI

<www.orica.com.au>

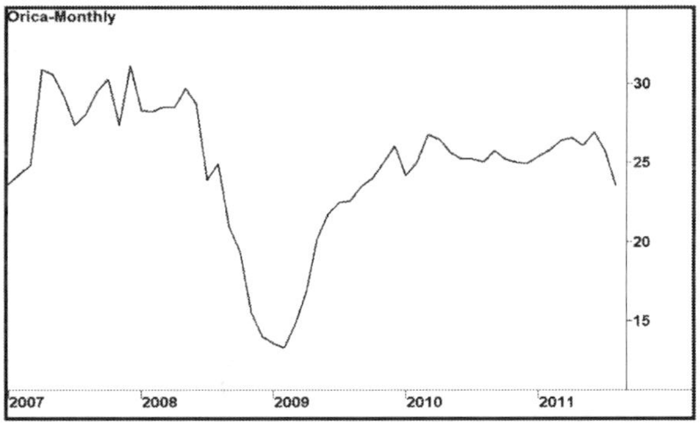

Share price ($)	23.52
12-month high ($)	28.10
12-month low ($)	22.25
Market capitalisation ($mn)	8558.3
Price-to-NTA-per-share ratio	8.2
5-year share price return (% p.a.)	6.3
Dividend reinvestment plan	Yes

Sector: Materials	Company	Sector
Price/earnings ratio (times)	15.8	12.3
Dividend yield (%)	4.0	2.2

Melbourne-based Orica was founded more than 130 years ago as a supplier of explosives for the mining industry, and for many years it was a subsidiary of Britain's Imperial Chemical Industries. Its Orica Mining Services business has become a global leader in commercial explosives for the mining, quarrying and construction sectors. Orica Chemicals is a major supplier and trader of chemicals, services and technology to the water treatment, mining chemical and industrial chemical markets. Its third division, Minova, is an international leader in chemicals and equipment associated with rock bolting, ground consolidation, ventilation and water control for underground mines and tunnels. In 2010 Orica spun off its consumer products operations into a new public company, DuluxGroup. Orica currently has operations in around 50 countries.

Latest business results (March 2011, half year)

Sales and profits fell, although this largely reflected the divestment in the previous year of Orica's consumer products businesses. Excluding this, sales were up 8 per cent and the after-tax profit rose 5 per cent, despite a $174 million hit from the strong dollar. The mining services business, now responsible for more than 60 per cent of total company turnover, saw sales up 10 per cent, although EBIT was up only 1 per cent. The chemicals business also saw a 1 per cent rise in profits, despite lower sales of sodium cyanide, as a result of the planned shutdown of one plant for an upgrade. Rising demand boosted Minova's sales, but intense competition in some of its markets led to a 16 per cent decline in profits.

Outlook

Following the separate listing of its consumer products division, Orica now has more than 85 per cent of its business geared towards the mining industry, and its fortunes will rise or fall accordingly. It is also highly dependent on commodity price and exchange rate trends. It is seeing strong demand in Australian and Asian coal markets and improving demand in metals markets, and expects these to underpin future growth. However, the Minova business continues to experience strong margin pressure in North America and parts of Europe, hurting profits. The chemicals business is seeing strong demand from mining markets, but challenging conditions elsewhere. During 2012 the company anticipates initial production from its new ammonium nitrate plant at Bontang, Indonesia, and from its $100 million detonator plant in Hunan province, China.

Year to 30 September	2009	2010
Revenues ($mn)	7411.0	6539.3
EBIT ($mn)	1082.2	1025.9
EBIT margin (%)	14.6	15.7
Profit before tax ($mn)	948.7	898.3

Year to 30 September	2009	2010
Profit after tax ($mn)	646.1	527.6
Earnings per share (¢)	182.6	148.4
Cash flow per share (¢)	252.6	215.8
Dividend (¢)	97	95
Percentage franked	35	74
Interest cover (times)	8.1	8.0
Return on equity (%)	16.0	14.3

Half year to 31 March	2010	2011
Revenues ($mn)	3226.0	2949.3
Profit before tax ($mn)	425.3	374.5
Profit after tax ($mn)	293.2	263.8
Earnings per share (¢)	82.6	71.1
Dividend (¢)	41	37
Percentage franked	39	49
Net tangible assets per share ($)	2.67	2.87
Debt-to-equity ratio (%)	33.1	40.1
Current ratio	1.0	1.4

OrotonGroup Limited

ORL

<www.orotongroup.com.au>

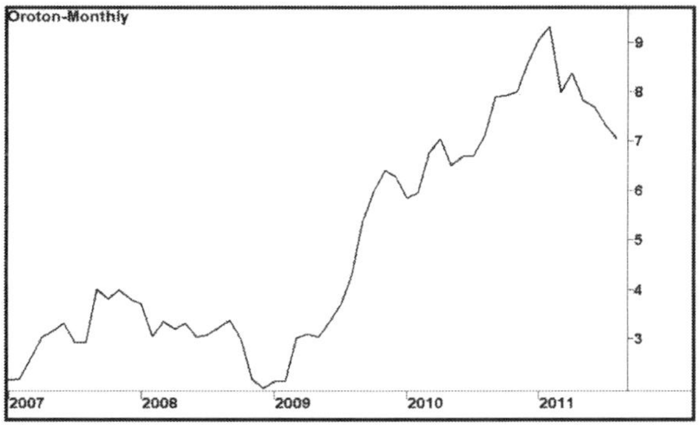

Share price ($)	7.05
12-month high ($)	9.50
12-month low ($)	5.95
Market capitalisation ($mn)	287.5
Price-to-NTA-per-share ratio	9.0
5-year share price return (% p.a.)	48.7
Dividend reinvestment plan	No

Sector: Consumer discretionary	Company	Sector
Price/earnings ratio (times)	12.5	13.1
Dividend yield (%)	6.8	3.5

Sydney-based fashion company OrotonGroup was established in 1938 as an importer of high-quality fabrics from Europe. Today it markets a wide range of fashion and sports clothing and accessories through two premium brands—Polo Ralph Lauren and Oroton—with a growing chain of outlets in Australia and New Zealand. It has also ventured into the Asian retail business.

Latest business results (January 2011, half year)

Sales rose and EBIT was also up, although the after-tax profit was flat, as the company at last felt the impact of a sluggish retail environment, following an extended period of growth. In fact, most of the rise in sales came through new store openings. On a like-for-like basis sales were similar to the January 2010 figure. Polo Ralph Lauren performed well in the circumstances, with 6 per cent sales growth, but the Oroton brand was down 5 per cent. The company was hit by higher expenses, partly due to sales being lower than expected, and also as a result of the cost of rebuilding Polo Ralph Lauren stock levels and some long-term growth and branding costs. The company's small online business saw sales more than double. It opened five new stores during the period, including its first two in Asia—in Hong Kong and Singapore—and at the end of January 2011 it operated a total of 81 stores.

Outlook

Over several years OrotonGroup was able to report a continuing series of strong profit increases through varying economic conditions, and it even appeared to sail through the global financial crisis relatively unscathed. However, it now faces very challenging conditions, with weak consumer sentiment, intense competition that includes some heavy discounting from rivals, and the growing threat of online marketing. In partial response, it has launched a new program of expansion to Asia, which it sees as a significant growth opportunity, although this is expected to entail a rise in costs. It has followed the initial two stores in Singapore and Hong Kong with a second Singapore presence and two further stores in Kuala Lumpur. It views its online presence as an important growth opportunity, as well as a new tool for customer communication and research. The company is also engaging in some strategic discounting, in response to market demands, but has also increased some prices, and sees long-term brand development as the more important strategy.

Year to 31 July*	2009	2010
Revenues ($mn)	135.6	146.4
EBIT ($mn)	28.0	32.0
EBIT margin (%)	20.6	21.9

Year to 31 July*	2009	2010
Gross margin (%)	67.2	68.3
Profit before tax ($mn)	27.5	31.4
Profit after tax ($mn)	19.4	23.0
Earnings per share (¢)	47.7	56.3
Cash flow per share (¢)	59.9	70.8
Dividend (¢)	38	48
Percentage franked	100	100
Interest cover (times)	61.2	50.6
Return on equity (%)	80.5	83.6

* 25 July 2009

Half year to 29 January**	2010	2011
Revenues ($mn)	81.6	87.4
Profit before tax ($mn)	21.3	22.0
Profit after tax ($mn)	15.4	15.4
Earnings per share (¢)	37.9	37.9
Dividend (¢)	22	22
Percentage franked	100	100
Net tangible assets per share ($)	0.74	0.78
Debt-to-equity ratio (%)	8.2	22.3
Current ratio	1.5	1.6

** 23 January 2010

Patties Foods Limited

PFL

<www.patties.com.au>

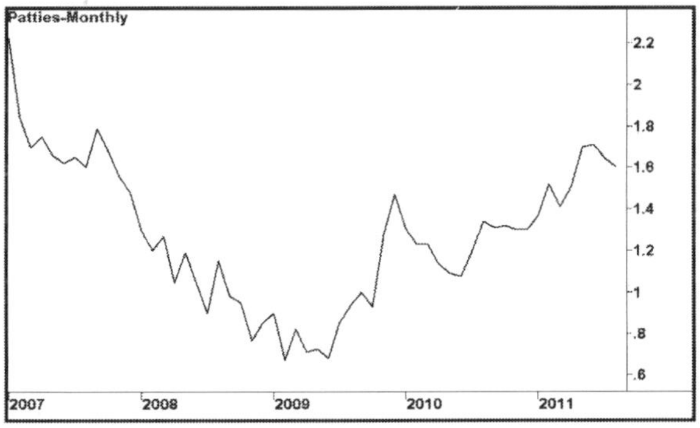

Share price ($)	1.60
12-month high ($)	1.83
12-month low ($)	1.24
Market capitalisation ($mn)	222.4
Price-to-NTA-per-share ratio	4.5
5-year share price return (% p.a.)	1.2
Dividend reinvestment plan	No

Sector: Consumer staples	Company	Sector
Price/earnings ratio (times)	12.1	16.5
Dividend yield (%)	4.8	4.8

Based in Bairnsdale in country Victoria, Patties Foods started life in 1966 as Patties Cake Shop. It has since expanded through acquisition and organic growth, and now incorporates a portfolio of brands, with a speciality in pies and bakery products. These brands include Four'N Twenty pies, Patties pies, Herbert Adams pies and pastries, Snowy River pies, Nanna's pies and pastries, Chefs Pride frozen fruits and purees, and Creative Gourmet frozen fruit. It also maintains a contract manufacturing business, supplying bakery products for a range of retailers and catering outlets.

Latest business results (June 2011, full year)

In difficult trading conditions Patties enjoyed another year of earnings growth. The company attributed this to the development and launch of a series of new products, as well as strong growth for many existing product lines. There was continuing success for Four'N Twenty's Angus range of meat pies, strong demand for Patties home party products, the successful launch of the Creative Gourmet Smoothie Cubes fruit drink and solid growth in frozen fruit sales. Continued manufacturing improvements at the company's Bairnsdale operation helped contain costs at a time of escalating commodities prices, though the company's gross margin edged down. Profits would have been higher but for an increase in marketing and advertising expenditure to support new product launches.

Outlook

Patties owns a series of near-iconic brands with high market shares, and this will help protect it in the event of any economic downturn. It believes that it can maintain growth in the June 2012 year, despite a slowdown in consumer spending and rising raw material costs, thanks to a pipeline of innovative new products, some new contracts and continuing improvements in manufacturing efficiencies. It has also been raising some prices. It has been working to upgrade and automate its Bairnsdale production plant, and now hopes to take advantage of its expanded capacity to boost its share of the out-of-home food products market. Since 2007 it has been supplying savoury pastry products to Retail Food Group for its Michel's Patisserie network of more than 300 stores. It has now signed a new agreement with the company to supply savoury pastry products to its Brumby's national franchise network of over 300 outlets. Deliveries are expected to begin by the end of 2011. Patties is also seeking further opportunities to supply Retail Food with both savoury and sweet products.

Year to 30 June	2010	2011
Revenues ($mn)	196.1	216.1
EBIT ($mn)	25.7	29.9

Year to 30 June	2010	2011
EBIT margin (%)	13.1	13.8
Gross margin (%)	39.4	39.1
Profit before tax ($mn)	21.2	25.1
Profit after tax ($mn)	15.7	18.4
Earnings per share (¢)	11.3	13.2
Cash flow per share (¢)	15.6	18.1
Dividend (¢)	6.5	7.7
Percentage franked	100	100
Net tangible assets per share ($)	0.30	0.36
Interest cover (times)	5.7	6.3
Return on equity (%)	13.6	14.8
Debt-to-equity ratio (%)	52.5	46.4
Current ratio	2.3	2.1

Perpetual Limited

PPT

<www.perpetual.com.au>

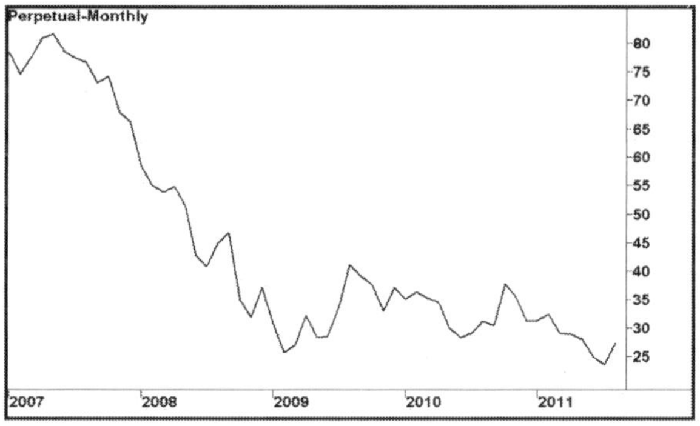

Share price ($)	27.35
12-month high ($)	39.39
12-month low ($)	19.52
Market capitalisation ($mn)	1221.8
Price-to-NTA-per-share ratio	5.6
5-year share price return (% p.a.)	−13.1
Dividend reinvestment plan	Yes

Sector: Financials	Company	Sector
Price/earnings ratio (times)	15.3	10.8
Dividend yield (%)	6.8	6.8

Sydney-based financial services company Perpetual was established in 1886 as Perpetual Trustees. It divides its operations into three broad areas. Perpetual Investments is a funds management business offering a range of managed investment products to the retail, wholesale and institutional markets. Perpetual Private Wealth is a specialist boutique financial services business aimed at high-net-worth individuals, and providing its clients access to tailored financial, tax, legal and estate planning advice. Perpetual Corporate Trust is a leading provider of corporate trustee and transaction support services to the financial services industry.

Latest business results (June 2011, full year)

Volatile markets hit the company, and business results were largely flat on the previous year. The best result came from the small Corporate Trust division, with revenues up 11 per cent for the year, though with a marked downturn in the second half as a contraction in housing market activity affected demand for mortgage lending services. The core Perpetual Investments division saw revenues slide, with net inflows turning negative, as investors remained cautious about the markets. The Private Wealth division also achieved some growth in revenues, with steady fund inflows, but higher costs led to a sharp drop in profits. At June 2011 the company had $27.2 billion in funds under management, up 1 per cent from a year before, although the company also reported that this had fallen to $25.4 billion at the end of July 2011. It also had $8.7 billion in private wealth funds under advice in June, up 5 per cent. Corporate Trust funds under administration totalled $205.8 billion, down 2 per cent.

Outlook

Perpetual retains its prominent position within Australia's booming wealth management business and the long-term outlook is positive as superannuation inflows continue to grow. However, most of its operations are highly sensitive to market volatility, which looks set to continue, with fears that many investors are losing confidence in equities. New management this year has implemented a major restructuring program, including staff layoffs, that it believes will deliver annual pre-tax savings of $9 million. It has closed Perpetual's struggling Dublin-based global equities management business. It has also sold its Smartsuper superannuation administration business, and is believed to be looking to sell other parts of its business. It is also establishing new funds, refining its growth strategies, putting a new focus on communications and reviewing all portfolios.

Year to 30 June	2010	2011
Revenues ($mn)	505.9	513.5
Perpetual Investments (%)	58	58
Private Wealth (%)	25	23
Corporate Trust (%)	17	19

Year to 30 June	2010	2011
EBIT ($mn)	97.3	96.8
EBIT margin (%)	19.2	18.9
Profit before tax ($mn)	107.7	105.4
Profit after tax ($mn)	72.8	72.5
Earnings per share (¢)	182.7	178.6
Cash flow per share (¢)	219.9	217.1
Dividend (¢)	210	185
Percentage franked	100	100
Net tangible assets per share ($)	4.89	4.87
Interest cover (times)	–	–
Return on equity (%)	22.4	20.0
Debt-to-equity ratio (%)	–	–
Current ratio	1.1	1.2

QBE Insurance Group Limited

QBE

<www.group.qbe.com>

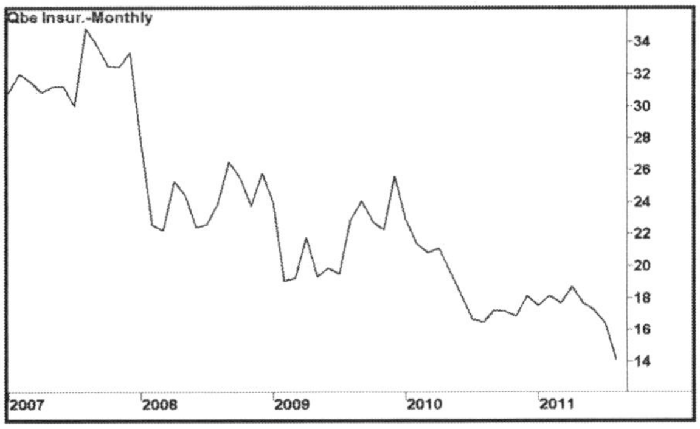

Share price ($)	14.11
12-month high ($)	19.60
12-month low ($)	12.25
Market capitalisation ($mn)	15415.9
Price-to-NTA-per-share ratio	3.3
5-year share price return (% p.a.)	–4.5
Dividend reinvestment plan	Yes

Sector: Financials	Company	Sector
Price/earnings ratio (times)	7.2	10.8
Dividend yield (%)	9.1	6.8

Sydney-based QBE—founded as North Queensland Insurance Company in 1886—is one of Australia's leading insurance companies, specialising in general insurance and reinsurance. Through a long series of acquisitions it has expanded globally to become one of the world's top 25 global insurers and reinsurers, with operations in around 50 countries. Its four operating divisions have headquarters in Sydney, London, New York and Singapore. Over three-quarters of business comes from abroad, with particular strength in Europe and the US.

Latest business results (June 2011, half year)

QBE reported a big rise in profits, reflecting strong growth in premium income, continuing solid underlying underwriting profitability and an improvement in investment yields. The good result came despite some particularly large claims at the end of the half-year, relating to Cyclone Yasi, a number of severe tornadoes in the US and a third earthquake in Christchurch. QBE now reports its results in US dollars, and the result was even better than in the table in this book, which provides the figures converted to Australian dollars. Gross written premium and net earned premium were up 30 per cent and 29 per cent respectively, thanks especially to some recent acquisitions, a high rate of customer retention and average premium rate increases of nearly 3 per cent. There was particular strength in the US and also in the relatively small Latin American market. Net investment income, which included operational foreign exchange gains of US$150 million, soared from US$116 million to US$657 million. Despite this, the company's insurance profit margin fell sharply, from 15.8 per cent to 11.2 per cent, due to the record catastrophe claims, which were up by US$590 million.

Outlook

QBE says that since 2005 over 90 per cent of the growth in its premium income has come from more than 50 acquisitions in numerous countries. This global diversification has also helped spread risk, and the company maintains its strategy of growth by acquisition. It fortuitously locked in three years of reinsurance arrangements in early 2011, before a high level of catastrophe claims that, according to some reports, were among the highest on record, and which are expected to lead to higher reinsurance fees. With a third of its investment assets in US dollar-denominated bonds, QBE's income looks set to be hit by falling bond yields.

Year to 31 December	2009	2010
Net earned premium ($mn)	12149.0	12350.0
Profit before tax ($mn)	2432.0	1685.9
Profit after tax ($mn)	1970.0	1389.1
Earnings per share (¢)	195.6	133.9
Dividend (¢)	128	128

Year to 31 December	2009	2010
Percentage franked	20	12
Return on equity (%)	18.1	13.1

Half year to 30 June	2010	2011
Net earned premium ($mn)	5887.6	6580.6
Profit before tax ($mn)	593.3	753.4
Profit after tax ($mn)	494.4	653.4
Earnings per share (¢)	48.2	61.0
Dividend (¢)	62	62
Percentage franked	15	10
Net tangible assets per share ($)	5.25	4.28
Debt-to-equity ratio (%)	10.2	28.8

Reckon Limited

RKN

<www.reckonlimited.com.au>

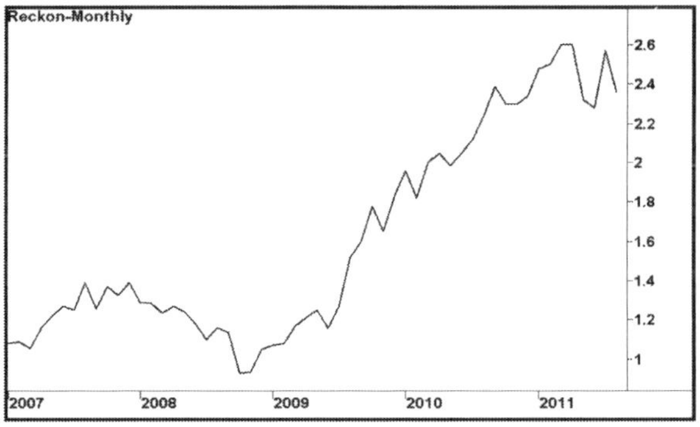

Share price ($)	2.36
12-month high ($)	2.74
12-month low ($)	1.96
Market capitalisation ($mn)	312.1
Price-to-NTA-per-share ratio	97.6
5-year share price return (% p.a.)	27.9
Dividend reinvestment plan	No

Sector: Information technology	Company	Sector
Price/earnings ratio (times)	19.0	18.2
Dividend yield (%)	3.4	3.9

Sydney-based software house Reckon was founded in 1987. In 1993 it began publishing and distributing

Quicken financial software in Australia, in an agreement with Intuit of the US. It now operates under three divisions, Business, Professional and nQueue Billback, and specialises in the provision of a wide range of financial and business software, under brands that include Quicken Australia, APS, Reckon Elite, Reckon Shelco and Reckon Espreon. It has operations throughout Australia and in New Zealand, Britain and the US.

Latest business results (June 2011, half year)

Profits rose on just a tiny increase in sales revenues, thanks especially to solid domestic demand for its software products. The Professional division, which incorporates the APS and Billback brands, and comprises about a quarter of total turnover, saw a healthy 15 per cent EBIT rise. Demand in Australia was particularly strong, easily offsetting weakness in Britain and New Zealand. The high-margin Business division, which is responsible for the Quicken and Reckon brands, saw EBIT up 9 per cent, despite some weakness in retail demand. The nQueue Billback division, which distributes specialised software to the British and US legal profession, and accounts for about 9 per cent of total company turnover, saw sales and profits down, hurt by weak economies abroad, the strong dollar and management changes. In addition, the company reported an after-tax non-operating deficit of $0.9 million, related mainly to a move to new premises.

Outlook

Reckon occupies a key place in the economy, supplying vital financial software to individuals and the small business sector. With just limited competition for some of its products, it enjoys a fair degree of pricing power. Many of its products require regular updates, and the company enjoys a high level of recurring revenues. Nevertheless, it is strongly geared to economic conditions. A slowing economy can lead to a postponement of new software purchases by corporate and retail customers. A new agreement with Intuit to develop professional practice management software for mid-size accounting firms, aimed at the giant North American market, has the potential to generate large royalty revenues. In May 2011 Reckon took a 5 per cent equity stake in online services company Melbourne IT, and has expressed a desire to work with that company to sell its software and other products through jointly developed online platforms.

Year to 31 December	2009	2010
Revenues ($mn)	85.2	90.0
EBIT ($mn)	18.0	22.4
EBIT margin (%)	21.2	24.9

Year to 31 December	2009	2010
Gross margin (%)	77.9	78.5
Profit before tax ($mn)	17.8	22.4
Profit after tax ($mn)	13.2	16.5
Earnings per share (¢)	9.9	12.4
Cash flow per share (¢)	15.1	18.3
Dividend (¢)	7	8
Percentage franked	100	90
Interest cover (times)	81.2	7467.3
Return on equity (%)	32.5	35.8

Half year to 30 June	2010	2011
Revenues ($mn)	46.5	46.7
Profit before tax ($mn)	11.4	12.3
Profit after tax ($mn)	8.4	9.3
Earnings per share (¢)	6.3	6.8
Dividend (¢)	3.5	3.5
Percentage franked	90	90
Net tangible assets per share ($)	–	0.02
Debt-to-equity ratio (%)	–	–
Current ratio	1.0	0.7

Reece Australia Limited

REH

<www.reece.com.au>

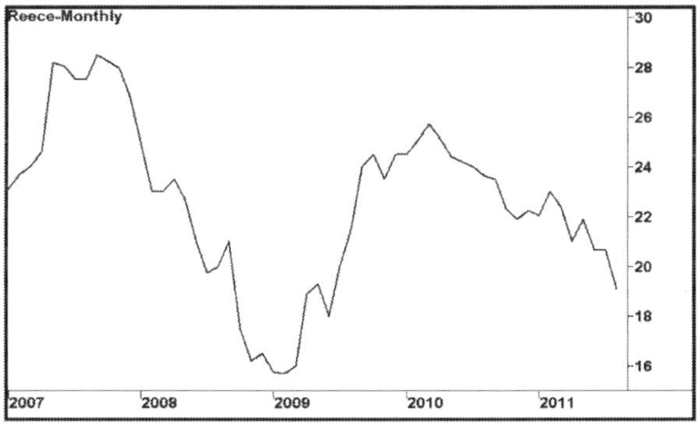

Share price ($)	19.10
12-month high ($)	24.00
12-month low ($)	18.13
Market capitalisation ($mn)	1902.4
Price-to-NTA-per-share ratio	2.9
5-year share price return (% p.a.)	7.5
Dividend reinvestment plan	No

Sector: Industrials	Company	Sector
Price/earnings ratio (times)	16.0	11.9
Dividend yield (%)	3.2	5.5

Melbourne-based plumbing supplies company Reece Australia traces its origins back to 1919, when Harold

Reece started selling his products from the back of a truck. It has gradually expanded from its Victorian roots, and is today one of the country's leading suppliers of plumbing products, with 434 stores and showrooms nationwide and six stores in New Zealand. It has also expanded into related fields. Its Reece hvac-r operation comprises a network of 37 branches offering products and support in the heating, ventilation, air conditioning and refrigeration spheres. The Reece Irrigation business consists of 34 specialist stores providing products and services for the landscape and agricultural industries. Reece Civil supplies products for underground pipe networks. The Reece Onsite operation caters to large domestic builders and commercial plumbers and developers. The controlling Wilson family own more than 60 per cent of the company's equity.

Latest business results (June 2011, full year)

Revenues and profits edged up in a difficult year for the company, with weakened consumer spending and the phasing out of several government incentive schemes affecting sales, and the impact of natural disasters hurting costs. During the year the company opened seven new stores in Australia and closed one, and it opened one new store in New Zealand. It also refurbished 40 of its trade and showroom outlets. At June 2011 the company had cash holdings of more than $134 million, up from $113 million a year earlier.

Outlook

Reece is heavily geared to the housing and renovations sector, with a particularly strong market position, and this has powered some superb long-term growth. However, it also led to a drop in profits in the June 2009 year—its first profit decline in eight years—as the economy faltered. In the face of a weakening economy and sluggish housing market the company has slowed down its rapid rate of expansion, though it continues investing heavily in upgrading its facilities. A new 42000-square-metre national distribution centre in Victoria is aimed at boosting operational efficiencies. A regional distribution centre under development in Queensland will be fully operational in early 2012. The entry by Woolworths to the hardware retail business—with its first Masters stores opening during 2011 and a target of 150 stores over five years—has led to concerns of a possible price war that could hurt the profitability of all retailers.

Year to 30 June	2010	2011
Revenues ($mn)	1503.5	1563.6
EBIT ($mn)	159.9	167.5
EBIT margin (%)	10.6	10.7

Year to 30 June	2010	2011
Gross margin (%)	31.2	31.3
Profit before tax ($mn)	161.8	171.0
Profit after tax ($mn)	114.3	118.6
Earnings per share (¢)	114.7	119.1
Cash flow per share (¢)	143.0	148.8
Dividend (¢)	58	61
Percentage franked	100	100
Net tangible assets per share ($)	5.97	6.57
Interest cover (times)	–	–
Return on equity (%)	20.3	19.0
Debt-to-equity ratio (%)	–	–
Current ratio	2.0	2.0

Retail Food Group Limited

RFG

<www.rfg.com.au>

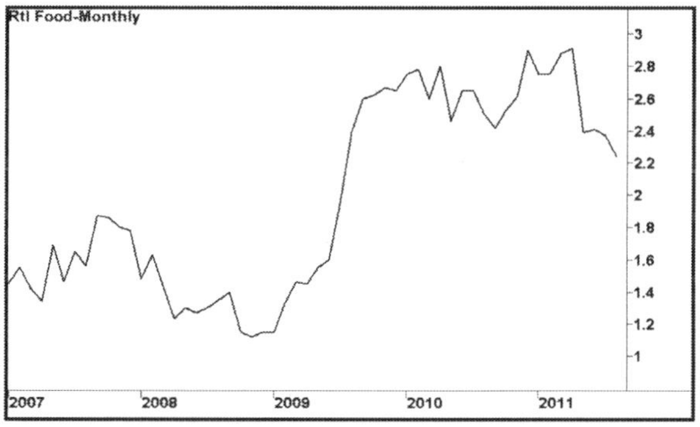

Share price ($)	2.24
12-month high ($)	3.00
12-month low ($)	2.00
Market capitalisation ($mn)	242.2
Price-to-NTA-per-share ratio	–
5-year share price return (% p.a.)	28.1
Dividend reinvestment plan	No

Sector: Consumer discretionary	Company	Sector
Price/earnings ratio (times)	8.8	13.1
Dividend yield (%)	6.5	3.5

Retail Food Group, based in Southport, Queensland, was established in 1989 to develop and manage the Donut King and the BBs Coffee and Croissants franchise systems. It has since expanded by acquisition and organic growth, and today incorporates Donut King, Michel's Patisserie, Brumby's Bakeries, bb's cafe and Big Dads Pies, along with New Zealand's Esquires Coffee Houses. At June 2011 it held 1044 franchise stores in Australia, 87 in New Zealand, 14 in China, two in Papua New Guinea and one in Saudi Arabia.

Latest business results (June 2011, full year)

Profits rose for the sixth straight year, although not at the stellar rate as in some previous years, and total franchise network sales of $651.1 million were up just 1.6 per cent from the June 2010 year. About 70 per cent of these sales came from Brumby's Bakery and Michel's Patisserie, and a further 25 per cent from Donut King. The continuing conversion of the Michel's Patisserie wholesale system to a royalty-based model led to a drop in Wholesale/Retail Operations revenues and a rise in Franchising Operations revenues. The company added a net total of 26 franchised outlets to its network. It said it would have achieved double-digit profit growth but for the floods in Australia and the Christchurch earthquakes, which together hurt business at more than 190 of its outlets. During the year it acquired the New Zealand master franchise for Esquires Coffee Houses business.

Outlook

Retail Food Group has expanded rapidly, thanks to both acquisition and organic growth. However, its business is quite dependent on trends in consumer spending, and it could be hurt by declines in this spending, despite a certain level of protection from the fact that it is generally selling low-priced foodstuffs. It sees coffee roasting and supply as one pathway to growth, and in the June 2011 year it delivered more than 620 tonnes of coffee to its franchise stores. It plans to expand the Esquires Coffee Houses business to Australia and it has also launched the Barista's Choice online coffee store. In July 2011 it announced the acquisition of Evolution Coffee Roasters, a New Zealand business that supplies 170 tonnes annually of premium coffee. Retail Food Group is also working to expand abroad, and has granted Michel's Patisserie licences to Indonesia, Brumby's Bakery licences to PNG and Donut King licences to PNG, New Zealand and Saudi Arabia.

Year to 30 June	2010	2011
Revenues ($mn)	133.8	125.3
Franchising Operations (%)	46	55
Wholesale/Retail Operations (%)	54	45

Year to 30 June	2010	2011
EBIT ($mn)	44.0	45.0
EBIT margin (%)	32.9	35.9
Gross margin (%)	33.3	35.3
Profit before tax ($mn)	36.6	38.4
Profit after tax ($mn)	26.0	27.2
Earnings per share (¢)	25.3	25.4
Cash flow per share (¢)	26.4	26.1
Dividend (¢)	11.75	14.5
Percentage franked	100	100
Net tangible assets per share ($)	–	–
Interest cover (times)	5.9	6.8
Return on equity (%)	21.2	18.4
Debt-to-equity ratio (%)	52.4	44.9
Current ratio	0.3	2.5

Ridley Corporation Limited

RIC

<www.ridley.com.au>

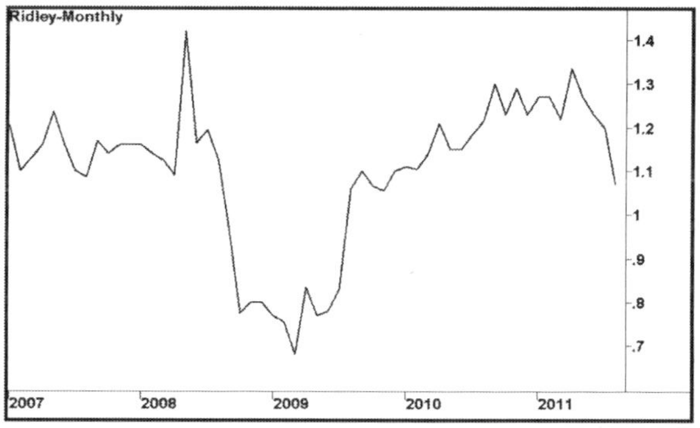

Share price ($)	1.07
12-month high ($)	1.37
12-month low ($)	1.02
Market capitalisation ($mn)	329.4
Price-to-NTA-per-share ratio	1.3
5-year share price return (% p.a.)	4.5
Dividend reinvestment plan	No

Sector: Consumer staples	Company	Sector
Price/earnings ratio (times)	11.2	16.5
Dividend yield (%)	7.0	4.8

Sydney-based Ridley, founded in 1987, is a leading producer of animal feed and salt. It operates through two businesses. Ridley AgriProducts is responsible for the manufacture of food products and supplements for livestock. It also makes Cobber dog foods and Ridley Aqua-Feed, for the aquaculture industry. Cheetham Salt, founded in 1888, is Australia's largest salt producer. It provides salt for a wide range of industrial and domestic applications from 10 solar salt fields and three refineries around Australia, with a production capacity of 1.4 million tonnes annually. It also operates a refinery in Indonesia, a sales office in Japan and a joint venture company, Dominion Salt, in New Zealand.

Latest business results (June 2011, full year)

In a difficult year for the company, due especially to heavy rains and floods in some eastern states, sales and profits were down. However, a significantly lower tax rate—the result of tax adjustments from previous years—meant that the after-tax profit edged up. In the AgriProducts division the dairy and the supplements segments suffered the most. The Aqua-Feed business also felt the impact of flooding. The salt business was hit by higher costs from the rains and floods, although the New Zealand joint venture continued to provide strong returns. Ridley's Salt division represents only 15 per cent of company revenues, but it generates almost as much profit as the AgriProducts division. In March 2011 Ridley acquired the niche poultry and fish rendering business of Camilleri Stockfeeds.

Outlook

Ridley has been engaged in an intense restructuring—including the sale of underperforming businesses and the paying down of debt—that lasted several years and it believed it was at last starting on a strong growth trajectory. However, the disastrous weather of the June 2011 year has hit the company, and it says that it believes it will take much of the June 2012 year to recover the operational volumes and margins that it has lost. It is also looking to expand, and it says that the Camilleri Stockfeeds acquisition—its first acquisition for several years—signals a new growth phase. It is also looking to build new businesses in Asia, based on its Indonesian salt operation. Ridley has substantial surplus land holdings, including some close to urban centres, and it is in the process of evaluating options for developing these to provide a new revenue stream.

Year to 30 June	2010	2011
Revenues ($mn)	728.0	723.7
AgriProducts (%)	85	85
Salt (%)	15	15
EBIT ($mn)	46.2	40.0

Year to 30 June	2010	2011
EBIT margin (%)	6.4	5.5
Gross margin (%)	10.8	10.3
Profit before tax ($mn)	38.1	30.2
Profit after tax ($mn)	29.1	29.3
Earnings per share (¢)	9.5	9.5
Cash flow per share (¢)	13.4	14.2
Dividend (¢)	7.25	7.5
Percentage franked	0	0
Net tangible assets per share ($)	0.83	0.80
Interest cover (times)	5.7	4.1
Return on equity (%)	10.4	10.2
Debt-to-equity ratio (%)	25.2	35.1
Current ratio	1.5	1.8

Rio Tinto Limited

RIO

<www.riotinto.com>

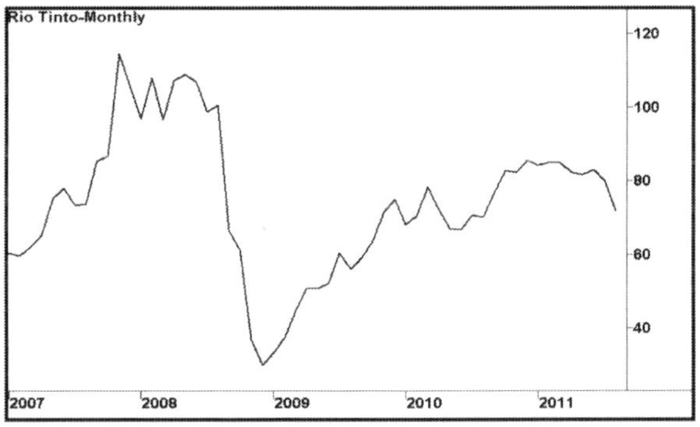

Share price ($)	71.79
12-month high ($)	89.04
12-month low ($)	63.85
Market capitalisation ($mn)	31281.9
Price-to-NTA-per-share ratio	3.8
5-year share price return (% p.a.)	6.5
Dividend reinvestment plan	Yes

Sector: Materials	Company	Sector
Price/earnings ratio (times)	9.0	12.3
Dividend yield (%)	1.5	2.2

British-based Rio Tinto, one of the world's largest mining companies, retains its ASX presence in a duallisting structure, and continues to pay franked dividends to Australian shareholders. Australian subsidiaries include Coal & Allied Industries and Energy Resources of Australia. Among its major products, it mines iron ore, copper, gold, industrial minerals, diamonds and coal, and is a large aluminium producer.

Latest business results (June 2011, half year)

Rio Tinto posted another solid gain in sales and profits, thanks to higher commodities prices and continuing strong Asian demand, although the result was more muted when converted to Australian dollars. (Rio Tinto reports its results in US dollars. The tables in this book are based on Australian dollar figures supplied by the company.) The result was also held back by fast-rising costs in some areas of operation. The company's major product groups all saw sales rise, with iron ore—responsible for more than 40 per cent of total company turnover—experiencing a 39 per cent jump in sales and a 45 per cent surge in profits. Aluminium and copper were also strong. However, the company's coal business was hit by major production problems, following heavy rains and flooding at several Australian sites, and profits fell, despite higher sales prices.

Outlook

Rio Tinto remains one of the foremost beneficiaries of the strength in Asian demand for commodities. Its own forecasts are that the Chinese economy will expand by 9.5 per cent in 2011. Longer term, it expects demand for iron ore, copper and aluminium to double over the coming 15 to 20 years. It is working to expand capacity at its Pilbara iron ore operation from 225 million tonnes per year to 283 million tonnes by the end of 2013, and proposes a further increase to 333 million tonnes by mid 2015. It is also working with China's Chinalco to develop iron ore resources at a giant project in Simandou, Guinea, at a cost that could reach US$15 billion. This has the potential to become the world's largest iron ore mine. First shipments could start by mid 2015. It is also a partner in the US$6 billion construction of a copper and gold mine in Oyu Tolgoi, Mongolia, with first production expected late in 2012. Nevertheless, the company faces many challenges, including slowing economies in some countries, currency volatility and escalating costs.

Year to 31 December	2009	2010
Revenues ($mn)	52943.0	61495.7
EBIT ($mn)	10405.1	23034.8
EBIT margin (%)	19.7	37.5

Year to 31 December	2009	2010
Profit before tax ($mn)	9381.0	22366.3
Profit after tax ($mn)	6167.0	15569.6
Earnings per share (¢)	349.7	794.0
Cash flow per share (¢)	595.7	984.5
Dividend (¢)	51.56	111.21
Percentage franked	100	100
Interest cover (times)	10.2	34.5
Return on equity (%)	15.6	29.3

Half year to 30 June	2010	2011
Revenues ($mn)	28325.0	30839.0
Profit before tax ($mn)	9903.0	10743.0
Profit after tax ($mn)	6480.0	7554.0
Earnings per share (¢)	330.4	387.7
Dividend (¢)	49.27	49.81
Percentage franked	100	100
Net tangible assets per share ($)	15.41	18.88
Debt-to-equity ratio (%)	25.4	15.4
Current ratio	1.5	1.6

SAI Global Limited

SAI

<www.saiglobal.com>

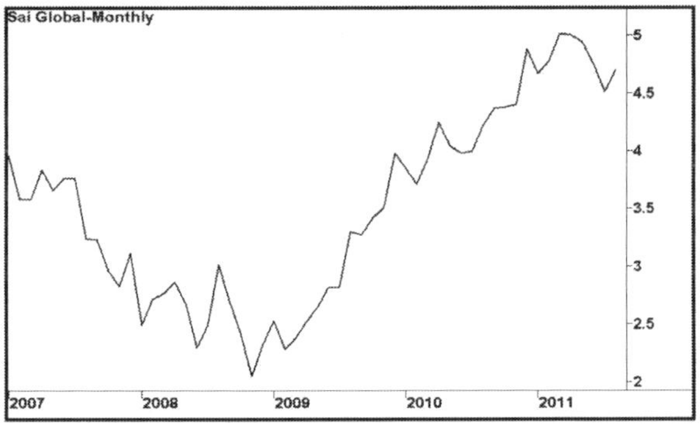

Share price ($)	4.70
12-month high ($)	5.15
12-month low ($)	3.95
Market capitalisation ($mn)	939.6
Price-to-NTA-per-share ratio	–
5-year share price return (% p.a.)	10.4
Dividend reinvestment plan	Yes

Sector: Industrials	Company	Sector
Price/earnings ratio (times)	19.0	11.9
Dividend yield (%)	3.0	5.5

Sydney corporate consultant SAI Global was spun off from Standards Australia—the body that develops and maintains some 7000 Australian standards—in

2003. It now provides a wide range of standards and related information to companies and organisations around the world. It divides its operations into three divisions. The Information Services division offers clients the information needed to comply with standards regulations, directives and legislation around the world. The Compliance Services division provides clients—predominantly legal, compliance, privacy and risk management professionals—with training and consultancy services in business risk, governance and compliance. The Assurance Services division helps clients manage risk through training, registration audits and supplier management programs.

Latest business results (June 2011, full year)

Once again, SAI achieved an excellent result, thanks to both acquisitions and continuing organic growth, and despite the negative impact of the strong dollar. The best result came from the Compliance Services division, thanks especially to the September 2010 US$170 million acquisition of Integrity Interactive, which has a particular specialty in ethics training in the US and Europe. This division saw revenues up 71.5 per cent, with profits surging nearly threefold, and the company reported US$7 million in annualised cost synergy benefits from the acquisition. By contrast, the company's largest division, Information Services, experienced a dip in revenues and profits, due mainly to a weak Australian property market, with other areas of the division's business generally strong. The Assurance Services division reported 4 per cent revenues growth, with profits up 20.8 per cent, both figures negatively affected by the strong dollar.

Outlook

SAI supplies products and services that many companies are obliged to purchase, offering a degree of protection at times of economic volatility, and it occupies a strong market position in many of its businesses. Despite concerns over the strong dollar, the company is forecasting further profit growth for the June 2012 year. It is working to strengthen its Information Services division, and has achieved success with a major new contract to provide national mortgage settlement services to ANZ from mid 2012. Its Compliance Services division sees particular potential in a new product suite to address issues posed by the new UK Bribery Act, and it is exploring similar opportunities in the US. The Assurance Services division is experiencing strong growth in the food business in America and Britain, and plans to expand this business throughout Europe.

Year to 30 June	2010	2011
Revenues ($mn)	388.9	423.1

Year to 30 June	2010	2011
Information Services (%)	50	45
Assurance Services (%)	38	36
Compliance Services (%)	12	19
EBIT ($mn)	56.6	77.0
EBIT margin (%)	14.6	18.2
Profit before tax ($mn)	47.8	65.3
Profit after tax ($mn)	33.7	48.0
Earnings per share (¢)	21.5	24.7
Cash flow per share (¢)	33.9	36.9
Dividend (¢)	12.8	14.3
Percentage franked	100	100
Net tangible assets per share ($)	–	–
Interest cover (times)	6.4	6.6
Return on equity (%)	16.1	17.9
Debt-to-equity ratio (%)	68.6	51.5
Current ratio	1.0	1.3

Sedgman Limited

SDM

<www.sedgman.com>

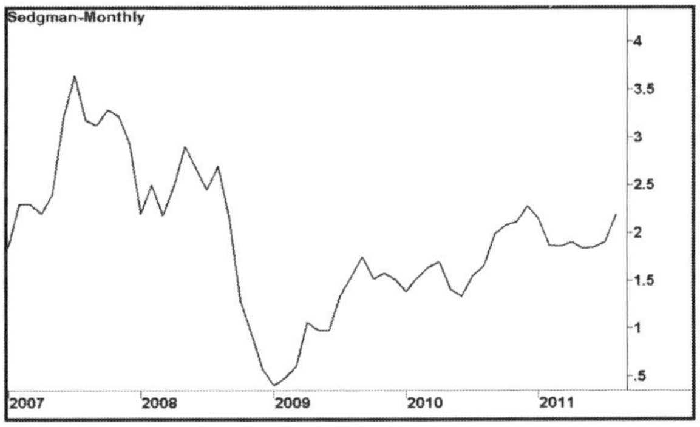

Share price ($)	2.19
12-month high ($)	2.37
12-month low ($)	1.44
Market capitalisation ($mn)	459.4
Price-to-NTA-per-share ratio	4.4
5-year share price return (% p.a.)	13.9
Dividend reinvestment plan	Yes

Sector: Industrials	Company	Sector
Price/earnings ratio (times)	17.5	11.9
Dividend yield (%)	3.2	5.5

Brisbane company Sedgman, established in 1979, supplies mineral processing equipment to the resources industry. It has a particular specialty in the design, construction and operation of coal handling and preparation plants. From its Queensland base it has expanded globally, and has offices in China, Chile and South Africa.

Latest business results (June 2011, full year)

A solid second half helped offset the problems of the first half—when the company's east coast coal projects were hurt by cyclones and floods—and revenues and profits rose. The company's Engineering Services division was responsible for the increase, with revenues jumping 86 per cent and profits up by more than 90 per cent. Major contracts secured during the year included a $145 million coal handling and preparation plant (CHPP) expansion contract for the Lake Vermont mine in Queensland, an $85 million CHPP upgrade at the Bengalla mine in New South Wales and a US$31 million CHPP and operations contract at the UHG coal mine in Mongolia. The Operations division saw revenues up 15 per cent, but with reported profits down, hit by the cyclones and floods and by asset writedowns. The company reported that 62 per cent of revenues derived from within Australia, with 22 per cent from South Africa. The June 2010 profit benefited from a highly favourable tax rate, due to significant R&D tax concessions and additional deductions relating to legislation changes.

Consequently, the June 2011 after-tax profit rose only slightly from the previous year.

Outlook

Sedgman is a leader in coal handling and preparation plants, and claims a domestic market share of more than 50 per cent. It will continue to benefit from growing Asian demand for Australian coal. It also gains recurring income from contracts for the processing of approximately 20 million tonnes of coal per annum, and it is expanding into metal processing operations, which it views as a significant growth opportunity. It also sees its global expansion as a key part of its strategy for growth, and in the June 2011 year it did business in South Africa, Mozambique, Botswana, China, Mongolia, Chile and Colombia. It expects overseas orders to become a rapidly growing portion of total business. The company had $606 million in orders at June 2011, down from $706 million a year earlier. With net cash holdings of around $14 million the company is seeking suitable acquisitions.

Year to 30 June	2010	2011
Revenues ($mn)	326.5	507.7
Engineering Services (%)	57	68
Operations (%)	43	32
EBIT ($mn)	28.5	35.6
EBIT margin (%)	8.7	7.0
Profit before tax ($mn)	27.0	34.5
Profit after tax ($mn)	25.0	26.0

Year to 30 June	2010	2011
Earnings per share (¢)	12.3	12.5
Cash flow per share (¢)	20.1	21.7
Dividend (¢)	6.5	7
Percentage franked	100	100
Net tangible assets per share ($)	0.43	0.49
Interest cover (times)	19.7	32.5
Return on equity (%)	22.9	18.4
Debt-to-equity ratio (%)	–	–
Current ratio	1.4	1.5

Seek Limited

SEK

<investors.seek.com.au>

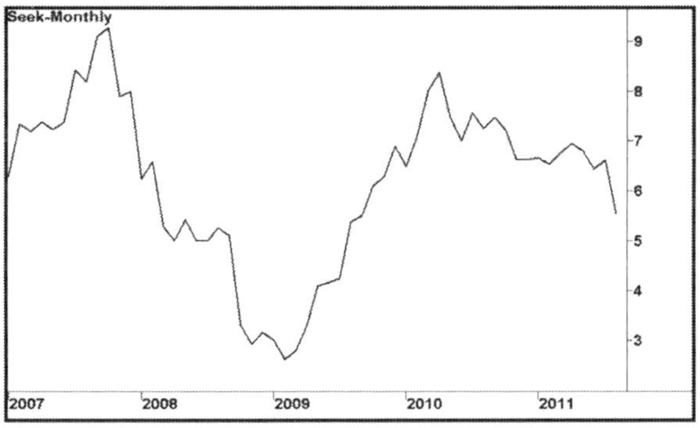

Share price ($)	5.55
12-month high ($)	7.86
12-month low ($)	5.21
Market capitalisation ($mn)	1870.6
Price-to-NTA-per-share ratio	–
5-year share price return (% p.a.)	3.3
Dividend reinvestment plan	No

Sector: Industrials	Company	Sector
Price/earnings ratio (times)	19.1	11.9
Dividend yield (%)	2.6	5.5

Melbourne-based Seek, founded in 1997, operates Australia's largest website for jobseekers. It has expanded to New Zealand and the UK, and also has equity stakes in online employment businesses in Asia and Latin America. In addition, the company operates in the education field, with Seek Learning and Think Group, which help jobseekers with career development by providing vocational education through partnerships with leading training providers, such as TAFE institutions and major universities. In a joint venture with Swinburne University, it plans online tertiary courses.

Latest business results (June 2011, full year)

Seek enjoyed another good year, with a strong recovery in employment advertising responsible for most of the gains. In a relatively tight labour market, the Seek Employment division achieved a 30 per cent rise in revenues, with profits jumping 43 per cent. It also benefited from the continuing move from print to online for job advertising. There was also a notable contribution from the company's rapidly expanding overseas employment businesses. These are operated as joint ventures, with Seek sharing in their after-tax profits, and in June 2011 it received a total of $16.9 million, compared to just $1.6 million a year earlier. In particular, the Zhaopin employment website in China—in which Seek has a 56.1 per cent holding—moved from loss to profit, and contributed $8.7 million to Seek. By contrast, Seek's Education division saw revenues up just 1 per cent, with profits plunging as the Think Group business fell into the red, due to reduced student numbers and higher costs.

Outlook

Seek has become one of the success stories of the internet revolution, and now claims to hold more than 50 per cent of the online jobs market in both Australia and New Zealand. With online advertising growing at a faster pace than traditional print media advertising in the employment sphere it has excellent prospects, although a slowing economy could also lead to a slowdown in job advertising. The company's overseas ventures now appear to have reached something of a tipping point—especially in China and Brazil—with their profitability growing rapidly, and Seek believes they could eventually grow to become as big as the Australian market. The company has invested heavily in restructuring its education businesses, and believes that they will achieve revenues and earnings growth in the June 2012 year.

Year to 30 June	2010	2011
Revenues ($mn)	280.7	343.1
Employment (%)	61	65
Education (%)	39	32

Year to 30 June	2010	2011
EBIT ($mn)	124.5	147.7
EBIT margin (%)	44.3	43.1
Profit before tax ($mn)	119.2	133.0
Profit after tax ($mn)	89.5	97.7
Earnings per share (¢)	26.6	29.0
Cash flow per share (¢)	29.5	32.8
Dividend (¢)	11.9	14.3
Percentage franked	100	100
Net tangible assets per share ($)	0.67	–
Interest cover (times)	23.4	10.0
Return on equity (%)	27.9	24.8
Debt-to-equity ratio (%)	17.0	40.8
Current ratio	1.5	0.7

Select Harvests Limited

SHV

<www.selectharvests.com.au>

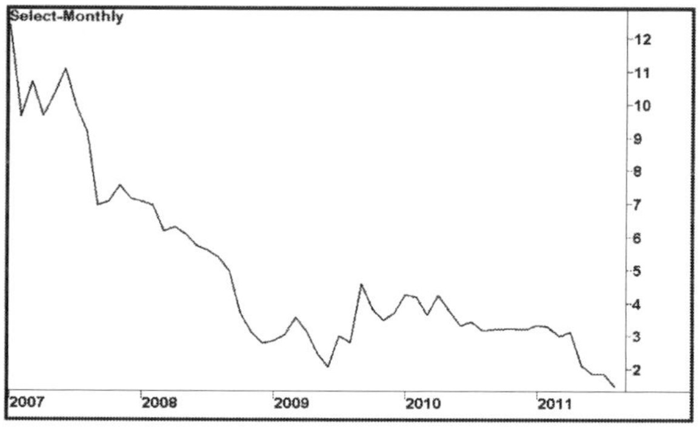

Share price ($)	1.48
12-month high ($)	3.49
12-month low ($)	1.40
Market capitalisation ($mn)	83.2
Price-to-NTA-per-share ratio	0.7
5-year share price return (% p.a.)	–30.5
Dividend reinvestment plan	No

Sector: Consumer staples	Company	Sector
Price/earnings ratio (times)	4.4	16.5
Dividend yield (%)	8.8	4.8

Melbourne-based Select Harvests, with origins dating back to the mid 1970s, is Australia's biggest almond grower and processor and one of the largest growers in the world. Following recent expansion it now owns 13100 acres of orchards in Victoria, New South Wales and Western Australia. It also manages 33900 acres of orchards for external investors, in Victoria's Sunraysia region, from which it derives set-up fees and annuity-style income. It is a substantial processor and exporter, and is also a leading supplier to Australian supermarkets of processed and packaged nuts, dried fruits and associated products, through the Lucky, Sunsol, Nu-Vit, Meriram and Soland brands.

Latest business results (June 2011, full year)

Sales rose but profits fell, hit by $1 million in costs relating to a product recall and other one-off expenses, along with a lower quality crop and the strong dollar. However, $2.3 million in R&D credits meant that the company paid substantially less tax than in the previous year, and the after-tax profit edged up. The crop for the year of an estimated 22600 tonnes—compared with 21400 tonnes in the previous year—was below forecasts. In addition, heavy rainfall before and during harvesting had a negative impact on quality. The Food Products division, though responsible for more than half of company sales, contributes less than 20 per cent of profits, and EBIT tumbled 27 per cent after an almond recall in April 2011. However, the company reported that underlying division profits rose 9 per cent, thanks especially to a range of new products.

Outlook

Select Harvests has been hit by inclement weather—first prolonged drought, which led to lower yields, and then heavy rains, which reduced almond quality. It expects both yields and quality to improve significantly in the June 2012 year, although rising costs—particularly fertiliser and power—and the strong dollar remain concerns. The company is rapidly expanding, through the acquisition of new tracts of land and the planting of new orchards, and expects a steady increase in output. With global almond consumption growing strongly, there are signs that demand could start to outstrip supply, with a positive impact on prices. It faces some loss of income from the June 2013 year with the ending of a three-year contract to manage 29500 acres of almond orchards for Olam, which took over the orchards from the financially troubled company Timbercorp.

Year to 30 June	2010	2011
Revenues ($mn)	238.4	248.3
Food Products (%)	55	54
Almond Operations (%)	45	46
EBIT ($mn)	26.0	22.6
EBIT margin (%)	10.9	9.1

Year to 30 June	2010	2011
Gross margin (%)	15.8	11.2
Profit before tax ($mn)	23.6	19.2
Profit after tax ($mn)	17.3	17.7
Earnings per share (¢)	43.4	33.7
Cash flow per share (¢)	55.8	43.6
Dividend (¢)	21	13
Percentage franked	100	100
Net tangible assets per share ($)	1.87	2.17
Interest cover (times)	10.7	6.7
Return on equity (%)	16.1	12.5
Debt-to-equity ratio (%)	39.6	43.3
Current ratio	1.4	2.0

SMS Management & Technology Ltd

SMX

<www.smsmt.com>

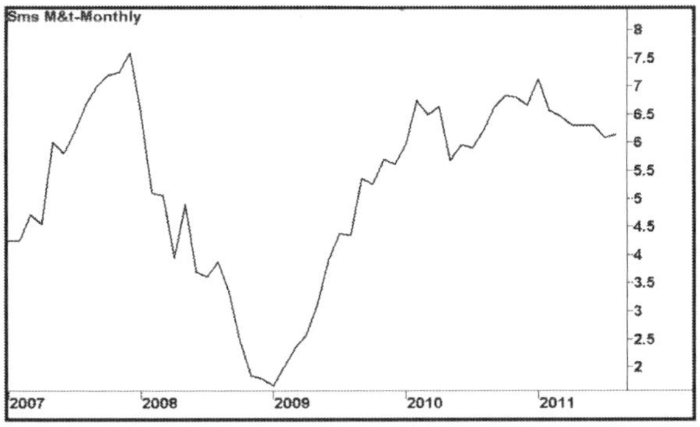

Share price ($)	6.14
12-month high ($)	7.44
12-month low ($)	5.16
Market capitalisation ($mn)	416.1
Price-to-NTA-per-share ratio	9.7
5-year share price return (% p.a.)	16.6
Dividend reinvestment plan	No

Sector: Information technology	Company	Sector
Price/earnings ratio (times)	13.9	18.2
Dividend yield (%)	4.9	3.9

Melbourne management services consultant SMS Management & Technology was founded in 1986. It provides management consulting and technology services to a wide range of blue-chip corporate and government clients. Among its specialised areas of expertise is defence, and it works for the defence and national security sectors in several countries. Its M&T Resources division specialises in recruitment for the IT and telecommunications industries. The company operates from offices throughout Australia. It also maintains offices in Hong Kong, Vietnam and Singapore.

Latest business results (June 2011, full year)

SMS enjoyed solid revenue growth, but higher costs—particularly for new staff—meant it could manage just a modest increase in its profits. The company also experienced some delayed sales from a newly acquired subsidiary, Renewtek, with this business contributing a small loss. The Queensland floods also had a negative impact on operations. About a third of the company's business was with federal and state governments, along with the defence and health sector. Demand from the financial services sector remained firm, though this business dipped from 24 per cent to 23 per cent of total company revenues. Revenues from the information and communications technology sector continued its decline, down to 16 per cent of the total, from 18 per cent in the previous year. In addition to Renewtek, the company made one other acquisition, Brisbane-based Microgenx, which specialises in Microsoft.NET and SharePoint development. During the year SMS signed new contracts worth $351 million, up from $303 million in the previous year and $245 million in the year before that.

Outlook

In an environment of skill shortages, SMS has adopted a policy of aggressively hiring new staff to help fuel growth. In the June 2011 year staff numbers rose 22 per cent to 1675, pushing staff utilisation rates down to 88 per cent, with a consequent negative impact on costs. Also as part of its growth strategies, SMS has launched a new infrastructure consultancy aimed at capitalising on emerging demand for cloud computing, which it sees as a significant growth area. It also expects continuing strong demand for business analytics services as clients increasingly invest in data management systems. In addition, it foresees growing demand from domestic clients for services to support their Asian activities. With no debt and around $25 million in cash holdings, SMS continues to seek acquisition opportunities.

Year to 30 June	2010	2011
Revenues ($mn)	247.4	306.1
EBIT ($mn)	37.7	41.3
EBIT margin (%)	15.2	13.5
Profit before tax ($mn)	38.5	41.7
Profit after tax ($mn)	27.9	29.8
Earnings per share (¢)	42.2	44.3
Cash flow per share (¢)	42.9	45.5
Dividend (¢)	29	30
Percentage franked	100	100
Net tangible assets per share ($)	0.71	0.63
Interest cover (times)	–	–
Return on equity (%)	32.4	30.2
Debt-to-equity ratio (%)	–	–
Current ratio	2.7	2.2

Sonic Healthcare Limited

SHL

<www.sonichealthcare.com>

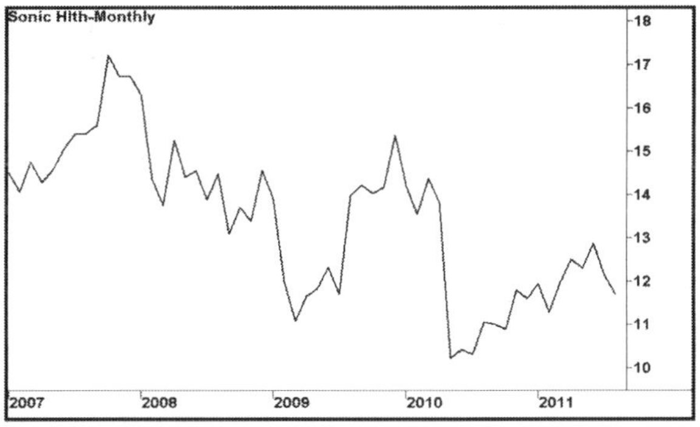

Share price ($)	11.70
12-month high ($)	13.14
12-month low ($)	10.33
Market capitalisation ($mn)	4563.5
Price-to-NTA-per-share ratio	–
5-year share price return (% p.a.)	3.1
Dividend reinvestment plan	No

Sector: Health care	Company	Sector
Price/earnings ratio (times)	15.4	17.5
Dividend yield (%)	5.0	2.6

Sydney-based Sonic Healthcare has its roots in the pathology practice of Douglass Laboratories that it acquired in 1987. It has since expanded dramatically through acquisition and organic growth, and now operates through numerous separate companies. It is one of the world's largest medical diagnostics companies, providing pathology and radiology services to medical practitioners, hospitals, community medical services and their patients, with operations in the US, Germany, Switzerland, Belgium, Britain, Ireland and New Zealand. These now account for more than half of company revenues. The company is Australia's largest private provider of pathology services and the second-largest provider of radiology services. It also operates the Independent Practitioner Network (IPN) group of medical practices.

Latest business results (June 2011, full year)

Sonic reversed the slide of the previous year, with sales and profits edging up. The result would have been stronger but for the strength of the dollar. On a constant-currency basis sales rose nearly 10 per cent, with the after-tax profit up 6 per cent. American and European operations were strong, with both organic growth and the contribution of a continuing series of acquisitions. During the year Sonic bought three laboratory groups in the US and two in Belgium. New Zealand business declined as a new contract came into force. Australian pathology and radiology operations experienced modest revenues growth. However, the company's IPN business saw revenues up 21.4 per cent, thanks to strong organic growth and the impact of some new acquisitions.

Outlook

Sonic has achieved sustained success through its drive to consolidate the once-fragmented Australian pathology industry. It is now doing the same in Germany, Switzerland, Belgium, Britain and the US, through a series of acquisitions. As it grows the synergies achieved boost margins even higher, and it believes it can achieve further profit growth of 10 per cent to 15 per cent in the June 2012 year, on a constant-currency basis. It has said it is not presently considering an entry to new markets, but will still pursue bolt-on acquisitions for its current areas of operation. After a period of volatility, it is experiencing solid growth again in its domestic pathology operations, with a new five-year government funding agreement underpinning business. It is believed to be interested in acquiring the $150 million St John of God pathology business. Also domestically, it has acquired the Allied Medical Group chain of GP clinics.

Year to 30 June	2010	2011
Revenues ($mn)	2972.6	3082.9
Pathology (%)	82	81
Radiology (%)	12	12

Year to 30 June	2010	2011
EBIT ($mn)	435.4	455.2
EBIT margin (%)	14.6	14.8
Profit before tax ($mn)	386.6	390.4
Profit after tax ($mn)	293.2	294.5
Earnings per share (¢)	75.5	75.8
Cash flow per share (¢)	99.5	100.9
Dividend (¢)	59	59
Percentage franked	35	28
Net tangible assets per share ($)	–	–
Interest cover (times)	8.9	7.0
Return on equity (%)	11.5	11.6
Debt-to-equity ratio (%)	58.7	61.0
Current ratio	0.9	1.7

STW Communications Group Ltd

SGN

<www.stwgroup.com.au>

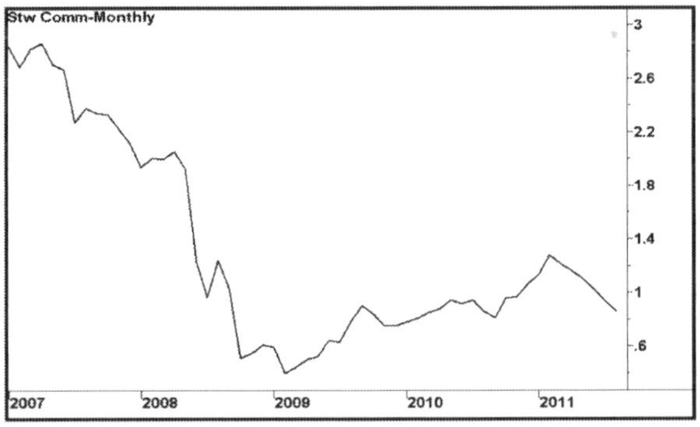

Share price ($)	0.86
12-month high ($)	1.38
12-month low ($)	0.70
Market capitalisation ($mn)	312.4
Price-to-NTA-per-share ratio	–
5-year share price return (% p.a.)	–13.2
Dividend reinvestment plan	No

Sector: Consumer discretionary	Company	Sector
Price/earnings ratio (times)	8.0	13.1
Dividend yield (%)	7.6	3.5

Sydney-based STW Communications Group, formerly called Singleton Group, was founded by entrepreneur John Singleton in the mid 1980s. It is a holding company, owning two-thirds of Singleton Ogilvy & Mather (Holdings), as well as a 49 per cent interest in the Australian and New Zealand operations of the advertising company J Walter Thompson. It has direct or indirect ownership of over 70 other smaller businesses in the marketing communications sphere, and the traditional advertising business accounts for less than half of company turnover. Its activities now encompass digital communication, production, branded content, retail and promotional marketing, sports sponsorship and management, brand and corporate design, business strategy, market research and insight, public relations, corporate communication, employee communication and multicultural communication. Its clients include some of the world's largest companies and many of Australia's best-known brands.

Latest business results (June 2011, half year)

As a holding company, STW presents its financial results in varying ways, and it can be difficult sometimes to make valid comparisons. Revenues and the after-tax profit edged up in a difficult environment. The company segments its many activities into two broad divisions: Advertising, Media and

Production, which accounts for around 55 per cent of company turnover, and Diversified Communications. All the company's growth came from the latter group of businesses, with revenues up 11 per cent. By contrast, the Advertising, Media and Production group of companies saw revenues slip nearly 7 per cent. During the period STW made four acquisitions, including the New Zealand full-service advertising agency Rolfe Limited and the Sydney advertising agency Tongue Pty Ltd. However, the company said its growth during the half was organic, rather than from the acquisition of new businesses.

Outlook

The advertising business can be volatile, and is heavily geared to economic conditions. The global financial crisis hit the industry hard, forcing STW into a major rationalisation of its operations, including reductions in staff numbers and the closing of some businesses. However, despite weak consumer spending and renewed volatility in global financial markets, the company forecasts that profits will rise 5 per cent to 10 per cent in the December 2011 year. It is also seeking new acquisitions, in order to help generate future growth. In particular, it is looking to make an acquisition in South-East Asia in the digital design field.

Year to 31 December	2009	2010
Revenues ($mn)	272.6	307.2
EBIT ($mn)	58.2	74.6

Year to 31 December	2009	2010
EBIT margin (%)	21.4	24.3
Profit before tax ($mn)	46.8	65.6
Profit after tax ($mn)	21.8	38.7
Earnings per share (¢)	7.3	10.8
Cash flow per share (¢)	9.3	12.5
Dividend (¢)	3.5	6.5
Percentage franked	100	100
Interest cover (times)	5.1	8.3
Return on equity (%)	7.6	11.5

Half year to 30 June	2010	2011
Revenues ($mn)	152.2	156.6
Profit before tax ($mn)	28.2	27.5
Profit after tax ($mn)	16.3	17.2
Earnings per share (¢)	4.6	4.8
Dividend (¢)	2.3	3
Percentage franked	100	100
Net tangible assets per share ($)	–	–
Debt-to-equity ratio (%)	12.5	23.1
Current ratio	0.7	0.9

Super Retail Group Limited

SUL

<www.superretailgroup.com.au>

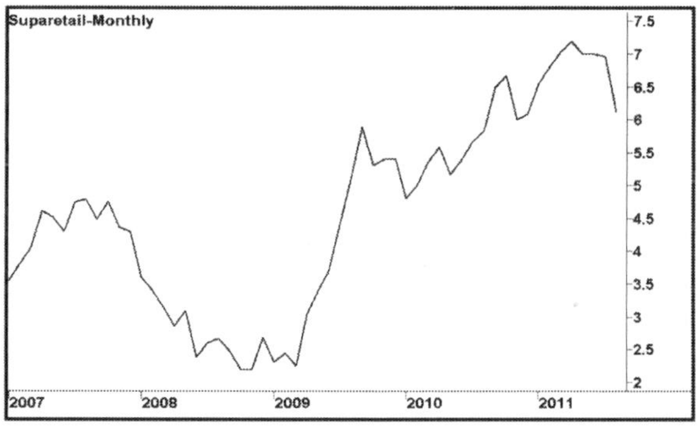

Share price ($)	6.13
12-month high ($)	7.49
12-month low ($)	5.48
Market capitalisation ($mn)	797.0
Price-to-NTA-per-share ratio	4.1
5-year share price return (% p.a.)	27.0
Dividend reinvestment plan	Yes

Sector: Consumer discretionary	Company	Sector
Price/earnings ratio (times)	14.2	13.1
Dividend yield (%)	4.7	3.5

Specialist retail chain Super Retail Group, formerly known as Super Cheap Auto, was established as a mail-order business in 1972, and has its headquarters in Lawnton, north of Brisbane. Today it operates more than 400 stores throughout Australia and New Zealand. It comprises four businesses. Supercheap Auto is a retailer of automotive spare parts and related products. BCF is a specialist retailer of boating, camping and fishing products. Goldcross Cycles is one of Melbourne's largest bicycle retailers, and has expanded into Queensland. Ray's Outdoors is an outdoor entertainment and camping goods supplier.

Latest business results (July 2011, full year)

A marked slowdown in consumer spending was not sufficient to stop Super Retail's growth, and it posted an excellent result, with strongly higher sales and profits. The result is even better when considering that the June 2011 financial year comprised 52 weeks, compared with 53 weeks for the previous financial year. Much of the increase came from the company's Leisure Retailing division, which comprises BCF and Ray's Outdoors. Sales and EBIT for this division were both up 50 per cent, largely reflecting a full year's contribution from Ray's, acquired in May 2010. BCF generated strong sales growth, up 4.6 per cent on a same-store basis. The other division, Auto and Cycle Retailing, comprises Supercheap Auto and Goldcross Cycles, although the latter represents just 2 per cent of company turnover. Sales for this division rose 3.4

per cent, with EBIT a sparkling 32 per cent higher. Supercheap maintained its growth, with sales up 4.8 per cent on a same-store basis. But Goldcross continued to underperform, with same-store sales down 14 per cent.

Outlook

Super Retail continues to grow, despite concerns about a prolonged slowdown in consumer spending. Though much of its expansion has come from the continual rollout of new stores, it also benefits from the economies of scale that come with its increasing size. Increasingly it is also working to develop its own brands and to source directly from manufacturers. It is a prominent beneficiary of the strength of the dollar. It plans to continue its vigorous expansion, with 20 to 25 new stores in the Leisure Retailing division in the June 2012 year and five new Supercheap Auto stores. It is exploring options for the future of its cycling business, which has been hit by strong competition from online retailers.

Year to 2 July*	2010	2011
Revenues ($mn)	938.0	1092.3
Auto and Cycle Retailing (%)	73	65
Leisure Retailing (%)	27	35
EBIT ($mn)	63.8	87.5
EBIT margin (%)	6.8	8.0
Gross margin (%)	42.9	45.2
Profit before tax ($mn)	53.9	77.7

Year to 2 July*	2010	2011
Profit after tax ($mn)	38.1	55.6
Earnings per share (¢)	34.0	43.1
Cash flow per share (¢)	54.3	60.8
Dividend (¢)	21.5	29
Percentage franked	100	100
Net tangible assets per share ($)	1.31	1.48
Interest cover (times)	6.5	8.8
Return on equity (%)	17.8	19.4
Debt-to-equity ratio (%)	29.1	24.2
Current ratio	2.4	2.3

* 3 July 2010

Tabcorp Holdings Limited

TAH

<www.tabcorp.com.au>

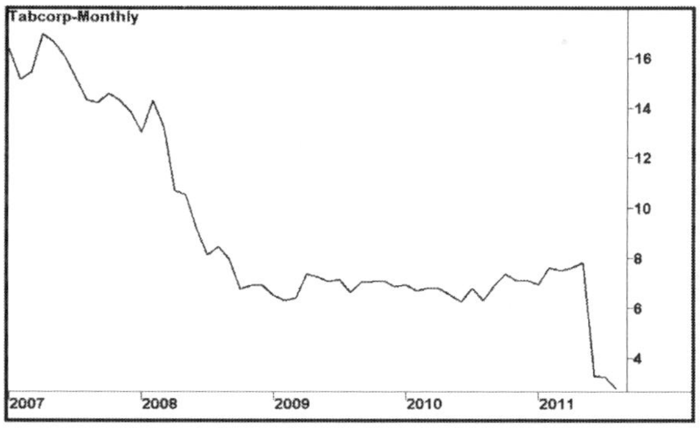

Share price ($)	2.79
12-month high ($)	3.76
12-month low ($)	2.74
Market capitalisation ($mn)	1919.0
Price-to-NTA-per-share ratio	–
5-year share price return (% p.a.)	–9.6
Dividend reinvestment plan	Yes

Sector: Consumer discretionary	Company	Sector
Price/earnings ratio (times)	3.4	13.1
Dividend yield (%)	15.4	3.5

Melbourne-based Tabcorp was established in 1994 with the privatisation of Victoria's TAB operations. It has since grown substantially through acquisition. It runs TAB operations in New South Wales and Victoria, as well as the Luxbet online wagering operation. It manages poker machines in Victoria and operates Keno games in Victoria, New South Wales and Queensland. It also runs Sky Racing—a subscription television channel focused on horseracing—and Sky Sports Radio. In June 2011 it completed the demerger of its casino business—comprising Star City in Sydney, Conrad Jupiters on the Gold Coast, Conrad Treasury in Brisbane, Jupiters Townsville, the Gold Coast Convention and Exhibition Centre and the Townsville Entertainment and Convention Centre—into a new company, Echo Entertainment Group.

Latest business results (June 2011, full year)

The demerger of Tabcorp's casino businesses in June 2011 means that comparisons of the latest financial results with those of the previous year do not have a lot of relevance. The now-demerged casinos business actually reported a sparkling result, with EBIT up by 33.6 per cent, thanks to an above-theoretical win rate from high-roller gamblers, leading to a gain of $79 million. In the previous year the casinos reported a below-theoretical win rate impact of $11 million. The Wagering division saw EBIT up by 4.5 per cent, despite just a 1 per cent rise in revenues. A substantial increase in fixed odds and online wagering more than offset a decline in totalisator revenues. The soccer World Cup in July 2010 also provided a boost. The Gaming division recorded a 7.1 per cent EBIT increase, with the company reporting a gain in market share. Keno division EBIT was up 4.7 per cent and EBIT for the Media and International division, which incorporates the Sky Racing television channels, rose 2.7 per cent.

Outlook

With the demerger of its casino operations, which follows some years of stagnation, Tabcorp is now working to restructure its operations. It has been awarded a renewal of its Victorian wagering and betting licence, for 12 years from August 2012, and it will launch Victorian Keno. It is also working to boost its horse racing television channels, with new international content. It has introduced betting applications for mobile phones and tablet devices. There has been speculation that Tabcorp and Tatts Group might seek to merge if allowed by the competition regulators.

Year to 30 June	2010	2011
Revenues ($mn)	4219.8	4469.5
Wagering (%)	39	35
Casinos (%)	32	34
Victorian Gambling	24	24
Keno (%)	3	4
Media and International (%)	2	3

Year to 30 June	2010	2011
EBIT ($mn)	794.4	905.0
EBIT margin (%)	18.8	20.2
Profit before tax ($mn)	640.2	770.6
Profit after tax ($mn)	469.5	541.6
Earnings per share (¢)	77.1	81.8
Cash flow per share (¢)	110.6	115.4
Dividend (¢)	55	43
Percentage franked	100	100
Net tangible assets per share ($)	–	–
Interest cover (times)	5.2	6.7
Return on equity (%)	13.9	23.2
Debt-to-equity ratio (%)	50.1	67.5
Current ratio	0.5	0.3

Tassal Group Limited

TGR

<www.tassal.com.au>

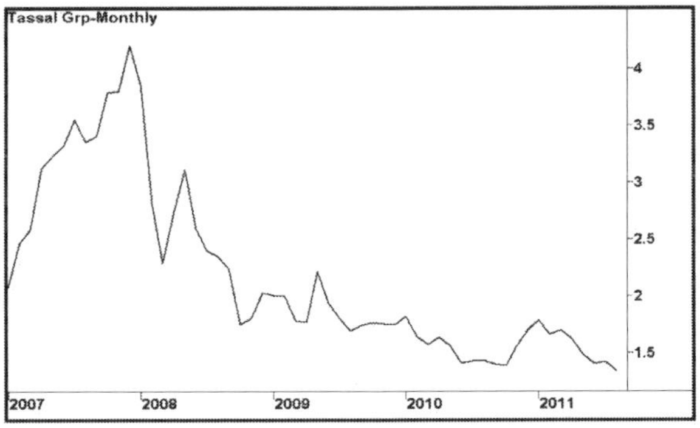

Share price ($)	1.34
12-month high ($)	1.81
12-month low ($)	1.18
Market capitalisation ($mn)	196.0
Price-to-NTA-per-share ratio	0.8
5-year share price return (% p.a.)	3.9
Dividend reinvestment plan	Yes

Sector: Consumer staples	Company	Sector
Price/earnings ratio (times)	6.4	16.5
Dividend yield (%)	1.5	4.8

Hobart-based salmon farmer Tassal was established in 1986 after government trials had established the viability of an Atlantic salmon industry in Tasmanian waters. It has grown steadily through merger, acquisition and restructuring, taking over some of the 11 companies that began salmon faming in the mid 1980s, and it now dominates the local industry with a market share of around 70 per cent and wide distribution of its products. It has opened the Smolt restaurant in Hobart and specialty salmon retail stores in Melbourne and Hobart.

Latest business results (June 2011, full year)

In difficult market conditions, characterised by strong competition, Tassal achieved modest growth in sales and profits. The company attributed this to a long-term farming program that delivered very strong growth in fish and harvest size, along with growth in retail sales—up 15.3 per cent to $127.8 million—and cost efficiency initiatives. This offset a weak wholesale market, with revenues down 23.4 per cent to $66.2 million. Exports nearly doubled, to $25.6 million, although export sales prices were weak. Tassal has changed its accounting method, with increases in the gross value of the company's fish holdings no longer included as revenue, and has restated its June 2010 revenues figure.

Outlook

Consumers in Australia and other Western countries are increasingly coming to recognise the health benefits of salmon, and demand is steadily rising, although Australian per capita consumption is substantially less than in some other Western countries. At a time when the world's fish beds are becoming depleted, there is also a growing acknowledgement of the importance of farmed fish. Tassal operates under a strategic plan stretching to 2016, by which time it predicts that it will be one of the world's 10 largest salmon producers. Having now completed a major three-year capital investment program, it believes it has established a platform for sustained growth, and in coming years it expects increased fish size, reduced feed prices and many cost efficiencies. It expects its best growth to come from high-margin retail sales, thanks to a major focus on marketing, strong brand recognition, new products and the addition of additional sales channels, including the Aldi chain. It also hopes to boost exports. With the company apparently now set for a period of sustained growth, several attempts have been made to initiate a takeover of the company, although Tassal has rebuffed these.

Year to 30 June	2010	2011
Revenues ($mn)	212.7	222.4
EBIT ($mn)	39.9	47.2

Year to 30 June	2010	2011
EBIT margin (%)	18.8	21.2
Gross margin (%)	3.4	2.2
Profit before tax ($mn)	34.6	40.6
Profit after tax ($mn)	28.0	30.3
Earnings per share (¢)	20.0	20.8
Cash flow per share (¢)	27.2	28.9
Dividend (¢)	6	2
Percentage franked	0	0
Net tangible assets per share ($)	1.43	1.62
Interest cover (times)	7.4	7.2
Return on equity (%)	12.3	11.6
Debt-to-equity ratio (%)	36.5	31.7
Current ratio	2.4	2.4

Tatts Group Limited

TTS

<www.tattsgroup.com>

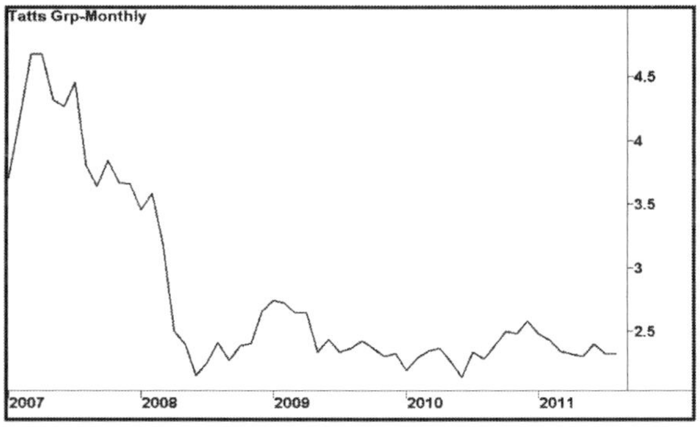

Share price ($)	2.32
12-month high ($)	2.60
12-month low ($)	2.08
Market capitalisation ($mn)	3058.9
Price-to-NTA-per-share ratio	–
5-year share price return (% p.a.)	0.2
Dividend reinvestment plan	Yes

Sector: Consumer discretionary	Company	Sector
Price/earnings ratio (times)	11.0	13.1
Dividend yield (%)	9.3	3.5

Melbourne-based gambling business Tatts Group traces its heritage back to 1891, when George Adams organised a public sweep on the Sydney Cup at the Tattersalls Hotel in Sydney. Today it operates under six broad groupings. Tatts Lotteries runs a lottery business in Victoria, New South Wales, Tasmania, Canberra and the Northern Territory. Tatts Pokies operates 13750 gaming machines at more than 240 venues in Victoria. TattsBet—formerly UNiTAB Wagering—runs a betting business in Queensland, South Australia and the Northern Territory. Maxgaming provides online gaming services to venues in New South Wales, Queensland and the Northern Territory. Bytecraft Systems provides technical support services to the gaming industry. Tatts also owns a British company, Talarius, which runs 7285 gaming machines at 170 venues.

Latest business results (June 2011, full year)

A full year's contribution from the acquisition of NSW Lotteries was behind a rise in revenues. However, profits were hit by floods in Queensland, which curtailed some horse racing, despite firm growth for the TattsBet business in South Australia and the Northern Territory. In addition, a sharp decline in Powerball and Oz Lotto jackpots—just three jackpots worth more than $20 million, compared with 11 in the previous year—led to reduced sales in the lotteries business. The company's Victorian pokies operation saw revenues and profits edge up, thanks to restructuring and some second-half growth. The small Bytecraft business reported a strong result, and the company's struggling Talarius operation in the UK moved from a loss to a break-even result.

Outlook

Tatts operates a portfolio of businesses that generally achieve solid, consistent returns and high cash flow. However, they are also heavily regulated and are quite dependent on levels of consumer discretionary spending. The company is optimistic about the outlook for June 2012. It has restructured its Tatts Pokies business in order to optimise returns before it loses its licence in August 2012, and expects higher profits. It continues to integrate the NSW Lotteries acquisition and believes this will be completed by the end of the June 2012 year, with a solid boost to profit margins. It is hopeful of winning a new licence to expand its lotteries into South Australia. TattsBet's investment in online betting and an expanded range of products is intended to boost revenues and profits. Market speculation continues that Tatts and Tabcorp might eventually merge, if allowed by the competition authorities.

Year to 30 June	2010	2011
Revenues ($mn)	3288.0	3657.0
Tatts Lotteries (%)	37	43
Tatts Pokies (%)	37	33
TattsBet (%)	18	16
Maxgaming (%)	4	3

Year to 30 June	2010	2011
Bytecraft Systems (%)	2	2
EBIT ($mn)	444.9	496.3
EBIT margin (%)	13.5	13.6
Profit before tax ($mn)	393.7	398.9
Profit after tax ($mn)	282.4	275.4
Earnings per share (¢)	22.1	21.2
Cash flow per share (¢)	32.8	30.4
Dividend (¢)	21	21.5
Percentage franked	100	100
Net tangible assets per share ($)	–	–
Interest cover (times)	8.7	5.1
Return on equity (%)	11.2	11.0
Debt-to-equity ratio (%)	48.1	39.5
Current ratio	0.4	0.7

Technology One Limited

TNE

<www.technologyonecorp.com>

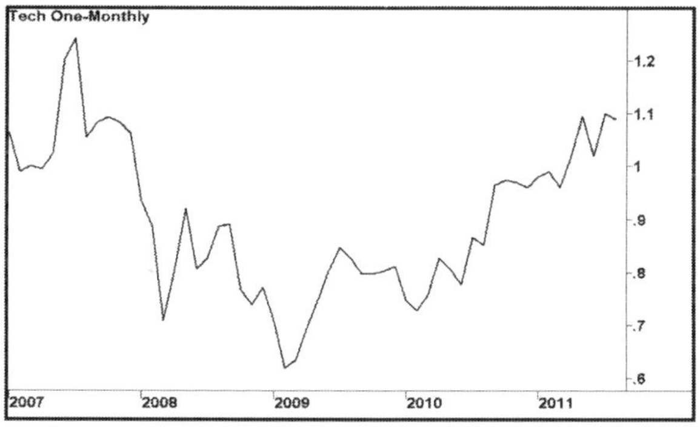

Share price ($)	1.09
12-month high ($)	1.18
12-month low ($)	0.85
Market capitalisation ($mn)	331.6
Price-to-NTA-per-share ratio	7.8
5-year share price return (% p.a.)	13.0
Dividend reinvestment plan	No

Sector: Information technology	Company	Sector
Price/earnings ratio (times)	18.4	18.2
Dividend yield (%)	5.2	3.9

Brisbane-based Technology One, founded in 1987, designs, develops, implements and supports a wide range of financial management, accounting and business software. It has gained success with its TechnologyOne Financials software product, and enjoys particular strength in local government. Its software is also used by many educational institutions, including half of all Australian universities. It derives revenues not only from the supply and support of its products but also from annual licence fees. It operates from offices in Australia, New Zealand, Malaysia and the UK.

Latest business results (March 2011, half year)

Technology One reported another excellent mid-year result, with sales and profits up strongly. The company's main revenue stream, annual licence fees, was up 16 per cent to $21.8 million. Consulting service fees rose 5 per cent to $19.6 million and initial licence fees increased 10 per cent to $15.6 million. The biggest gain came from the company's TechnologyOne Plus project services business, with revenues soaring 82 per cent to $10.3 million. Research and development expenses rose from $12.7 million in the March 2010 period to $14.9 million. The company also incurred development costs of $6.8 million for a range of projects intended to promote future expansion. The result was hurt by a further loss on British operations.

Outlook

Technology One is involved in a range of initiatives that it believes will deliver significant growth in future years. It has opened a new R&D centre in Brisbane with more than 500 staff members. It has established a new Mobility Group to develop applications for iPhones, iPads and other smart mobile devices, and expects strong demand from its customer base for these. It is completing research into its next generation platform—to be used to build new versions of its software products—called the Technology One Cloud Computing (C2) suite. It sees much of its future growth deriving from developments related to C2. The company has put in place a new strategy for its struggling UK operation and it is investigating the possibility of finding a partner for this business. It has expressed its confidence that the UK will eventually provide excellent profit growth. It is also considering the launch of a new offshore R&D centre. In March 2011 Technology One had more than $22 million in net cash holdings, giving it a significant level of resources for future expansion.

Year to 30 September	2009	2010
Revenues ($mn)	120.7	134.0
EBIT ($mn)	19.7	22.4
EBIT margin (%)	16.3	16.7
Profit before tax ($mn)	20.3	23.3

Year to 30 September	2009	2010
Profit after tax ($mn)	15.7	17.8
Earnings per share (¢)	5.2	5.9
Cash flow per share (¢)	6.4	7.2
Dividend (¢)	3.75	5.7
Percentage franked	100	100
Interest cover (times)	–	–
Return on equity (%)	29.1	29.6

Half year to 31 March	2010	2011
Revenues ($mn)	58.5	70.3
Profit before tax ($mn)	6.9	9.1
Profit after tax ($mn)	5.7	7.4
Earnings per share (¢)	1.9	2.4
Dividend (¢)	1.33	1.46
Percentage franked	100	100
Net tangible assets per share ($)	0.13	0.14
Debt-to-equity ratio (%)	–	–
Current ratio	2.0	2.1

Ten Network Holdings Limited

TEN

<www.tencorporate.com.au>

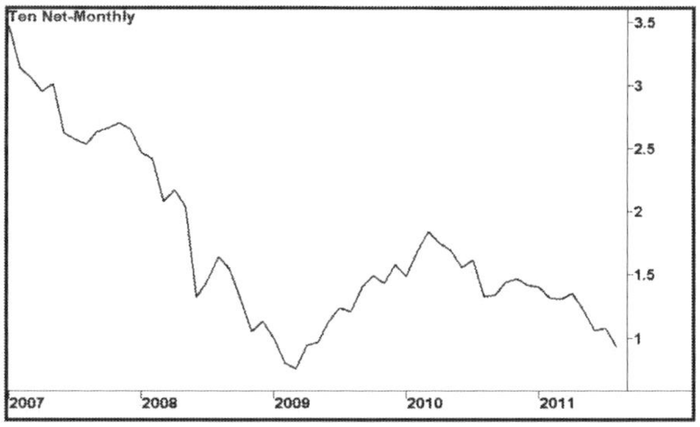

Share price ($)	0.94
12-month high ($)	1.66
12-month low ($)	0.81
Market capitalisation ($mn)	978.1
Price-to-NTA-per-share ratio	–
5-year share price return (% p.a.)	−15.8
Dividend reinvestment plan	No

Sector: Consumer discretionary	Company	Sector
Price/earnings ratio (times)	10.1	13.1
Dividend yield (%)	6.4	3.5

Sydney-based Ten Network Holdings is a television company, with its roots in the Independent Television System, launched in 1965. It operates three free-to-air television channels in Sydney, Melbourne, Adelaide, Brisbane and Perth. Its programming is also carried by affiliates in other parts of the country. Its channels are Channel Ten, which is broadcast in analogue and digital, and Channels One and Eleven, which are digital channels. The company also manages the EYE outdoor advertising business, which operates in Australia, New Zealand, Indonesia, Britain and the US.

Latest business results (February 2011, half year)

Sales revenues rose but profits fell, in a result that the company described as not acceptable. Television revenues rose 2.2 per cent to $404.0 million, but profits were hit by higher expenses. In particular, the company spent $25 million on broadcasting the Delhi Commonwealth Games, which performed below expectations. It also invested heavily in its new early evening news program and the launch in January 2011 of the new Eleven channel. The EYE outdoor advertising business saw revenues up 2 per cent to $80.2 million, and with a big jump in profits. In addition to the figures in the table, the company was hit by a pre-tax charge of $7.1 million for restructuring its television businesses.

Outlook

Ten Network has been experiencing some upheavals since late 2010 when James Packer, Lachlan Murdoch and iron ore billionaire Gina Rinehart all took equity stakes in the company. Murdoch has become interim chief executive, and has announced a series of measures to boost profitability, including the cutting of more than 100 staff jobs and a decision to stop coverage of Australian Football League matches from 2012. The company has also relaunched its digital One channel, to reduce its reliance on sport, and it is actively seeking new programming. However, despite hit shows that include *MasterChef* and *The Biggest Loser,* the company's share of television advertising booked through media agencies fell in the June 2011 half to 29.2 per cent. Rival channels Seven and Nine both showed increases, to 38.4 per cent and 32.4 per cent respectively. The company's much smaller EYE division is showing some solid growth, and has become the market leader in outdoor/billboard advertising for airports and shopping malls in Australia and New Zealand, and it is working to boost its shopping mall business in the US.

Year to 31 August	2009	2010
Revenues ($mn)	901.5	990.5
EBIT ($mn)	117.6	178.9
EBIT margin (%)	13.0	18.1
Profit before tax ($mn)	67.8	141.5

Year to 31 August	2009	2010
Profit after tax ($mn)	47.2	96.9
Earnings per share (¢)	5.1	9.3
Cash flow per share (¢)	8.7	12.1
Dividend (¢)	2	6
Percentage franked	100	0
Interest cover (times)	2.4	4.8
Return on equity (%)	6.0	11.7

Half year to 28 February	2010	2011
Revenues ($mn)	473.4	483.3
Profit before tax ($mn)	85.3	78.9
Profit after tax ($mn)	58.7	54.6
Earnings per share (¢)	5.6	4.8
Dividend (¢)	0	0
Percentage franked	–	–
Net tangible assets per share ($)	–	–
Debt-to-equity ratio (%)	50.5	48.6
Current ratio	1.5	1.6

Thorn Group Limited

TGA

<www.thorn.com.au>

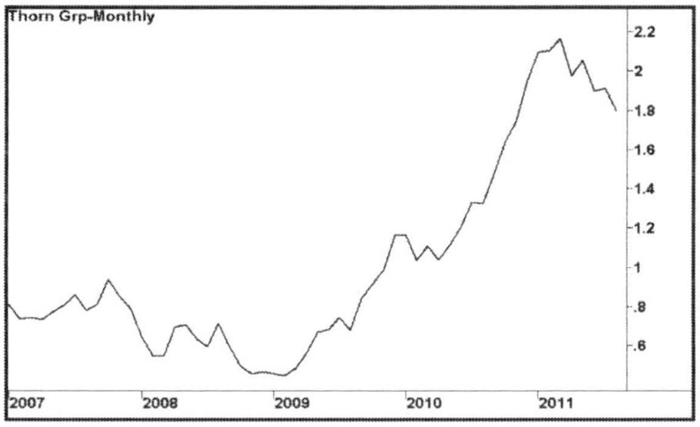

Share price ($)	1.80
12-month high ($)	2.27
12-month low ($)	1.31
Market capitalisation ($mn)	262.8
Price-to-NTA-per-share ratio	4.2
5-year share price return (% p.a.)	23.9
Dividend reinvestment plan	No

Sector: Consumer discretionary	Company	Sector
Price/earnings ratio (times)	10.6	13.1
Dividend yield (%)	4.7	3.5

Sydney-based Thorn Group dates back to the opening of an electrical appliance store in 1937. It is today a leader in the household goods rental market through its Radio Rentals and Rentlo national network of stores. Its Thorn Business Services division provides commercial rental services to companies and government. The company has also moved into the provision of consumer credit with its Cashfirst personal loans business. In March 2011 it acquired National Credit Management (NCM), a national provider of credit and receivables management services.

Latest business results (March 2011, full year)

A 7.5 per cent increase in customer numbers for the company's core Radio Rentals and Rentlo businesses, and a 4.6 per cent rise in the average monthly payment per customer, to $133.76, helped generate a strong jump in profits. The after-tax profit would have risen by about 40 per cent had it not been for costs of about $1 million involved in the acquisition of NCM. The company attributed its new 'Rent, Try, $1 Buy!' promotion, offering customers the chance to try a product before buying it, as a key factor in the good result. Furniture demand was particularly strong, with 36 per cent growth from the previous year, and whitegoods rentals were up 10 per cent. The Cashfirst loan book doubled to $12 million, with 11.4 per cent of loan value written off as bad debt, down from 14.5 per cent in the previous year.

Outlook

Thorn is a beneficiary of a tight economic environment and a slowdown in consumer spending, with a growing number of householders now looking to rent electrical goods and home appliances, rather than buy. The company has more than 95000 customers, and expects soon to reach 100000. Each customer rents an average of 2.3 products, and around 40 per cent of them enter into a new contract when an existing contract expires. To attract more business the company is redeveloping existing stores and it is looking to open new showrooms in key metropolitan areas. The fast-growing Cashfirst business has an account base of over 7000 customers, with the company using a national television advertising campaign to attract new business. Thorn believes its $31.4 million purchase of NCM will help it achieve strong sales and profit growth in March 2012, and it also believes the acquisition will enable it to move into new areas of business.

Year to 31 March	2010	2011
Revenues ($mn)	145.1	157.6
EBIT ($mn)	24.6	32.7
EBIT margin (%)	17.0	20.7
Profit before tax ($mn)	24.0	32.3

Year to 31 March	2010	2011
Profit after tax ($mn)	19.5	22.0
Earnings per share (¢)	15.1	17.0
Cash flow per share (¢)	16.2	18.2
Dividend (¢)	6.32	8.49
Percentage franked	100	100
Net tangible assets per share ($)	0.51	0.43
Interest cover (times)	40.5	88.6
Return on equity (%)	25.8	24.9
Debt-to-equity ratio (%)	0.3	28.4
Current ratio	0.9	1.3

Toll Holdings Limited

TOL

<www.tollgroup.com>

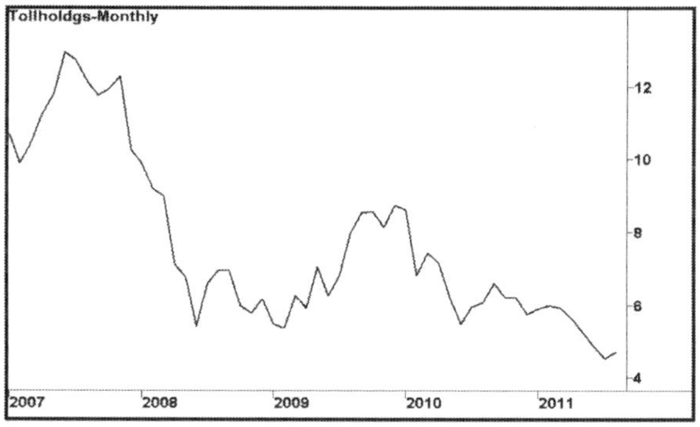

Share price ($)	4.72
12-month high ($)	7.04
12-month low ($)	3.70
Market capitalisation ($mn)	3351.8
Price-to-NTA-per-share ratio	3.6
5-year share price return (% p.a.)	–5.5
Dividend reinvestment plan	Yes

Sector: Industrials	Company	Sector
Price/earnings ratio (times)	11.8	11.9
Dividend yield (%)	5.3	5.5

Melbourne-based transportation giant Toll Holdings was founded in Newcastle in 1888. It has grown through a large series of acquisitions, and is today one of the Asia-Pacific region's largest providers of integrated logistics services. Its many varied businesses incorporate road fleets, air and marine transport, warehousing, ports and railways, with operations in more than 50 countries.

Latest business results (June 2011, full year)

Toll achieved an increase in revenues, due especially to the impact of various acquisitions, but profits were little changed. The company segments its many activities into six big groups. The largest of these, Toll Global Express, saw a healthy rise in revenues and profits, with a good domestic performance, despite weakness in some business segments. Toll Global Forwarding is now the second-largest division, with a big jump in revenues and profits, but this mainly reflected acquisitions, and profit margins remained low. Toll Specialised and Domestic Freight enjoyed a strong year, thanks in particular to strong demand from the resources sector. However, both Toll Global Logistics and Toll Domestic Forwarding saw revenues edge up but profits decline.

Outlook

Toll is heavily geared to global economic conditions, as well as to the individual economies of the many countries in which it operates. As a hugely diverse company it is also highly dependent on the quality of its management. Its initial success came from acquiring numerous related businesses in Australia, so that it became able to offer a full range of logistics services to almost any client. It is now working to extend that strategy to Asia and beyond, through the acquisition of a series of companies. For the time being domestic business remains responsible for about two-thirds of revenues, but this is steadily changing as the company realises its expansion ambitions, and the strongest growth recently has derived from Asian operations, which now represent more than 20 per cent of turnover. But with a third of its business geared to domestic consumer spending trends, Toll will be hurt by the weak spending environment. Its $110 million acquisition of Western Australian transportation company Mitchell Corporation in May 2011 is intended to boost its exposure to the mining sector, where it has been seen as relatively weak. A sagging share price has led to speculation that the company could be acquired, perhaps by a private equity group, and broken up.

Year to 30 June	2010	2011
Revenues ($mn)	6944.0	8224.5
Toll Global Express (%)	26	26
Toll Global Forwarding (%)	15	20
Toll Global Logistics (%)	18	17
Toll Specialised and Domestic Freight (%)	15	15

Year to 30 June	2010	2011
Toll Domestic Forwarding (%)	15	13
EBIT ($mn)	406.7	446.2
EBIT margin (%)	5.9	5.4
Profit before tax ($mn)	369.3	410.8
Profit after tax ($mn)	292.9	281.4
Earnings per share (¢)	41.9	39.8
Cash flow per share (¢)	75.2	74.3
Dividend (¢)	25	25
Percentage franked	100	100
Net tangible assets per share ($)	1.34	1.30
Interest cover (times)	10.9	12.6
Return on equity (%)	11.1	10.3
Debt-to-equity ratio (%)	34.4	36.4
Current ratio	1.3	0.8

Treasury Group Limited

TRG

<www.treasurygroup.com>

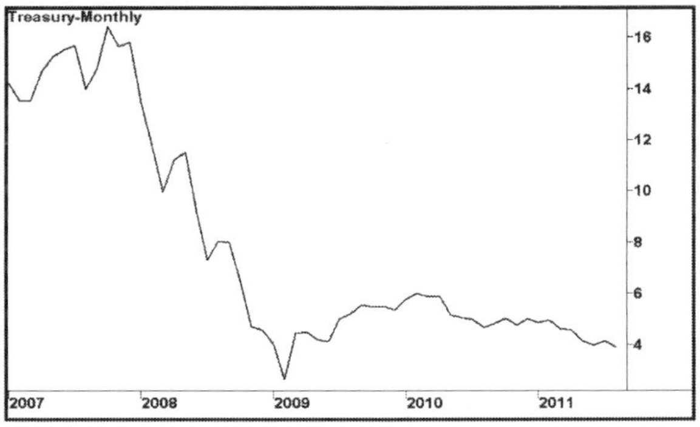

Share price ($)	3.90
12-month high ($)	5.20
12-month low ($)	3.40
Market capitalisation ($mn)	90.0
Price-to-NTA-per-share ratio	1.5
5-year share price return (% p.a.)	−13.5
Dividend reinvestment plan	No

Sector: Financials	Company	Sector
Price/earnings ratio (times)	9.0	10.8
Dividend yield (%)	8.7	6.8

Melbourne financial company Treasury Group provides specialist back-office services—including risk and compliance services and a responsible entity function—for boutique fund management companies. Not only does it take a fee for its services—based on the amount of funds under management—but it also takes an equity stake in the companies with which it works. It owns 48 per cent of the equity of Investors Mutual, 40 per cent of IML Investment Partners, 42 per cent of Orion Asset Management, 40 per cent of RARE Infrastructure, 49 per cent of Global Value Investors, 40 per cent of Treasury Asia Asset Management (TAAM), 40 per cent of RARE IP Trust, 39 per cent of Celeste Funds Management and 30 per cent of AR Capital Management, as well as redeemable preference shares entitling it to 20 per cent of the equity in Aubrey Capital Management.

Latest business results (June 2011, full year)

Volatile financial markets caught up with the company, and revenues and profits were down. Despite this, total funds under management at June 2011 of $16.76 billion represented a 13.9 per cent rise on a year earlier. The first half saw net fund outflow, but this was easily offset by very strong fund inflows in the second half, with notable strength for the defensive RARE Infrastructure fund, and net fund inflows for the year totalled $787 million. Institutional business rose further, from 77 per cent of funds under management to 79 per cent, while retail business fell from 23 per cent to 21 per cent, leading to a decline in margins. Just five years earlier institutional investors comprised just 61 per cent of the total.

Outlook

Thanks to the rapid growth in Australia of the boutique funds management business, Treasury Group has had many requests to provide back-room services, and it has been able to select only those fund managers it believes offer the best long-term growth potential. Nevertheless, the fortunes of the funds management industry are strongly leveraged to stock market fluctuations, and the company recognises that investor sentiment remains volatile. In the present financial environment many retail investors are withdrawing their money from equities, with the result that the company's reliance on lower margin institutional investors continues to rise. Treasury Group has no debt and more than $10 million in cash holdings, and is in a position to consider a variety of growth options.

Year to 30 June	2010	2011
Revenues ($mn)	19.6	18.5
EBIT ($mn)	10.4	9.0

Year to 30 June	2010	2011
EBIT margin (%)	52.7	48.9
Profit before tax ($mn)	11.5	9.9
Profit after tax ($mn)	11.7	10.0
Earnings per share (¢)	50.6	43.4
Cash flow per share (¢)	50.9	43.7
Dividend (¢)	26	34
Percentage franked	100	100
Net tangible assets per share ($)	2.43	2.56
Interest cover (times)	–	–
Return on equity (%)	22.0	17.4
Debt-to-equity ratio (%)	–	–
Current ratio	3.2	4.8

The Trust Company Limited

TRU

<www.trust.com.au>

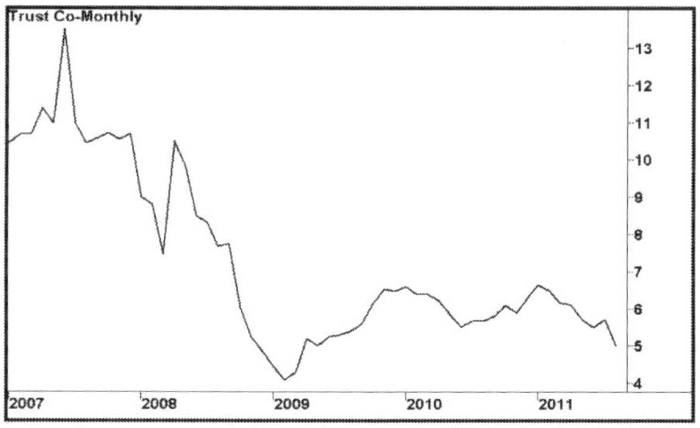

Share price ($)	5.00
12-month high ($)	6.85
12-month low ($)	4.90
Market capitalisation ($mn)	161.8
Price-to-NTA-per-share ratio	2.2
5-year share price return (% p.a.)	–7.1
Dividend reinvestment plan	No

Sector: Financials	Company	Sector
Price/earnings ratio (times)	11.7	10.8
Dividend yield (%)	7.0	6.8

Sydney-based The Trust Company was founded in 1885, and is one of Australia's oldest trustee companies. It divides its businesses into two divisions. The Personal Client Services division provides estate and trust planning, health and personal injury assistance, funds management and financial planning. The Corporate Client Services division provides trustee and custodian services for the property and infrastructure asset sectors, and securities and debenture issues and approved trustee services for corporate superannuation funds. It has a particular specialty in philanthropy, and administers more than 300 charitable trusts, including the Miles Franklin Literary Award. In 2011 it acquired New Zealand Guardian Trust. It has offices in Australia, Singapore and New Zealand.

Latest business results (February 2011, full year)

Profits rose after three years of decline, thanks to a sparkling performance from the company's Corporate Client Services division, which won several large new mandates during the year. This offset a poor result from Personal Client Services, which saw revenues flat for the year and profits down. The company's estates and trusts business administered lower estate numbers and estate values during the year, with a decline in revenues. In addition, the cash management trust experienced significant outflow as competition for deposits intensified during the year. Income from term deposits and investments rose 28 per cent. Corporate Client Services division assets under management reversed the downturn of the previous year and rose 1 per cent to $117 billion. Personal Client Services division assets under management were flat at $3.4 billion, having risen sharply in the previous year.

Outlook

With much of its revenue base exposed to financial market fluctuations, Trust Company could continue to experience volatility in its earnings. Nevertheless, it remains well placed to take advantage of the growing needs of Australians for a wide range of financial advice, and of the growing complexity of financial regulations. The $31.5 million acquisition of New Zealand's Guardian Trust is one of the company's most significant investments in some years, and it will contribute to some firm growth. It will also transform the company's business. Guardian Trustee, with a 128-year history, is a leader in the New Zealand corporate and personal trustee markets, though with a marked leaning towards corporate business. This work will thus become more important for Trust Company. In addition, Trust Company anticipates some strong client synergy opportunities to develop.

Year to 28 February	2010	2011
Revenues ($mn)	57.1	60.3
Personal Client Services (%)	56	53
Corporate Client Services (%)	38	40

Year to 28 February	2010	2011
EBIT ($mn)	16.3	17.9
EBIT margin (%)	28.5	29.7
Profit before tax ($mn)	17.2	19.8
Profit after tax ($mn)	11.7	13.8
Earnings per share (¢)	36.3	42.7
Cash flow per share (¢)	39.4	46.1
Dividend (¢)	33.7	35
Percentage franked	100	100
Net tangible assets per share ($)	2.27	2.31
Interest cover (times)	–	–
Return on equity (%)	10.3	12.2
Debt-to-equity ratio (%)	–	–
Current ratio	5.0	6.1

UGL Limited

UGL

<www.ugllimited.com.au>

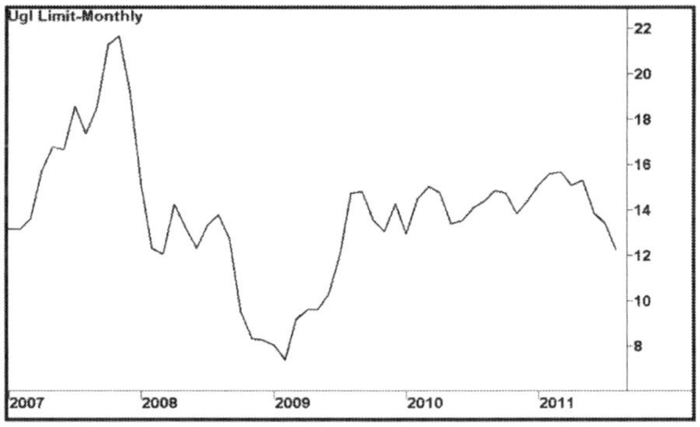

Share price ($)	12.25
12-month high ($)	16.48
12-month low ($)	11.25
Market capitalisation ($mn)	2024.9
Price-to-NTA-per-share ratio	16.0
5-year share price return (% p.a.)	2.3
Dividend reinvestment plan	No

Sector: Industrials	Company	Sector
Price/earnings ratio (times)	12.8	11.9
Dividend yield (%)	5.7	5.5

Sydney-based UGL, founded in the 1970s and formerly known as United Group, is a leading engineering and property services company, operating throughout Australia, New Zealand, Asia, North America and parts of the Middle East, under four divisions. Its Services division provides outsourcing expertise in such areas as corporate real estate, property management and project management. The Rail division designs and manufactures rail rolling stock and also maintains railway networks. The Infrastructure division provides construction and maintenance services to the water, power, transport, communications and defence sectors. The Resources division provides construction and maintenance services to the resources and manufacturing sectors.

Latest business results (June 2011, full year)

In a difficult environment UGL achieved a solid result, its 10th straight year of higher profits. Property services has become UGLs biggest division, and revenues were down, although this largely reflected the strong dollar, and profits rose. The Rail division had an excellent year, with a full-year contribution from the MTM train franchise in Melbourne and success with Sydney's Oscar 3 passenger rail contract, and EBIT soared 53 per cent. The Infrastructure division also saw sales and profits higher, with strength across all key business segments. The Resources division had a mixed performance, despite a second-half recovery, with revenues up but EBIT slumping 26 per cent, and already-low profit margins falling further. During the year the company received new contracts and extensions worth more than $4 billion. This was down from the $5.3 billion of the previous year, and at June 2011 UGL held an order book of $8.2 billion, compared to $9.1 billion at June 2010.

Outlook

UGL has expressed its belief that it can continue its growth momentum in the June 2012 year despite a reduced order book. It views its rail business as offering particular potential, as Australian cities boost their investment in local train services. It also sees the resources sector offering growth opportunities in rail, and it is assessing international markets. Its infrastructure work is spread across three main market segments—transport and communications, water, and power—and here too the outlook is positive. However, the Services division remains quite dependent on both American economic trends and currency movements, although domestic business is strong, and the company's Resources division is struggling to boost margins. UGL has been rebuffed in attempts to arrange a friendly takeover of engineering company Transfield Services.

Year to 30 June	2010	2011
Revenues ($mn)	4359.1	4583.6
Services (%)	31	29
Rail (%)	26	27
Infrastructure (%)	25	23
Resources (%)	17	21
EBIT ($mn)	223.0	243.3
EBIT margin (%)	5.1	5.3
Profit before tax ($mn)	196.3	215.8
Profit after tax ($mn)	144.5	158.5
Earnings per share (¢)	87.7	95.5
Cash flow per share (¢)	123.6	131.5
Dividend (¢)	64	70
Percentage franked	100	100
Net tangible assets per share ($)	–	0.76
Interest cover (times)	8.4	8.9
Return on equity (%)	12.7	13.6
Debt-to-equity ratio (%)	20.1	15.2
Current ratio	1.4	1.5

Webjet Limited

WEB

<www.webjet.com.au>

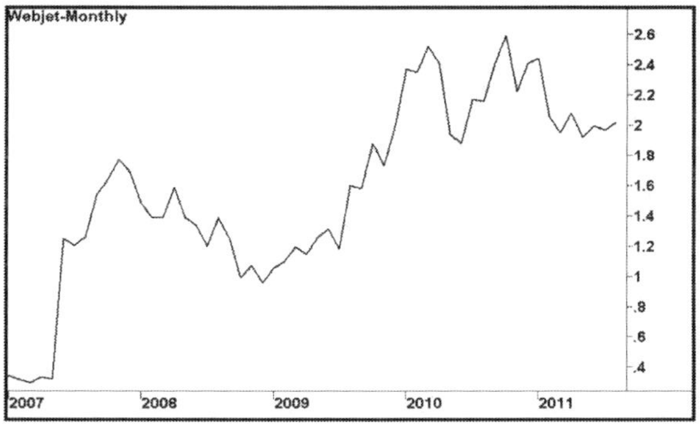

Share price ($)	2.02
12-month high ($)	2.71
12-month low ($)	1.50
Market capitalisation ($mn)	153.1
Price-to-NTA-per-share ratio	4.7
5-year share price return (% p.a.)	12.0
Dividend reinvestment plan	No

Sector: Consumer discretionary	Company	Sector
Price/earnings ratio (times)	14.0	13.1
Dividend yield (%)	5.4	3.5

Melbourne-based Webjet, established in 1998, is an online travel agency. It specialises in airline bookings, hotel reservations, travel insurance and rental cars. It has launched business operations in the US, Canada, New Zealand, Singapore and Hong Kong, and has been planning to enter Europe.

Latest business results (June 2011, full year)

Webjet was a beneficiary of the strong dollar and a buoyant travel market, as it posted a rise in sales and profits. The total transaction value of all business transacted through Webjet during the year was $592 million, up 17 per cent from the previous year, with the number of transactions up 13 per cent and unit prices up 4 per cent. The good result came despite a $0.7 million loss from new businesses the company has launched in the US and Asia.

Outlook

Webjet is one of the beneficiaries of the migration of business to online platforms, and it has become a leader in the online air travel market. It has been seeing particularly strong growth in bookings from mobile devices, with compound monthly growth of 27 per cent for iPhone bookings in the June 2011 year. It is helped by the strong dollar, which means that spending on travel has generally remained firm in the midst of a weak consumer spending environment. From its dominant position in Australia it is now working to replicate its model abroad, with new businesses in several countries. This has held back profits, although, if successful, such initiatives have the potential to generate sustained long-term profit growth. However, its moves abroad mean the company faces considerable competition from well-entrenched rivals such as Expedia, and its success is not assured. In the face of global financial volatility, it has postponed plans to enter Europe. It views the US$545 billion global hotel booking business as another key growth opportunity, given that travellers often book flights first and then hotels. It is working to boost its exposure to this market, and expects to be offering reservations to more than 100000 hotels around the world by January 2012. However, here too it faces many established rivals. Webjet is forecasting profit growth of at least 10 per cent in the June 2012 year. The company has no debt and more than $31 million in cash holdings, allowing considerable scope for growth through acquisition or from launching new businesses.

Year to 30 June	2010	2011
Revenues ($mn)	37.1	43.5
EBIT ($mn)	12.8	13.3
EBIT margin (%)	34.4	30.5
Profit before tax ($mn)	14.5	15.4
Profit after tax ($mn)	10.6	11.1

Year to 30 June	2010	2011
Earnings per share (¢)	13.9	14.4
Cash flow per share (¢)	14.3	15.0
Dividend (¢)	10.5	11
Percentage franked	100	100
Net tangible assets per share ($)	0.44	0.43
Interest cover (times)	–	–
Return on equity (%)	28.6	27.8
Debt-to-equity ratio (%)	–	–
Current ratio	4.3	3.4

Westpac Banking Corporation

WBC

<www.westpac.com.au>

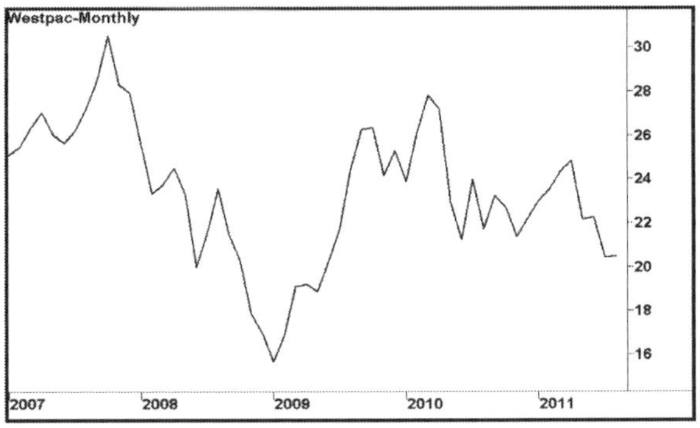

Share price ($)	20.48
12-month high ($)	25.60
12-month low ($)	17.84
Market capitalisation ($mn)	62057.1
Price-to-NTA-per-share ratio	2.1
5-year share price return (% p.a.)	3.2
Dividend reinvestment plan	Yes

Sector: Financials	Company	Sector
Price/earnings ratio (times)	9.6	10.8
Dividend yield (%)	6.8	6.8

Sydney-based Westpac, which began trading in 1817 as the Bank of New South Wales, is one of Australias big four banks, with interests in most areas of financial services. It is also one of New Zealand's leading banks, and has some smaller businesses in the Pacific region. It owns St George Bank, BankSA and Bank of Melbourne. Its wealth management arm, BT Financial Group, incorporates brands that include Securitor Financial Group, Asgard, Advance and Ascalon Capital Managers. It also owns Hastings Funds Management and has a 60 per cent holding in the publicly listed funds manager BT Investment Management.

Latest business results (March 2011, half year)

Profits rose strongly from the March 2010 period, although this largely reflected a one-off tax benefit associated with the acquisition of St George Bank. Excluding this, profit growth was a more modest 7 per cent. The bank was a beneficiary of a solid decline in provisioning for bad debts and also of some stringent cost control. Mortgage lending grew 6 per cent from a year earlier, but business lending dipped 4 per cent. Thanks to the decision to raise interest rates late in 2010 by more than the Reserve Bank increase in the official rate, Westpac's net interest margin rose from 2.17 per cent in the September 2010 half to 2.21 per cent. New Zealand operations provided good growth, despite the Christchurch earthquake. The BT Financial Group division achieved modest profit growth, with improved funds management earnings more than offsetting higher natural disaster-related claims for the insurance business.

Outlook

Westpac is strongly geared to the domestic economy. It has expressed a belief that the business environment remains broadly supportive, thanks to a low unemployment rate and the likelihood of continuing strong capital spending, and despite consumer and business caution and the impact of natural disasters. As a result, it expects consumer and business sentiment to improve during the remainder of 2011, and it forecasts a recovery in business credit growth. In order to boost growth in Victoria, it has relaunched its Bank of Melbourne brand, with a string of new branches. It is also working to expand insurance sales through existing networks and via independent financial advisers. It is increasing its activities in Asia with the upgrade of its Beijing office to a full branch. It expects further benefits from the acquisition of St George through the cross-selling of products such as insurance and superannuation.

Year to 30 September	2009	2010
Operating income ($mn)	16505.0	16910.0
Net interest income ($mn)	11646.0	11842.0

Year to 30 September	2009	2010
Operating expenses ($mn)	7171.0	7416.0
Profit before tax ($mn)	6096.0	8038.0
Profit after tax ($mn)	3446.0	6346.0
Earnings per share (¢)	125.4	214.4
Dividend (¢)	116	139
Percentage franked	100	100
Non-interest income to total income (%)	29.4	30.0
Cost-to-income ratio (%)	43.4	43.9
Return on equity (%)	13.2	17.4
Return on assets (%)	0.7	1.1

Half year to 31 March	2010	2011
Operating income ($mn)	8581.0	8347.0
Profit before tax ($mn)	4010.0	4231.0
Profit after tax ($mn)	2875.0	3961.0
Earnings per share (¢)	97.5	132.5
Dividend (¢)	65	76
Percentage franked	100	100
Net tangible assets per share ($)	8.42	9.55

Wide Bay Australia Limited

WBB

<www.widebayaust.com.au>

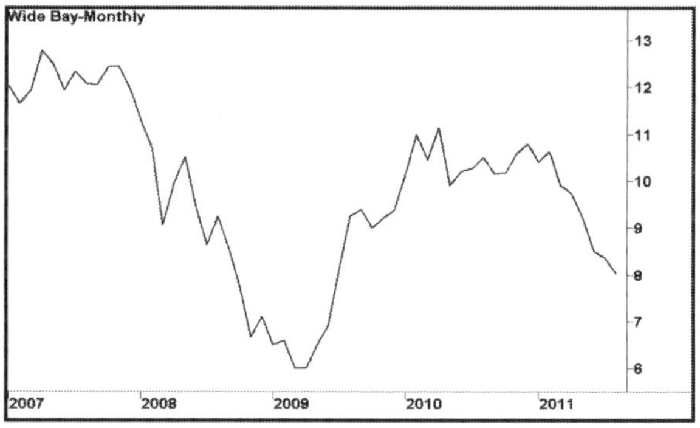

Share price ($)	8.03
12-month high ($)	11.10
12-month low ($)	7.35
Market capitalisation ($mn)	283.9
Price-to-NTA-per-share ratio	1.9
5-year share price return (% p.a.)	–0.3
Dividend reinvestment plan	Yes

Sector: Financials	Company	Sector
Price/earnings ratio (times)	12.1	10.8
Dividend yield (%)	7.5	6.8

Based in Bundaberg in Queensland, Wide Bay Australia was founded in 1979 from the merger of two building societies, both of which had histories dating back to the early 1960s. It subsequently merged with two more building societies, and in 2008 it acquired Mackay Permanent Building Society. It is a leading provider of financial services in Queensland, with a network of 43 branches and agencies—mainly in coastal locations between the Gold Coast and Cairns—and is one of the state's largest non-bank deposit-taking institutions. It has expanded interstate, with one branch in Sydney and another in Melbourne, and a lending outlet in Adelaide. It owns the mortgage insurer Mortgage Risk Management (MRM), a 51 per cent share in the leasing and finance provider Wide Bay Australia Mini Lease and 25 per cent of the financial planning firm Financial Technology Securities.

Latest business results (June 2011, full year)

Profits edged up, a solid result in a volatile financial environment, with business affected by the effects of Cyclone Yasi and the Queensland floods, along with a weak housing market. Loan approvals fell to $308 million, down from $369 million in the previous year and $531 million in the year before that. However, the total loan portfolio edged up from $2.25 billion to $2.28 billion. The result included an after-tax profit of $2.3 million from MRM, down from $2.9 million in the previous year.

Financial Technology Securities contributed an after-tax profit of $875000, up from $700000 in the previous year.

Outlook

As the largest financial institution based north of Brisbane, Wide Bay is at the heart of a buoyant region with solid growth prospects. Some major infrastructure projects are expected in this area, notably LNG developments around Gladstone, with the potential to generate tens of thousands of jobs. Wide Bay's essential business is taking customer deposits and arranging home loans in its areas of operations. However, with the housing market now weak it is working to develop a secured commercial lending program. It is also looking at other initiatives to increase lending, including the wider use of brokers, which in the past have accounted for around 20 per cent of total loan approvals. Wide Bay has decided to wind down the operations of Wide Bay Australia Mini Lease as its existing contracts are paid out. It is also seeking other growth opportunities, including more acquisitions and the possibility of developing partnerships with other institutions.

Year to 30 June	2010	2011
Operating income ($mn)	71.0	72.7
Net interest income ($mn)	54.7	56.8

Year to 30 June	2010	2011
Operating expenses ($mn)	38.5	39.8
Profit before tax ($mn)	31.9	32.6
Profit after tax ($mn)	22.3	22.6
Earnings per share (¢)	70.4	66.2
Dividend (¢)	63	60
Percentage franked	100	100
Non-interest income to total income (%)	22.9	21.9
Net tangible assets per share ($)	3.72	4.33
Cost-to-income ratio (%)	54.2	54.8
Return on equity (%)	14.3	12.7
Return on assets (%)	0.9	0.8

Woodside Petroleum Limited

WPL

<www.woodside.com.au>

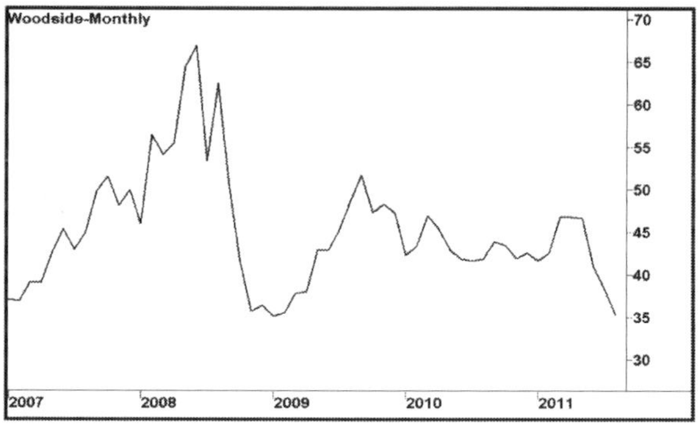

Share price ($)	35.33
12-month high ($)	50.85
12-month low ($)	30.53
Market capitalisation ($mn)	28024.8
Price-to-NTA-per-share ratio	2.5
5-year share price return (% p.a.)	–0.5
Dividend reinvestment plan	Yes

Sector: Energy	Company	Sector
Price/earnings ratio (times)	16.0	20.4
Dividend yield (%)	3.1	2.7

Perth-based Woodside, founded in 1954, is a leading specialist energy company. It is one of Australia's largest producers of oil and gas and one of the world's largest producers of liquefied natural gas (LNG). It is part owner and operator of Australia's largest resources project, the North West Shelf Venture in Western Australia, which produces about 40 per cent of Australia's oil and gas. It is engaged in construction of the Pluto LNG project near Karratha, Western Australia, and it is working on plans to start LNG development at the Sunrise project in the Timor Sea and the Browse project in northern Western Australia. It also maintains a portfolio of non-LNG projects. Shell Australia owns 24 per cent of Woodside's equity.

Latest business results (June 2011, half year)

Woodside now reports its results in US dollars, and on that basis higher oil prices offset a 13.1 per cent decline in production, and the company recorded a 7.2 per cent rise in sales revenues, with underlying after-tax profit up 3.6 per cent. However, the figures in this book have been converted to Australian dollars, using prevailing exchange rates; on that basis sales and profits fell. Production of 31.9 million barrels of oil equivalent (mmboe) declined, due mainly to scheduled maintenance, although there were also some weather interruptions. The company delivered 132 cargoes of LNG, up from 127 cargoes a year earlier.

Outlook

For 2011 Woodside believes it is on target for total production of 62 to 64 mmboe. For the longer term it has extremely high hopes for its massive $14.9 billion Pluto LNG project, although this has been subject to delays, with the first deliveries not now expected until March 2012. The company has also postponed any decision on a second Pluto project. It is now seen as unlikely to make a decision before mid 2012 on whether to proceed with the Browse project. Its partners in this venture, including BP, BHP Billiton, Chevron and Royal Dutch Shell, are still seeking a sufficient number of customers to make the project viable. The company is seeking to win the approval of the East Timor government in order to begin work on the Sunrise project. Late in 2010 Shell sold down its holding in Woodside from 34 per cent to 24 per cent, and there has been speculation that BHP Billiton might try to acquire Woodside.

Year to 31 December	2009	2010
Revenues ($mn)	4352.0	4557.6
EBIT ($mn)	2864.0	2452.2
EBIT margin (%)	65.8	53.8
Gross margin (%)	56.9	60.2

Year to 31 December	2009	2010
Profit before tax ($mn)	2848.0	2471.7
Profit after tax ($mn)	1824.0	1712.0
Earnings per share (¢)	259.3	221.4
Cash flow per share (¢)	394.3	326.6
Dividend (¢)	110	110.84
Percentage franked	100	100
Interest cover (times)	179.0	–
Return on equity (%)	22.0	16.5

Half year to 30 June	2010	2011
Revenues ($mn)	2361.8	2187.4
Profit before tax ($mn)	1395.5	1183.5
Profit after tax ($mn)	1014.6	803.9
Earnings per share (¢)	131.5	101.9
Dividend (¢)	56.34	52.44
Percentage franked	100	100
Net tangible assets per share ($)	16.02	14.11
Debt-to-equity ratio (%)	28.1	34.6
Current ratio	2.0	0.7

Woolworths Limited

WOW

<www.woolworthslimited.com.au>

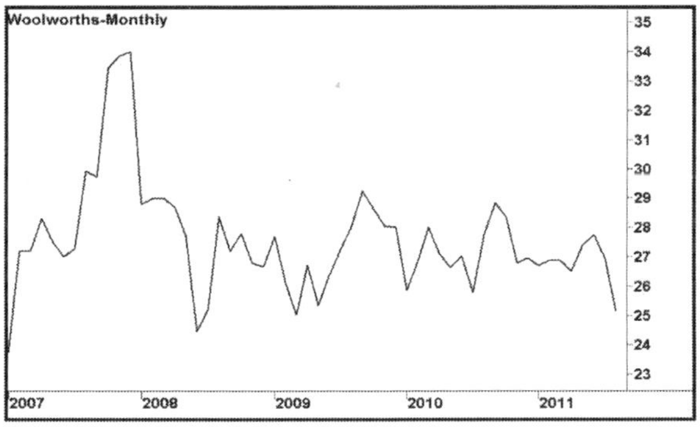

Share price ($)	25.15
12-month high ($)	30.18
12-month low ($)	23.70
Market capitalisation ($mn)	30593.2
Price-to-NTA-per-share ratio	12.9
5-year share price return (% p.a.)	7.5
Dividend reinvestment plan	Yes

Sector: Consumer staples	Company	Sector
Price/earnings ratio (times)	14.4	16.5
Dividend yield (%)	4.9	4.8

Woolworths, founded in Sydney in 1924, is one of Australia's retail giants. Its more than 3200 outlets across Australia and New Zealand include Woolworths, Thomas Dux, Countdown, Foodtown, SuperValue and Fresh Choice supermarkets, Big W mixed good stores, Dick Smith and Tandy electronics stores, Dan Murphy's and BWS liquor stores, Langton's wine auctions and Caltex/Woolworths petrol outlets. To support its new Masters chain of hardware stores it has acquired the Danks hardware wholesaler. It has also entered into a small consumer electronics joint retail venture with the Tata Group in India, comprising 64 stores.

Latest business results (June 2011, full year)

Woolworths' 11-year record of double-digit profit growth ended as the company was hit by a combination of subdued consumer spending, the impact of natural disasters, price deflation and enhanced competition. Revenues and profits rose, but only modestly, although the rise in profits outstripped that for sales, as the company again achieved success in boosting margins. The company said the 5.1 per cent increase in after-tax profit would have been 6.4 per cent but for natural disaster costs. It also said its domestic supermarkets increased their share of the market, in the face of heavy competition. Petrol sales were strong, with EBIT up 18.2 per cent. New Zealand supermarket sales and profits edged up in New Zealand dollars.

But Big W and the consumer electronics business both had a bad year, with profits well down due to a sluggish sales environment, online competition and price deflation.

Outlook

Woolworths occupies a central position in the Australian economy, with more than a 30 per cent market share for food, liquor and groceries. However, these are essentially mature businesses, and with consumer spending down the company sees June 2012 profits rising by just 2 per cent to 6 per cent. It has particularly high hopes for its new Masters hardware stores, with the first stores opening during 2011 and with a target of 150 stores over five years. However, start-up costs of $100 million will hurt company profits. It has announced a new move into insurance, in a partnership with Swiss Re and Hollard Group. Its May 2011 acquisition of Cellarmasters helps it move into liquor direct marketing. It is also increasingly introducing its own liquor brands to its stores. It is working to rejuvenate its underperforming consumer electronics business with new store formats.

Year to 26 June*	2010	2011
Revenues ($mn)	51694.3	54142.9
Australian Food and Liquor (%)	67	67
Petrol (%)	11	11
Big W (%)	8	8

Year to 26 June*	2010	2011
New Zealand Supermarkets (%)	8	8
EBIT ($mn)	3082.1	3276.4
EBIT margin (%)	6.0	6.1
Gross margin (%)	25.7	25.8
Profit before tax ($mn)	2870.6	3014.9
Profit after tax ($mn)	2020.8	2124.0
Earnings per share (¢)	164.0	174.6
Cash flow per share (¢)	228.8	245.2
Dividend (¢)	115	122
Percentage franked	100	100
Net tangible assets per share ($)	2.04	1.95
Interest cover (times)	14.6	12.5
Return on equity (%)	28.1	28.0
Debt-to-equity ratio (%)	36.2	42.4
Current ratio	0.7	0.8

* 27 June 2010

WorleyParsons Limited

WOR

<www.worleyparsons.com>

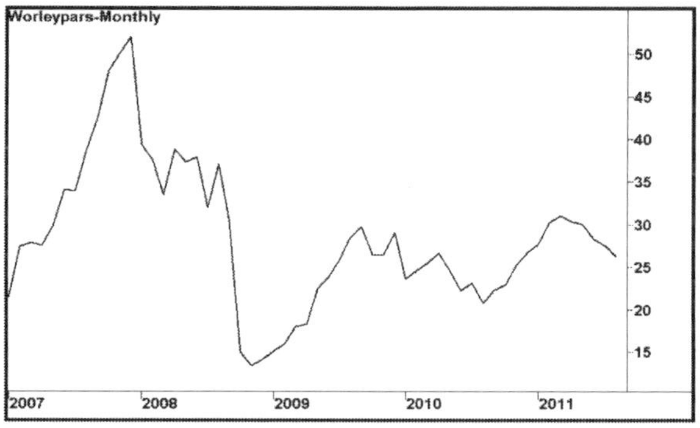

Share price ($)	26.27
12-month high ($)	33.61
12-month low ($)	20.74
Market capitalisation ($mn)	6454.5
Price-to-NTA-per-share ratio	44.6
5-year share price return (% p.a.)	11.3
Dividend reinvestment plan	No

Sector: Energy	Company	Sector
Price/earnings ratio (times)	17.7	20.4
Dividend yield (%)	3.3	2.7

Sydney-based WorleyParsons started in 1971 as a structural engineering consultancy, later acquiring the Australian engineering operations of the American firm of Worley. It has grown into a major global provider of professional services—including feasibility studies, design, project management, facility start-up services and maintenance contracts—for large engineering projects in the oil and gas, minerals and metals, power and infrastructure sectors. It operates in more than 40 countries, and international business is responsible for about three-quarters of turnover.

Latest business results (June 2011, full year)

Profits rebounded sharply from the drop of the previous year, although this largely reflected accounting changes. Excluding these, the after-tax profit rose just 2.5 per cent, to $298.5 million, although the company also reported a negative impact of $31.5 million from the strength of the dollar and a further $15 million from Mideast instability and natural disasters. Hydrocarbons projects are the company's mainstay, and this division reported a 17 per cent rise in revenues, with EBIT up 10 per cent, on the back of a growing number of both upstream and downstream work. The company's three other divisions all reported higher revenues, with Infrastructure and Environment especially strong. There was a notable turnaround for the company's businesses in the second half, with underlying profits 50 per cent higher than in the first half. During the year it was awarded 68 significant new long-term contracts. With strong prospects of further good business to come, the company boosted its workforce during the year from 30000 to 35100.

Outlook

WorleyParsons is seeing a growing number of orders across all its spheres of operations, and it is forecasting good growth in the June 2012 year. It is increasingly seeking work in the developing world, and the 2011 acquisition of Kwezi V3 Engineers in South Africa is part of that strategy. It has become one of China's largest engineering and construction management providers, and it is starting to win orders from Chinese customers who are developing projects abroad. It is also seeking to gain a bigger position in the booming natural gas sector, while maintaining its strong role in crude oil and oil sands developments. It is also expecting solid growth in infrastructure work, particularly in Africa, following the Kwezi V3 acquisition, and it has been winning some major contracts in Latin America.

Year to 30 June	2010	2011
Revenues ($mn)	5059.7	5605.1
Hydrocarbons (%)	67	68
Infrastructure and Environment (%)	10	12
Minerals and Metals (%)	12	11
Power (%)	11	9
EBIT ($mn)	427.4	539.9
EBIT margin (%)	8.4	9.6

Year to 30 June	2010	2011
Profit before tax ($mn)	393.3	498.4
Profit after tax ($mn)	291.1	364.2
Earnings per share (¢)	118.5	148.3
Cash flow per share (¢)	155.9	187.2
Dividend (¢)	75.5	86
Percentage franked	72	57
Net tangible assets per share ($)	0.20	0.59
Interest cover (times)	12.5	13.0
Return on equity (%)	16.7	19.8
Debt-to-equity ratio (%)	34.7	27.2
Current ratio	1.6	1.5

Wotif.com Holdings Limited

WTF

<www.wotifgroup.com>

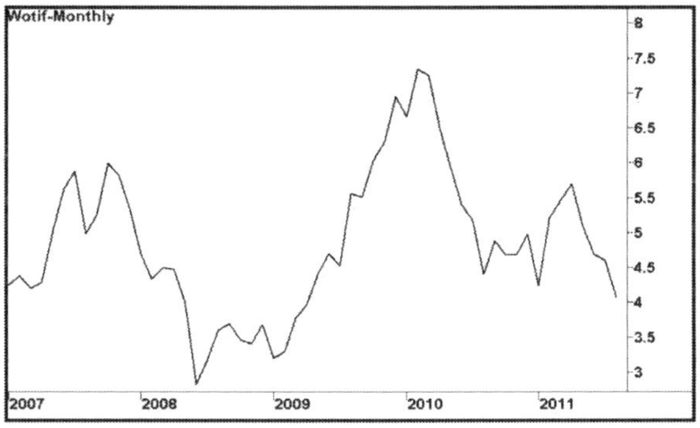

Share price ($)	4.08
12-month high ($)	5.94
12-month low ($)	3.96
Market capitalisation ($mn)	861.7
Price-to-NTA-per-share ratio	255.4
5-year share price return (% p.a.)	5.5
Dividend reinvestment plan	No

Sector: Consumer discretionary	Company	Sector
Price/earnings ratio (times)	16.9	13.1
Dividend yield (%)	5.4	3.5

Wotif.com Holdings, based in Brisbane and founded in 2000, is a leader in online hotel bookings. It has grown rapidly, offering a wide range of accommodation in 66 countries. It has offices in Britain, Canada, China, Indonesia, Hong Kong, Malaysia, New Zealand, Singapore and Thailand. Its new Wotflight business is a flight booking service that handles Australian domestic travel and flights to New Zealand. Its other brands include leisure and activities provider GoDo, leisure travel agency travel.com.au, travel and booking agency <lastminute.com.au>, Asian travel service Asia Web Direct, accommodation agency <latestays.com> and corporate travel booking system Arnold Travel Technology.

Latest business results (June 2011, full year)

Profits edged down on a slight increase in revenues. It was the company's first profit decline since its 2006 ASX listing, and was attributed to a rush of overseas travel by Australians, restricting growth in demand for hotel rooms within Australia, which is the company's main source of business. In addition, in a competitive market environment the company boosted its marketing expenditure by $2.1 million. During the year the company took $1.01 billion in hotel bookings, up from $1.00 billion in the previous year, with 6.97 million room nights sold, down from 7.12 million. Of the room nights sold, 5.82 million were in

Australia and New Zealand, with 0.97 million in Asia. The number of flight transactions rose from 102000 to 137000, with transaction revenues essentially flat at $93.7 million.

Outlook

Wotif.com has grown to be the leader in Australia and New Zealand for online hotel bookings, with a high level of brand awareness. It is now able to offer stays in more than 19600 hotels and other accommodation properties, a number that has grown 12 per cent in a year. In the face of some heavy competition, the company has been boosting its marketing efforts. It has been achieving success with its Wot Deal of the Day, which offers special daily deals to its Australian base of 1.3 million email subscribers. It is seeing very strong growth for various mobile applications for its services, and intends to expand these. It is also working to achieve greater cross-selling of flight bookings from its large base of hotel customers. A new joint venture in Vietnam could be the first of several in Asia. <Wotif.com> is sometimes spoken of as a possible takeover target for a US online travel giant such as Expedia, Priceline or Orbitz.

Year to 30 June	2010	2011
Revenues ($mn)	133.2	134.2
EBIT ($mn)	70.7	67.4

Year to 30 June	2010	2011
EBIT margin (%)	53.1	50.2
Profit before tax ($mn)	73.6	71.6
Profit after tax ($mn)	53.0	51.0
Earnings per share (¢)	25.3	24.2
Cash flow per share (¢)	28.1	27.1
Dividend (¢)	21.5	22
Percentage franked	100	100
Net tangible assets per share ($)	–	0.02
Interest cover (times)	–	–
Return on equity (%)	67.4	58.4
Debt-to-equity ratio (%)	–	–
Current ratio	0.8	0.9

Part II

The tables

Table A

Market capitalisation

A company's market capitalisation is determined by multiplying the share price by the number of shares. To be included in this book, a company must be in the All Ordinaries index, which comprises the 500 largest companies by market capitalisation.

	$mn
BHP Billiton	126372.2
Commonwealth Bank	74400.5
Westpac Banking	62057.1
ANZ Banking	52395.9
National Australia Bank	52078.3
Rio Tinto	31281.9
Woolworths	30593.2
Newcrest Mining	30354.2
Woodside Petroleum	28024.8
QBE Insurance Group	15415.9
CSL	14926.5
Coal & Allied Industries	10632.6
Orica	8558.3
WorleyParsons	6454.5
Incitec Pivot	6058.8
ASX	5015.9

	$mn
Macarthur Coal	4791.2
Lend Lease Group	4709.9
Sonic Healthcare	4563.5
Cochlear	4300.2
Computershare	4196.3
Toll Holdings	3351.8
Campbell Brothers	3097.7
Metcash	3090.8
Tatts Group	3058.9
Caltex Australia	3005.1
Mineral Resources	2190.5
Harvey Norman Holdings	2124.6
UGL	2024.9
Flight Centre	1997.1
Tabcorp Holdings	1919.0
Reece Australia	1902.4
Seek	1870.6
Ansell	1811.6
Adelaide Brighton	1775.3
Monadelphous Group	1760.3
David Jones	1521.5
IOOF Holdings	1437.8
Navitas	1426.6
Consolidated Media	1309.1
Bradken	1233.2
Perpetual	1221.8
IRESS	1034.4
Ausdrill	1012.9
Ten Network Holdings	978.1
SAI Global	939.6
Wotif.com Holdings	861.7

	$mn
Super Retail Group	797.0
GWA Group	693.5
Mermaid Marine Australia	691.4
Fleetwood Corporation	638.8
ARB Corporation	620.4
Amcom Telecom.	605.7
Cardno	572.3
Cabcharge Australia	551.9
APN News & Media	513.4
GUD Holdings	510.6
Domino's Pizza	496.6
Blackmores	492.3
Industrea	478.4
Sedgman	459.4
SMS Management & Tech.	416.1
Count Financial	372.4
iiNet	360.4
M2 Telecommunications	343.7
Austbrokers Holdings	338.9
Technology One	331.6
Ridley Corp	329.4
STW Communications	312.4
Reckon	312.1
Austin Engineering	304.0
OrotonGroup	287.5
Wide Bay Australia	283.9
Thorn Group	262.8
Lycopodium	249.3
Cedar Woods Properties	246.0
Retail Food Group	242.2
Little World Beverages	238.1

	$mn
Fantastic Holdings	226.4
Patties Foods	222.4
Country Road	221.0
Codan	211.7
Euroz	205.9
Data#3	205.1
Tassal Group	196.0
Credit Corp Group	192.1
Cash Converters	191.2
IMF (Australia)	182.3
Oakton	180.1
DWS Advanced Business	179.3
Finbar Group	173.6
Trust Company	161.8
ASG Group	160.7
Mortgage Choice	156.3
Webjet	153.1
Nick Scali	133.7
Hunter Hall	123.0
Melbourne IT	119.6
Equity Trustees	102.8
Treasury Group	90.0
Select Harvests	83.2
Infomedia	66.7

Table B

Revenues

This list ranks the companies in the book according to their most recent full-year revenues figures (operating income for the banks). The figures include revenues from sales and services, but other revenues—such as interest receipts and investment income—are not generally included.

	$mn
BHP Billiton	70332.4
Rio Tinto	61495.7
Woolworths	54142.9
Commonwealth Bank	19397.0
Caltex Australia	18671.9
National Australia Bank	17008.0
Westpac Banking	16910.0
ANZ Banking	15692.0
Metcash	12364.0
QBE Insurance Group	12350.0
Lend Lease Group	8926.7
Toll Holdings	8224.5
Orica	6539.3
WorleyParsons	5605.1
UGL	4583.6
Woodside Petroleum	4557.6

	$mn
Tabcorp Holdings	4469.5
CSL	4187.6
Newcrest Mining	4102.0
Tatts Group	3657.0
Sonic Healthcare	3082.9
Incitec Pivot	2931.7
Harvey Norman Holdings	2645.4
Coal & Allied Industries	2098.3
David Jones	2053.1
Flight Centre	1816.9
Computershare	1567.6
Reece Australia	1563.6
Monadelphous Group	1443.9
Ansell	1219.8
Bradken	1147.5
Campbell Brothers	1108.3
Super Retail Group	1092.3
Adelaide Brighton	1072.9
APN News & Media	1059.1
Ten Network Holdings	990.5
Ausdrill	834.6
Cardno	827.7
Cochlear	809.6
GWA Group	726.4
Ridley Corp	723.7
iiNet	697.2
Data#3	696.2
Macarthur Coal	687.3
IOOF Holdings	642.6
Navitas	641.8
ASX	617.6

	$mn
Mineral Resources	609.5
GUD Holdings	592.8
Perpetual	513.5
Sedgman	507.7
Fleetwood Corporation	465.8
Fantastic Holdings	436.7
M2 Telecommunications	426.8
SAI Global	423.1
Country Road	420.1
Industrea	356.6
Seek	343.1
STW Communications	307.2
SMS Management & Tech.	306.1
Mermaid Marine Australia	285.3
ARB Corporation	254.2
Select Harvests	248.3
Domino's Pizza	245.3
Blackmores	235.3
Tassal Group	222.4
Patties Foods	216.1
Austin Engineering	205.9
Melbourne IT	189.2
Cash Converters	186.1
Oakton	181.3
IRESS	179.8
Cabcharge Australia	171.0
Codan	169.6
Mortgage Choice	169.0
Lycopodium	168.5
Thorn Group	157.6
ASG Group	153.3

	$mn
OrotonGroup	146.4
Wotif.com Holdings	134.2
Technology One	134.0
Cedar Woods Properties	129.8
Count Financial	126.0
Retail Food Group	125.3
Credit Corp Group	113.5
Consolidated Media	104.0
Nick Scali	100.0
DWS Advanced Business	98.4
Finbar Group	97.4
Austbrokers Holdings	92.3
Reckon	90.0
Amcom Telecom.	86.7
Euroz	77.8
Wide Bay Australia	72.7
Little World Beverages	68.8
Trust Company	60.3
Infomedia	48.9
Webjet	43.5
IMF (Australia)	40.6
Equity Trustees	38.6
Hunter Hall	35.5
Treasury Group	18.5

Table C

Year-on-year revenues growth

Companies generally strive for growth, though profit growth is usually of far more significance than a boost in revenues. In fact, it is possible for a company to increase its revenues by all kinds of means—including cutting profit margins or acquiring other companies—and year-on-year revenues growth is of little relevance if other ratios are not also improving. The figures used for this calculation are the latest full-year figures.

	%
Mineral Resources	95.0
IMF (Australia)	87.6
Cardno	74.7
Fleetwood Corporation	60.0
Sedgman	55.5
iiNet	47.3
Mermaid Marine Australia	47.2
Newcrest Mining	46.4
Cash Converters	45.6
Austin Engineering	43.7
Lycopodium	40.9
Amcom Telecom.	39.4
Campbell Brothers	34.3

	%
Ausdrill	32.3
ASG Group	26.9
GUD Holdings	24.9
Little World Beverages	24.4
SMS Management & Tech.	23.7
Seek	22.2
Credit Corp Group	21.7
Cedar Woods Properties	21.4
Toll Holdings	18.4
Webjet	17.3
BHP Billiton	17.2
Super Retail Group	16.5
Data#3	16.3
Rio Tinto	16.2
Navitas	15.6
ANZ Banking	15.3
Equity Trustees	14.7
Bradken	14.3
Industrea	14.1
Monadelphous Group	13.2
STW Communications	12.7
ARB Corporation	11.5
Tatts Group	11.2
Technology One	11.0
WorleyParsons	10.8
Country Road	10.3
Cochlear	10.2
Patties Foods	10.2
Ten Network Holdings	9.9
Harvey Norman Holdings	9.4
Blackmores	9.0

	%
SAI Global	8.8
Adelaide Brighton	8.7
Thorn Group	8.6
OrotonGroup	8.0
Metcash	7.4
Consolidated Media	7.0
IRESS	6.1
Austbrokers Holdings	6.0
Tabcorp Holdings	5.9
Cabcharge Australia	5.8
Reckon	5.6
Trust Company	5.5
Caltex Australia	5.3
UGL	5.2
M2 Telecommunications	5.1
ASX	5.0
Woolworths	4.7
Woodside Petroleum	4.7
Tassal Group	4.6
Domino's Pizza	4.5
Fantastic Holdings	4.2
Select Harvests	4.2
Reece Australia	4.0
Nick Scali	3.8
GWA Group	3.7
Sonic Healthcare	3.7
David Jones	3.4
Flight Centre	3.0
DWS Advanced Business	2.9
APN News & Media	2.8
IOOF Holdings	2.5

	%
Macarthur Coal	2.5
Westpac Banking	2.5
Wide Bay Australia	2.4
Count Financial	1.7
Euroz	1.7
QBE Insurance Group	1.7
Perpetual	1.5
National Australia Bank	1.4
Wotif.com Holdings	0.8
Commonwealth Bank	0.6
Hunter Hall	0.0
Ridley Corp	−0.6
Ansell	−0.9
Mortgage Choice	−0.9
Oakton	−2.8
Infomedia	−3.2
Melbourne IT	−4.9
Treasury Group	−5.8
CSL	−6.0
Retail Food Group	−6.4
Coal & Allied Industries	−9.5
Codan	−10.4
Orica	−11.8
Computershare	−13.8
Lend Lease Group	−13.8
Incitec Pivot	−14.3
Finbar Group	−51.0

Table D

EBIT margin

A company's earnings before interest and taxation (EBIT) is sometimes regarded as a better measure of its profitability than the straight pre-tax or post-tax profit figure. EBIT is derived by adding net interest payments (that is, interest payments minus interest receipts) to the pre-tax profit. Different companies choose different methods of financing their operations; by adding back interest payments to their profits we can help minimise these differences and make comparisons between companies more valid.

The EBIT margin is the EBIT figure as a percentage of annual sales. Clearly a high figure is to be desired, though of course this can be achieved artificially by inflating borrowings (and hence interest payments). And it is noteworthy that efficient companies such as some of the giant retailers can operate most satisfactorily on low margins.

The EBIT margin figure has little relevance for banks—whose high interest payments to their customers mean they have virtually no EBIT—and they have been excluded, as have insurance companies.

	%
Consolidated Media	86.2

	%
IMF (Australia)	79.1
ASX	75.9
Hunter Hall	61.1
Woodside Petroleum	53.8
Wotif.com Holdings	50.2
Treasury Group	48.9
Coal & Allied Industries	46.7
Macarthur Coal	45.0
BHP Billiton	44.3
Seek	43.1
Cabcharge Australia	41.4
Euroz	40.5
Newcrest Mining	37.6
Rio Tinto	37.5
Amcom Telecom.	37.1
Retail Food Group	35.9
IRESS	35.8
Count Financial	35.1
Mineral Resources	34.3
Finbar Group	33.4
Austbrokers Holdings	32.6
Credit Corp Group	31.2
Webjet	30.5
Cedar Woods Properties	30.4
Trust Company	29.7
Cochlear	29.7
Equity Trustees	29.0
CSL	28.3
Infomedia	26.9
DWS Advanced Business	24.9
Reckon	24.9

	%
Computershare	24.8
STW Communications	24.3
Mermaid Marine Australia	23.6
Industrea	23.3
Mortgage Choice	22.9
IOOF Holdings	22.4
Incitec Pivot	22.1
OrotonGroup	21.9
Tassal Group	21.2
Cash Converters	21.1
Thorn Group	20.7
Codan	20.7
Little World Beverages	20.4
Tabcorp Holdings	20.2
Adelaide Brighton	20.2
ARB Corporation	19.8
APN News & Media	19.4
Perpetual	18.9
SAI Global	18.2
Ten Network Holdings	18.1
Blackmores	17.7
Campbell Brothers	17.6
Technology One	16.7
Navitas	16.6
Nick Scali	16.1
Fleetwood Corporation	16.0
Orica	15.7
Harvey Norman Holdings	15.5
Austin Engineering	15.3
Sonic Healthcare	14.8
GWA Group	14.8

	%
ASG Group	14.6
Lycopodium	14.2
Patties Foods	13.8
Bradken	13.6
Tatts Group	13.6
Ausdrill	13.5
SMS Management & Tech.	13.5
Oakton	13.1
GUD Holdings	13.0
David Jones	12.1
Domino's Pizza	11.8
Flight Centre	11.4
Ansell	11.4
Melbourne IT	11.2
Reece Australia	10.7
Cardno	10.5
M2 Telecommunications	9.7
WorleyParsons	9.6
Select Harvests	9.1
Monadelphous Group	8.9
Super Retail Group	8.0
iiNet	7.8
Lend Lease Group	7.5
Sedgman	7.0
Fantastic Holdings	6.4
Woolworths	6.1
Ridley Corp	5.5
Country Road	5.5
Toll Holdings	5.4
UGL	5.3

	%
Metcash	3.4
Data#3	2.9
Caltex Australia	2.7

Table E

Year-on-year EBIT margin growth

The EBIT (earnings before interest and taxation) margin is one of the measures of a company's efficiency. So a rising margin is much to be desired, as it suggests that a company is achieving success in cutting its costs. This table does not include banks or insurance companies.

	%
Finbar Group	125.9
Rio Tinto	90.6
Macarthur Coal	76.5
Lend Lease Group	63.0
M2 Telecommunications	49.9
IOOF Holdings	40.4
Coal & Allied Industries	38.7
Ten Network Holdings	38.5
Count Financial	30.8
Cedar Woods Properties	28.4
Mineral Resources	27.2
Newcrest Mining	26.8
Incitec Pivot	25.2
SAI Global	25.0

	%
Campbell Brothers	24.4
Thorn Group	22.2
Domino's Pizza	20.2
Mortgage Choice	18.1
Super Retail Group	17.9
Consolidated Media	17.9
Reckon	17.6
Country Road	17.3
BHP Billiton	16.9
Hunter Hall	16.5
Data#3	15.2
WorleyParsons	14.0
IMF (Australia)	14.0
STW Communications	13.6
Tassal Group	13.0
IRESS	11.9
Cardno	9.7
Retail Food Group	9.2
GWA Group	8.8
Bradken	7.6
Tabcorp Holdings	7.6
Orica	7.4
Adelaide Brighton	7.4
Little World Beverages	7.0
David Jones	6.7
OrotonGroup	6.1
Ausdrill	6.0
ASG Group	5.9
APN News & Media	5.8
Patties Foods	5.8
Austbrokers Holdings	5.6

	%
Credit Corp Group	5.1
Fantastic Holdings	4.6
Trust Company	4.4
Industrea	3.9
Navitas	3.8
UGL	3.8
Blackmores	3.7
Technology One	2.7
ASX	2.2
Woolworths	1.5
ARB Corporation	1.4
Monadelphous Group	1.1
Nick Scali	0.9
Sonic Healthcare	0.8
Reece Australia	0.7
Tatts Group	0.3
Metcash	0.2
Caltex Australia	–0.2
Cochlear	–0.6
Euroz	–1.2
Flight Centre	–1.3
Amcom Telecom.	–1.4
Perpetual	–1.9
Ansell	–2.1
Seek	–2.9
Melbourne IT	–4.8
Wotif.com Holdings	–5.4
Infomedia	–5.7
CSL	–7.1
Treasury Group	–7.4
Toll Holdings	–7.4

	%
Computershare	–7.8
Lycopodium	–9.6
Harvey Norman Holdings	–9.7
DWS Advanced Business	–10.0
Mermaid Marine Australia	–10.0
iiNet	–10.2
Equity Trustees	–10.9
Webjet	–11.4
SMS Management & Tech.	–11.4
Cash Converters	–12.7
Ridley Corp	–13.0
GUD Holdings	–13.8
Codan	–14.7
Fleetwood Corporation	–14.8
Select Harvests	–16.6
Austin Engineering	–17.2
Cabcharge Australia	–17.4
Woodside Petroleum	–18.2
Oakton	–18.8
Sedgman	–19.5

Table F

After-tax profit

This table ranks all the companies according to their most recent full-year after-tax profit.

	$mn
BHP Billiton	23184.3
Rio Tinto	15569.6

	$mn
Commonwealth Bank	6394.0
Westpac Banking	6346.0
ANZ Banking	4501.0
National Australia Bank	4224.0
Woolworths	2124.0
Woodside Petroleum	1712.0
QBE Insurance Group	1389.1
Newcrest Mining	1058.0
CSL	940.6
Coal & Allied Industries	703.6
Tabcorp Holdings	541.6
Orica	527.6
Lend Lease Group	492.8
Incitec Pivot	442.8
WorleyParsons	364.2
ASX	356.6
Caltex Australia	317.0
Sonic Healthcare	294.5
Toll Holdings	281.4
Tatts Group	275.4
Computershare	258.9
Harvey Norman Holdings	252.3
Metcash	241.4
Macarthur Coal	241.4
Cochlear	180.1
David Jones	170.8
UGL	158.5
Adelaide Brighton	151.4
Mineral Resources	151.0
Flight Centre	139.8
Campbell Brothers	132.3

	$mn
Ansell	122.7
Reece Australia	118.6
IOOF Holdings	99.5
APN News & Media	98.2
Seek	97.7
Ten Network Holdings	96.9
Monadelphous Group	95.1
Consolidated Media	94.8
Bradken	87.1
Navitas	77.4
Ausdrill	73.4
Perpetual	72.5
GWA Group	63.4
Cardno	58.8
Super Retail Group	55.6
Fleetwood Corporation	51.3
Wotif.com Holdings	51.0
IRESS	50.5
GUD Holdings	49.0
SAI Global	48.0
Industrea	47.9
Cabcharge Australia	46.1
Mermaid Marine Australia	43.2
iiNet	39.0
STW Communications	38.7
ARB Corporation	37.9
Tassal Group	30.3
SMS Management & Tech.	29.8
Ridley Corp	29.3
Cedar Woods Properties	28.1
M2 Telecommunications	27.7

	$mn
Cash Converters	27.6
Mortgage Choice	27.5
Blackmores	27.3
Retail Food Group	27.2
Euroz	26.6
Amcom Telecom.	26.1
Sedgman	26.0
Count Financial	25.6
Finbar Group	24.0
Codan	23.4
OrotonGroup	23.0
IMF (Australia)	22.9
Wide Bay Australia	22.6
Thorn Group	22.0
Austin Engineering	21.5
Domino's Pizza	21.4
Austbrokers Holdings	21.4
Credit Corp Group	21.0
Fantastic Holdings	19.5
Patties Foods	18.4
Country Road	18.2
Technology One	17.8
Select Harvests	17.7
DWS Advanced Business	17.4
Lycopodium	17.1
Oakton	16.8
Reckon	16.5
Melbourne IT	16.1
ASG Group	15.7
Data#3	15.0
Trust Company	13.8

	$mn
Hunter Hall	12.3
Nick Scali	11.6
Webjet	11.1
Infomedia	10.0
Treasury Group	10.0
Little World Beverages	9.2
Equity Trustees	8.2

Table G

Year-on-year earnings-per-share growth

The earnings per share (EPS) figure is a crucial one. It tells you—the shareholder—what your part is of the company's profits, for each of your shares. So investors invariably look for EPS growth in a stock. The year-on-year EPS growth figure is often one of the first ratios that investors look to when evaluating a stock. The figures used for this calculation are the latest full-year figures.

	%
Rio Tinto	127.1
Mineral Resources	104.4
IMF (Australia)	89.9
Ten Network Holdings	83.1
Westpac Banking	70.9

	%
Macarthur Coal	67.9
BHP Billiton	61.9
Credit Corp Group	59.7
Cedar Woods Properties	58.3
Campbell Brothers	58.2
M2 Telecommunications	54.9
National Australia Bank	47.9
Country Road	47.7
STW Communications	47.7
Data#3	37.4
ANZ Banking	35.4
Cardno	28.3
IOOF Holdings	28.2
Newcrest Mining	27.9
Super Retail Group	26.8
Lend Lease Group	25.7
Little World Beverages	25.2
WorleyParsons	25.1
Reckon	24.9
Amcom Telecom.	24.3
Fleetwood Corporation	24.0
Coal & Allied Industries	20.2
Domino's Pizza	19.6
Consolidated Media	19.1
OrotonGroup	18.1
Trust Company	17.9
Adelaide Brighton	17.0
Patties Foods	16.8
Mortgage Choice	16.5
Incitec Pivot	16.2

	%
IRESS	16.0
Navitas	15.6
Cochlear	15.4
SAI Global	15.1
Ausdrill	14.4
Bradken	13.5
Technology One	13.2
ARB Corporation	12.9
GWA Group	12.8
iiNet	12.6
Thorn Group	12.5
Monadelphous Group	12.4
Austbrokers Holdings	12.2
Commonwealth Bank	11.6
Blackmores	11.2
Cash Converters	10.3
ASG Group	10.3
Harvey Norman Holdings	9.0
Seek	8.9
UGL	8.9
David Jones	8.0
Austin Engineering	7.5
ASX	7.2
Woolworths	6.5
Lycopodium	6.5
Tabcorp Holdings	6.0
Metcash	5.7
Count Financial	5.2
Hunter Hall	5.0
Fantastic Holdings	4.8

	%
SMS Management & Tech.	4.8
Tassal Group	4.1
Reece Australia	3.8
Webjet	3.5
Mermaid Marine Australia	3.4
Nick Scali	3.1
Ansell	3.1
Sedgman	1.5
Ridley Corp	0.8
Caltex Australia	0.7
Retail Food Group	0.5
Equity Trustees	0.4
Sonic Healthcare	0.4
Flight Centre	−0.2
Perpetual	−2.2
APN News & Media	−2.3
Euroz	−3.4
Tatts Group	−4.3
Wotif.com Holdings	−4.5
Toll Holdings	−4.9
Melbourne IT	−5.7
Wide Bay Australia	−6.0
GUD Holdings	−6.2
DWS Advanced Business	−6.2
CSL	−6.3
Infomedia	−9.6
Treasury Group	−14.3
Woodside Petroleum	−14.6
Orica	−18.7
Oakton	−18.7

	%
Finbar Group	–19.2
Cabcharge Australia	–19.9
Select Harvests	–22.4
Computershare	–22.7
Codan	–24.8
Industrea	–26.1
QBE Insurance Group	–31.5

Table H

Return on equity

Shareholders' equity is the company's assets minus its liabilities. It is, in theory, the amount owned by the shareholders of the company. Return on equity is the after-tax profit expressed as a percentage of that equity. Thus, it is the amount of profit that the company managers made for you—the shareholder—from your assets. For many investors it is one of the most important gauges of how well a company is doing. It is one of the requirements for inclusion in this book that all companies have a return on equity of at least 10 per cent in their latest financial year.

	%
OrotonGroup	83.6
Wotif.com Holdings	58.4
Monadelphous Group	56.3
Data#3	53.3

	%
Hunter Hall	51.0
Nick Scali	49.3
Coal & Allied Industries	46.6
Navitas	44.7
BHP Billiton	42.1
IRESS	38.6
Cochlear	38.3
Lycopodium	36.2
Blackmores	36.2
Reckon	35.8
Codan	34.2
Mortgage Choice	32.8
Count Financial	32.5
M2 Telecommunications	32.4
ARB Corporation	31.5
DWS Advanced Business	30.6
SMS Management & Tech.	30.2
Technology One	29.6
Rio Tinto	29.3
Infomedia	28.9
IMF (Australia)	28.6
Mineral Resources	28.3
Fleetwood Corporation	28.2
Woolworths	28.0
Webjet	27.8
Thorn Group	24.9
Seek	24.8
Little World Beverages	24.4
Consolidated Media	24.4
CSL	23.9
David Jones	23.9

	%
Cedar Woods Properties	23.5
Euroz	23.3
Tabcorp Holdings	23.2
Austin Engineering	22.5
Credit Corp Group	21.8
Computershare	21.6
Domino's Pizza	20.9
Country Road	20.6
GUD Holdings	20.6
Fantastic Holdings	20.3
Perpetual	20.0
WorleyParsons	19.8
Super Retail Group	19.4
Flight Centre	19.3
Reece Australia	19.0
Ansell	18.7
Mermaid Marine Australia	18.5
Retail Food Group	18.4
Sedgman	18.4
Campbell Brothers	18.2
Melbourne IT	17.9
Metcash	17.9
Cardno	17.9
SAI Global	17.9
Commonwealth Bank	17.8
Westpac Banking	17.4
Treasury Group	17.4
Industrea	17.2
Finbar Group	17.0
Amcom Telecom.	16.7

	%
iiNet	16.7
Adelaide Brighton	16.6
Macarthur Coal	16.5
Oakton	16.5
Woodside Petroleum	16.5
Cash Converters	16.4
Austbrokers Holdings	16.2
ASG Group	16.1
Bradken	15.5
Cabcharge Australia	15.3
Equity Trustees	15.0
Patties Foods	14.8
GWA Group	14.5
Orica	14.3
Lend Lease Group	14.2
UGL	13.6
ANZ Banking	13.5
QBE Insurance Group	13.1
Incitec Pivot	12.7
Ausdrill	12.7
Wide Bay Australia	12.7
Select Harvests	12.5
Trust Company	12.2
ASX	12.0
Harvey Norman Holdings	11.7
Ten Network Holdings	11.7
Tassal Group	11.6
Sonic Healthcare	11.6
STW Communications	11.5
IOOF Holdings	11.3

	%
Newcrest Mining	11.3
National Australia Bank	11.0
Tatts Group	11.0
Caltex Australia	10.6
APN News & Media	10.4
Toll Holdings	10.3
Ridley Corp	10.2

Table I

Year-on-year return on equity growth

Company managers have a variety of strategies they can use to boost profits. It is much harder to lift the return on equity (ROE). Find a company with a high ROE figure, and one that is growing year by year, and it is possible that you have found a real growth stock.

	%
Ten Network Holdings	95.6
Rio Tinto	87.8
Tabcorp Holdings	66.4
IMF (Australia)	65.1
BHP Billiton	51.5
STW Communications	50.1
National Australia Bank	50.1
Macarthur Coal	41.2

	%
Cedar Woods Properties	38.0
Mineral Resources	37.0
Credit Corp Group	36.4
ANZ Banking	35.4
Cardno	34.7
Country Road	33.7
Westpac Banking	32.0
IOOF Holdings	27.4
Campbell Brothers	26.5
M2 Telecommunications	25.8
Consolidated Media	22.5
Data#3	20.8
Coal & Allied Industries	18.9
Lend Lease Group	18.6
WorleyParsons	18.5
Trust Company	18.0
Hunter Hall	17.7
Amcom Telecom.	17.0
Incitec Pivot	15.1
Domino's Pizza	14.5
Little World Beverages	14.4
GWA Group	11.5
SAI Global	11.1
Reckon	10.0
CSL	10.0
Fleetwood Corporation	9.0
Patties Foods	8.6
Super Retail Group	8.6
IRESS	8.3
UGL	7.4
Adelaide Brighton	7.3

	%
Ausdrill	6.2
Harvey Norman Holdings	4.3
ASX	4.1
OrotonGroup	3.9
Commonwealth Bank	3.7
iiNet	3.1
Metcash	2.2
Technology One	1.4
Sonic Healthcare	0.8
Austbrokers Holdings	0.7
Mortgage Choice	0.3
Equity Trustees	−0.1
David Jones	−0.2
Woolworths	−0.3
Ansell	−0.3
Cochlear	−1.1
ASG Group	−1.6
Tatts Group	−1.7
Ridley Corp	−1.8
ARB Corporation	−1.9
APN News & Media	−2.4
Webjet	−2.9
Blackmores	−2.9
Thorn Group	−3.4
Tassal Group	−5.3
Lycopodium	−5.4
Newcrest Mining	−6.0
Reece Australia	−6.3
Fantastic Holdings	−6.6
SMS Management & Tech.	−7.0

	%
Caltex Australia	−7.4
Cash Converters	−7.4
Toll Holdings	−7.6
Melbourne IT	−8.3
Euroz	−8.9
Flight Centre	−9.0
Monadelphous Group	−9.7
Bradken	−9.9
DWS Advanced Business	−10.6
Orica	−10.6
Perpetual	−10.8
Mermaid Marine Australia	−10.9
Wide Bay Australia	−10.9
Seek	−11.0
Infomedia	−11.6
Nick Scali	−12.7
Retail Food Group	−13.0
Wotif.com Holdings	−13.3
Austin Engineering	−18.9
Sedgman	−19.6
Treasury Group	−21.2
Select Harvests	−22.2
GUD Holdings	−22.5
Cabcharge Australia	−23.5
Woodside Petroleum	−25.0
Computershare	−25.9
QBE Insurance Group	−27.6
Count Financial	−28.3
Navitas	−29.1

Codan	–29.1
Oakton	–30.2
Finbar Group	–31.8
Industrea	–40.2

Table J

Debt-to-equity ratio

A company's borrowings as a percentage of its shareholders' equity is one of the most common measures of corporate debt. Many investors will be wary of a company with a ratio that is too high. However, a company with a steady business and a regular income flow—such as an electric power company or a large supermarket chain—is generally considered relatively safe with a high level of debt, whereas a small company in a new business field might be thought at risk with even moderate debt levels. Much depends on surrounding circumstances, including the prevailing interest rates. Of course, it is often from borrowing that a company grows, and some investors are not happy buying shares in a company with little or no debt.

There are various ways to calculate the ratio, but for this book the net debt position is used. That is, a company's cash has been deducted from its borrowings. For inclusion in this book no company was allowed a debt-to-equity ratio of more than 70 per cent. Some of the companies had no net debt—their cash position was greater than the amount of their borrowings—and so have been assigned a zero figure in this table. The ratio has no relevance for banks, so they have been excluded.

	%
Amcom Telecom.	0.0
Ansell	0.0
ARB Corporation	0.0
ASX	0.0
Austbrokers Holdings	0.0
Cash Converters	0.0
Coal & Allied Industries	0.0
Cochlear	0.0
Consolidated Media	0.0
Country Road	0.0
CSL	0.0
Data#3	0.0
Domino's Pizza	0.0
DWS Advanced Business	0.0
Equity Trustees	0.0
Euroz	0.0
Flight Centre	0.0
Hunter Hall	0.0
IMF (Australia)	0.0
Infomedia	0.0
IOOF Holdings	0.0
IRESS	0.0
Lycopodium	0.0
Macarthur Coal	0.0

	%
Mineral Resources	0.0
Monadelphous Group	0.0
Mortgage Choice	0.0
Nick Scali	0.0
Perpetual	0.0
Reckon	0.0
Reece Australia	0.0
Sedgman	0.0
SMS Management & Tech.	0.0
Technology One	0.0
Treasury Group	0.0
Trust Company	0.0
Webjet	0.0
Wotif.com Holdings	0.0
Fleetwood Corporation	1.6
Oakton	4.2
Newcrest Mining	4.4
Cardno	6.3
Fantastic Holdings	7.7
David Jones	9.8
BHP Billiton	10.1
ASG Group	10.6
Ausdrill	12.7
Austin Engineering	13.2
Campbell Brothers	13.5
UGL	15.2
Count Financial	15.4
Rio Tinto	15.4
Lend Lease Group	17.8
M2 Telecommunications	18.3
Finbar Group	19.0

	%
Caltex Australia	20.7
Harvey Norman Holdings	21.9
OrotonGroup	22.3
Credit Corp Group	22.8
STW Communications	23.1
Melbourne IT	23.8
Adelaide Brighton	23.9
Super Retail Group	24.2
WorleyParsons	27.2
Thorn Group	28.4
QBE Insurance Group	28.8
Mermaid Marine Australia	29.4
Tassal Group	31.7
Woodside Petroleum	34.6
Bradken	34.7
Ridley Corp	35.1
Codan	35.5
Toll Holdings	36.4
Little World Beverages	36.8
Blackmores	37.7
Incitec Pivot	38.1
Tatts Group	39.5
GUD Holdings	39.6
iiNet	39.7
Orica	40.1
Cabcharge Australia	40.4
Seek	40.8
Woolworths	42.4
Cedar Woods Properties	42.5
Navitas	43.0
Select Harvests	43.3

	%
Retail Food Group	44.9
GWA Group	45.0
Patties Foods	46.4
Metcash	47.3
Ten Network Holdings	48.6
Industrea	50.1
SAI Global	51.5
Computershare	53.5
APN News & Media	60.6
Sonic Healthcare	61.0
Tabcorp Holdings	67.5

Table K

Current ratio

The current ratio is simply the company's current assets divided by its current liabilities. Current assets are cash or assets that can, in theory, be converted quickly into cash. Current liabilities are normally those payable within a year. The current ratio measures the ability of a company to repay in a hurry its short-term debt, should the need arise. Banks and insurance companies are not included.

Macarthur Coal	9.1
IMF (Australia)	6.9
Trust Company	6.1
Treasury Group	4.8

DWS Advanced Business	4.0
Amcom Telecom.	3.5
Webjet	3.4
Cash Converters	3.1
Equity Trustees	3.1
ARB Corporation	3.0
CSL	2.9
Infomedia	2.8
Bradken	2.8
Euroz	2.7
Retail Food Group	2.5
Adelaide Brighton	2.5
Hunter Hall	2.4
Tassal Group	2.4
Blackmores	2.4
Super Retail Group	2.3
GWA Group	2.3
SMS Management & Tech.	2.2
Lycopodium	2.1
Patties Foods	2.1
Technology One	2.1
Select Harvests	2.0
Reece Australia	2.0
Fantastic Holdings	2.0
Cochlear	1.9
IRESS	1.9
Campbell Brothers	1.9
GUD Holdings	1.9
Newcrest Mining	1.9
Fleetwood Corporation	1.9
Ridley Corp	1.8

Oakton	1.7
Ausdrill	1.7
Industrea	1.7
Sonic Healthcare	1.7
Harvey Norman Holdings	1.6
Mineral Resources	1.6
Nick Scali	1.6
Ten Network Holdings	1.6
Mortgage Choice	1.6
Rio Tinto	1.6
Finbar Group	1.6
OrotonGroup	1.6
WorleyParsons	1.5
Mermaid Marine Australia	1.5
Caltex Australia	1.5
UGL	1.5
Sedgman	1.5
Ansell	1.5
Metcash	1.4
Country Road	1.4
Austin Engineering	1.4
Cedar Woods Properties	1.4
Incitec Pivot	1.4
Computershare	1.4
Cardno	1.4
Codan	1.4
ASG Group	1.4
Orica	1.4
Coal & Allied Industries	1.3
ASX	1.3

BHP Billiton	1.3
SAI Global	1.3
Flight Centre	1.3
Thorn Group	1.3
Credit Corp Group	1.2
APN News & Media	1.2
Perpetual	1.2
Monadelphous Group	1.2
Data#3	1.2
Austbrokers Holdings	1.2
Domino's Pizza	1.1
David Jones	1.1
Count Financial	1.1
Cabcharge Australia	1.0
Melbourne IT	1.0
STW Communications	0.9
M2 Telecommunications	0.9
Wotif.com Holdings	0.9
Woolworths	0.8
Toll Holdings	0.8
Reckon	0.7
Lend Lease Group	0.7
Woodside Petroleum	0.7
Consolidated Media	0.7
Tatts Group	0.7
Seek	0.7
iiNet	0.6
Navitas	0.5
Little World Beverages	0.4
Tabcorp Holdings	0.3

Tabcorp Holdings	0.3

Table L

Price/earnings ratio

The price/earnings ratio (PER)—the current share price divided by the earnings per share figure—is one of the best known of all sharemarket ratios. Essentially it expresses the amount of money investors are ready to pay for each cent or dollar of a company's profits, and it allows you to compare the share prices of different companies with widely different profits. A high PER suggests the market has a high regard for the company and its growth prospects; a low ratio may mean that investors are disdainful of the stock. The figures in this table are based on share prices as of 31 August 2011.

Tabcorp Holdings	3.4
Select Harvests	4.4
APN News & Media	5.1
Mortgage Choice	5.8
Tassal Group	6.4
Finbar Group	6.5
Infomedia	6.7
Cash Converters	6.9
QBE Insurance Group	7.2
Melbourne IT	7.4
Euroz	7.4

STW Communications	8.0
IMF (Australia)	8.0
Harvey Norman Holdings	8.4
Cedar Woods Properties	8.7
David Jones	8.8
Retail Food Group	8.8
Treasury Group	9.0
Lend Lease Group	9.0
Rio Tinto	9.0
Codan	9.0
Credit Corp Group	9.1
iiNet	9.2
Cardno	9.3
BHP Billiton	9.4
Caltex Australia	9.5
Westpac Banking	9.6
Industrea	9.6
ASG Group	9.8
Hunter Hall	9.9
Ten Network Holdings	10.1
DWS Advanced Business	10.3
GUD Holdings	10.3
Thorn Group	10.6
Oakton	10.7
GWA Group	10.9
Tatts Group	11.0
Ridley Corp	11.2
ANZ Banking	11.3
Nick Scali	11.5
Commonwealth Bank	11.6
National Australia Bank	11.6

Fantastic Holdings	11.6
Trust Company	11.7
Adelaide Brighton	11.7
Toll Holdings	11.8
Cabcharge Australia	12.0
Patties Foods	12.1
Wide Bay Australia	12.1
Country Road	12.1
Fleetwood Corporation	12.2
M2 Telecommunications	12.3
Equity Trustees	12.4
Ausdrill	12.4
Bradken	12.4
OrotonGroup	12.5
Metcash	12.8
UGL	12.8
Mineral Resources	13.2
Incitec Pivot	13.6
Data#3	13.7
SMS Management & Tech.	13.9
Austin Engineering	13.9
Webjet	14.0
Consolidated Media	14.0
ASX	14.0
Super Retail Group	14.2
Flight Centre	14.3
IOOF Holdings	14.4
Woolworths	14.4
Count Financial	14.5
Lycopodium	14.6

Ansell	14.7
Coal & Allied Industries	15.1
Mermaid Marine Australia	15.2
Perpetual	15.3
Sonic Healthcare	15.4
Austbrokers Holdings	15.6
Orica	15.8
Woodside Petroleum	16.0
Reece Australia	16.0
Computershare	16.2
CSL	16.3
ARB Corporation	16.4
Wotif.com Holdings	16.9
Sedgman	17.5
Navitas	17.5
WorleyParsons	17.7
Blackmores	18.0
Technology One	18.4
Monadelphous Group	18.5
SAI Global	19.0
Reckon	19.0
Seek	19.1
Macarthur Coal	19.2
IRESS	20.2
Campbell Brothers	22.6
Domino's Pizza	23.2
Amcom Telecom.	23.2
Cochlear	23.8
Little World Beverages	25.3

Newcrest Mining	26.9

Table M

Price-to-NTA-per-share ratio

The NTA-per-share figure expresses the worth of a company's net tangible assets—that is, its assets minus its liabilities and intangible assets—for each share of the company. Intangible assets, such as goodwill or the value of newspaper mastheads, are excluded because it is deemed difficult to place a value on them (though this proposition is debatable), and also because they might not have much worth if separated from the company. The price-to-NTA-per-share ratio relates this figure to the share price.

A ratio of one means that the company is valued exactly according to the value of its assets. A ratio below one suggests that the shares are a bargain, though usually there is a good reason for this. Profits are more important than assets.

In some respects this is an 'old economy' ratio. For many high-tech companies in the 'new economy' the most important assets are human ones whose worth does not appear on the balance sheet.

Companies with a negative NTA-per-share figure, as a result of having intangible assets valued at more than their remaining net assets, have been omitted from this table.

Select Harvests	0.7

Tassal Group	0.8
Caltex Australia	0.9
Harvey Norman Holdings	1.0
Finbar Group	1.0
Ridley Corp	1.3
Treasury Group	1.5
Ausdrill	1.6
Euroz	1.7
Mortgage Choice	1.8
ANZ Banking	1.8
National Australia Bank	1.8
Wide Bay Australia	1.9
Credit Corp Group	1.9
Cedar Woods Properties	1.9
David Jones	2.0
Lend Lease Group	2.1
Westpac Banking	2.1
Trust Company	2.2
Cash Converters	2.2
Adelaide Brighton	2.4
Cabcharge Australia	2.4
Fantastic Holdings	2.5
Woodside Petroleum	2.5
Mermaid Marine Australia	2.6
Bradken	2.6
Macarthur Coal	2.7
Commonwealth Bank	2.7
Country Road	2.7
Reece Australia	2.9
Newcrest Mining	3.0
Fleetwood Corporation	3.1
QBE Insurance Group	3.3

Mineral Resources	3.6
Toll Holdings	3.6
Rio Tinto	3.8
Count Financial	3.9
BHP Billiton	4.0
Consolidated Media	4.0
Industrea	4.1
Super Retail Group	4.1
Thorn Group	4.2
Amcom Telecom.	4.3
Sedgman	4.4
Patties Foods	4.5
Equity Trustees	4.6
Webjet	4.7
Flight Centre	5.1
Austbrokers Holdings	5.1
ARB Corporation	5.3
CSL	5.5
Ansell	5.6
Perpetual	5.6
Lycopodium	5.7
Nick Scali	5.7
Little World Beverages	5.8
DWS Advanced Business	5.9
GUD Holdings	5.9
Hunter Hall	5.9
Blackmores	6.4
IMF (Australia)	6.6
Coal & Allied Industries	6.7
Oakton	6.8
ASX	7.1

Technology One	7.8
Data#3	8.0
Orica	8.2
Incitec Pivot	8.3
OrotonGroup	9.0
Austin Engineering	9.3
Monadelphous Group	9.4
Campbell Brothers	9.7
SMS Management & Tech.	9.7
Infomedia	9.8
Domino's Pizza	10.2
IOOF Holdings	10.7
Woolworths	12.9
IRESS	13.4
Cochlear	14.6
Codan	15.1
UGL	16.0
GWA Group	16.6
Metcash	36.8
WorleyParsons	44.6
Reckon	97.6
Wotif.com Holdings	255.4
Cardno	376.3

Table N

Dividend yield

Many investors buy shares for income, rather than for capital growth. They look for companies that offer a high dividend yield (the dividend expressed as a percentage of the share price). This table ranks the companies in this book according to their historic dividend yields. Note that the franking credits available from some companies can make the dividend yield substantially higher. The dividend yield changes with the share price. The figures in this table are based on share prices as of 31 August 2011.

	%
Tabcorp Holdings	15.4
APN News & Media	14.5
Euroz	12.5
Infomedia	10.9
IMF (Australia)	10.1
Finbar Group	10.1
David Jones	10.1
Melbourne IT	10.1
Mortgage Choice	9.8
Hunter Hall	9.6
Tatts Group	9.3
QBE Insurance Group	9.1
DWS Advanced Business	8.9
Select Harvests	8.8
Treasury Group	8.7
GUD Holdings	8.7
Equity Trustees	8.3
ASG Group	7.9
GWA Group	7.8
STW Communications	7.6
Wide Bay Australia	7.5

	%
Consolidated Media	7.1
Count Financial	7.0
Ridley Corp	7.0
Cash Converters	7.0
Trust Company	7.0
Codan	7.0
IOOF Holdings	6.9
OrotonGroup	6.8
Westpac Banking	6.8
Perpetual	6.8
Metcash	6.7
Commonwealth Bank	6.7
Fleetwood Corporation	6.6
Cabcharge Australia	6.6
Cardno	6.5
Retail Food Group	6.5
National Australia Bank	6.4
ASX	6.4
Ten Network Holdings	6.4
ANZ Banking	6.2
Harvey Norman Holdings	6.0
Adelaide Brighton	5.9
Country Road	5.8
Data#3	5.8
Cedar Woods Properties	5.8
M2 Telecommunications	5.8
UGL	5.7
Nick Scali	5.5
Navitas	5.4
Webjet	5.4

	%
Wotif.com Holdings	5.4
Caltex Australia	5.4
Toll Holdings	5.3
Technology One	5.2
Bradken	5.2
iiNet	5.1
Sonic Healthcare	5.0
Fantastic Holdings	5.0
SMS Management & Tech.	4.9
Woolworths	4.9
Patties Foods	4.8
Coal & Allied Industries	4.8
Super Retail Group	4.7
Monadelphous Group	4.7
Thorn Group	4.7
Credit Corp Group	4.7
IRESS	4.7
Lycopodium	4.7
Oakton	4.4
Blackmores	4.2
Lend Lease Group	4.2
Flight Centre	4.2
Austbrokers Holdings	4.1
Orica	4.0
Computershare	3.7
Ausdrill	3.6
Mineral Resources	3.5
Reckon	3.4
WorleyParsons	3.3
Sedgman	3.2

	%
Reece Australia	3.2
Woodside Petroleum	3.1
Industrea	3.1
Campbell Brothers	3.1
SAI Global	3.0
Domino's Pizza	3.0
Cochlear	3.0
CSL	2.8
Mermaid Marine Australia	2.8
Little World Beverages	2.7
Austin Engineering	2.7
ARB Corporation	2.7
Seek	2.6
Macarthur Coal	2.5
BHP Billiton	2.5
Ansell	2.4
Incitec Pivot	2.1
Amcom Telecom.	1.9
Rio Tinto	1.5
Tassal Group	1.5
Newcrest Mining	0.8

Table O

Year-on-year dividend growth

Most investors hope for a rising dividend, and this table tells how much each company raised (or lowered) its dividend in its latest financial year.

	%
APN News & Media	200.0
IMF (Australia)	200.0
Ten Network Holdings	200.0
Credit Corp Group	150.0
Caltex Australia	140.0
Rio Tinto	115.7
Country Road	110.8
Mineral Resources	110.0
STW Communications	85.7
Incitec Pivot	77.3
Cedar Woods Properties	76.9
Macarthur Coal	73.9
M2 Telecommunications	60.0
Technology One	52.0
Euroz	50.0
Adelaide Brighton	40.7
Campbell Brothers	40.0
Data#3	37.5
Super Retail Group	34.9
Thorn Group	34.3
iiNet	33.3
Oakton	30.8
Treasury Group	30.8
OrotonGroup	26.3
Count Financial	25.0
ANZ Banking	23.5
Retail Food Group	23.4
Domino's Pizza	23.0
IOOF Holdings	22.9
Austin Engineering	21.1

	%
Seek	20.2
Flight Centre	20.0
Newcrest Mining	20.0
Westpac Banking	19.8
Patties Foods	18.5
ARB Corporation	17.9
Cardno	17.2
Cash Converters	16.7
Bradken	16.2
ASG Group	15.4
Coal & Allied Industries	15.3
Monadelphous Group	14.5
Amcom Telecom.	14.3
Reckon	14.3
WorleyParsons	13.9
Austbrokers Holdings	13.3
Finbar Group	13.3
Cochlear	12.5
Codan	12.5
Mermaid Marine Australia	12.5
IRESS	11.8
SAI Global	11.7
Lycopodium	11.1
Commonwealth Bank	10.3
Navitas	10.1
UGL	9.4
Ausdrill	9.1
Lend Lease Group	9.0
Blackmores	8.9
Mortgage Choice	8.3
Ansell	8.2

	%
Sedgman	7.7
Fleetwood Corporation	7.4
Fantastic Holdings	7.3
David Jones	7.1
DWS Advanced Business	6.7
Woolworths	6.1
ASX	5.8
Little World Beverages	5.3
Reece Australia	5.2
Webjet	4.8
National Australia Bank	4.1
Trust Company	3.9
Metcash	3.8
Ridley Corp	3.4
SMS Management & Tech.	3.4
GUD Holdings	3.2
Industrea	2.6
Tatts Group	2.4
Wotif.com Holdings	2.3
Woodside Petroleum	0.8
Computershare	0.0
Consolidated Media	0.0
CSL	0.0
GWA Group	0.0
Infomedia	0.0
Melbourne IT	0.0
Nick Scali	0.0
QBE Insurance Group	0.0
Sonic Healthcare	0.0
Toll Holdings	0.0

	%
BHP Billiton	–0.8
Hunter Hall	–0.9
Orica	–2.1
Wide Bay Australia	–4.8
Equity Trustees	–9.1
Cabcharge Australia	–11.8
Perpetual	–11.9
Harvey Norman Holdings	–14.3
Tabcorp Holdings	–21.8
Select Harvests	–38.1
Tassal Group	–66.7

Table P

Five-year share-price return

This table ranks the annual average return to investors from a five-year investment in each of the companies in the book. It is the accumulated return, which means it incorporates not only capital gain but also reinvested dividends, bonus stock and rights issues.

	% p.a.
M2 Telecommunications	63.5
Mineral Resources	60.0
Austin Engineering	59.9
OrotonGroup	48.7
Mermaid Marine Australia	41.2

	% p.a.
iiNet	36.1
Data#3	33.8
Monadelphous Group	31.3
Incitec Pivot	31.0
Macarthur Coal	29.6
IMF (Australia)	28.7
Retail Food Group	28.1
Reckon	27.9
Little World Beverages	27.5
Industrea	27.4
Super Retail Group	27.0
ARB Corporation	26.5
Amcom Telecom.	25.9
Campbell Brothers	25.4
Lycopodium	24.2
Thorn Group	23.9
Ausdrill	23.5
Blackmores	20.9
Navitas	20.9
Austbrokers Holdings	20.4
Fleetwood Corporation	19.5
Domino's Pizza	17.8
Newcrest Mining	17.7
SMS Management & Tech.	16.6
Flight Centre	15.4
Coal & Allied Industries	14.1
Sedgman	13.9
CSL	13.1
Technology One	13.0
Country Road	12.4
Webjet	12.0

	% p.a.
Bradken	11.8
Cochlear	11.5
IRESS	11.5
WorleyParsons	11.3
Ansell	10.5
ASG Group	10.5
Adelaide Brighton	10.4
Euroz	10.4
SAI Global	10.4
BHP Billiton	9.8
DWS Advanced Business	9.6
Finbar Group	9.4
GUD Holdings	8.8
Cardno	7.9
Codan	7.5
Reece Australia	7.5
Woolworths	7.5
Nick Scali	7.4
Commonwealth Bank	7.1
Rio Tinto	6.5
Cash Converters	6.3
Orica	6.3
Wotif.com Holdings	5.5
Ridley Corp	4.5
Metcash	4.3
Tassal Group	3.9
Seek	3.3
Westpac Banking	3.2
Sonic Healthcare	3.1
David Jones	2.9
UGL	2.3

	% p.a.
ASX	2.2
Computershare	2.2
Cedar Woods Properties	1.8
Patties Foods	1.2
GWA Group	0.2
Tatts Group	0.2
ANZ Banking	−0.3
Wide Bay Australia	−0.3
Woodside Petroleum	−0.5
Melbourne IT	−1.5
IOOF Holdings	−2.0
Equity Trustees	−2.2
National Australia Bank	−2.6
Fantastic Holdings	−2.7
Consolidated Media	−2.9
Count Financial	−3.6
Hunter Hall	−4.5
Mortgage Choice	−4.5
QBE Insurance Group	−4.5
Cabcharge Australia	−5.3
Toll Holdings	−5.5
Harvey Norman Holdings	−7.1
Trust Company	−7.1
Lend Lease Group	−8.2
Credit Corp Group	−8.7
Oakton	−9.2
Tabcorp Holdings	−9.6
Caltex Australia	−9.9
Perpetual	−13.1
STW Communications	−13.2

Infomedia	−13.5
Treasury Group	−13.5
Ten Network Holdings	−15.8
APN News & Media	−24.6
Select Harvests	−30.5

Table Q

Non-interest income to total income

The final three tables rank the banks only. Most of the banks are working to diversify away from their traditional lending business into other operations, such as insurance and funds management. This table ranks them according to their success, showing how much of their income derives from non-interest sources.

	%
Commonwealth Bank	35.0
ANZ Banking	30.7
Westpac Banking	30.0
National Australia Bank	27.9
Wide Bay Australia	21.9

Table R

Cost-to-income ratio

All the banks are working to reduce their high costs. The cost-to-income ratio—expressing costs as a percentage of operating income—is one of the measures commonly used by analysts to ascertain their success.

	%
Westpac Banking	43.9
ANZ Banking	46.5
Commonwealth Bank	46.7
National Australia Bank	50.2
Wide Bay Australia	54.8

Table S

Return on assets

Banks have large assets, and the return-on-assets ratio—after-tax profit as a percentage of average total assets—is another popular measure of their efficiency.

	%
Westpac Banking	1.1
Commonwealth Bank	1.0
ANZ Banking	0.9
Wide Bay Australia	0.8
National Australia Bank	0.6

MARTIN ROTH
FINDING THE TOP STOCKS
Strategies for Success
TOP STOCKS 2012

Active Investing revised edition

Grow your portfolio using low-risk tried-and-tested techniques—without having to pay a broker or fund manager big bucks, and without the risk of losing it all on a gamble.

In this fully revised Australian sharemarket classic, best-selling author and professional trader Alan Hull shows you how to manage your portfolio like a professional in less than one hour a week.

Inside you'll discover:

- how to make your money work for you in all market climates—even downtrends
- how Alan's non-speculative and low-risk tips and tricks can help you
- how to protect your portfolio from market risk
- why blue-chip stocks are best
- which shares to buy, when to sell, how to take profits and how to withdraw cash from your portfolio
- how to grow your portfolio, even with a conservative approach.

By following Alan's strategies and techniques, you will discover how to create wealth in every possible market condition—all in less than one hour a week!

<www.alanhull.com>

<www.wiley.com>

Notes:

[Space left intentionally blank in original book]

Back Cover Material

A mid a weak economy, slowing corporate profitability, a limping sharemarket and growing investor caution, the 18th edition of Australia's most trusted and sought after sharemarket reference, *Top Stocks,* returns. Despite the current financial climate, a surprisingly large number of Australian companies continue to race ahead with surging profits. *Top Stocks 2012* guides investors with the latest information on the companies that will help them build a successful portfolio.

Respected financial journalist Martin Roth puts his rigorous, independent selection criteria to work on the top 500 Australian companies, once more delivering detailed and crucial analysis on Australia's best public companies. In *Top Stocks 2012* you will discover which firms pose the lowest risk and the greatest long-term investment value.

Inside, you'll find:

- individual, unbiased analysis of the latest results from 102 top Australian companies
- comparative sales and profits data, and in-depth ratio analysis
- comprehensive research detailing each company's overall outlook
- 19 tables that rank all of the companies according to financial data.

***

Martin Roth is an internationally successful financial journalist. Based in Melbourne, he is one of Australia's leading authors of investment books.

Books For ALL Kinds of Readers

Printed in Dunstable, United Kingdom

91342612R00288